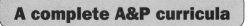

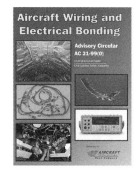

Airframe & Powerplant Mechanics

Powerplant

Test Guide

written, oral & practical FAA exam prep with PTS

Tom Forenz; chief editor

Produced and Distributed by:

Aircraft Technical Book Company
Tabernash, CO 80478 USA
1-970-726-5111
www.ACtechbooks.com

isbn 978-0-98386588-9

=AIRCRAFT
TECHNICAL
Book Company

TABLE OF CONTENTS

How To Use This Test Guide

This book is designed to help you pass your FAA knowledge test. But, even more importantly, it's designed to help reinforce your understanding of the subjects you've been studying in the classroom or on your own with textbooks and other tools. Therefore, rather than this being the first book you pick up, it should be the last. When you take this route, you will find the questions in this book easy and obvious. If instead you take the "fast" approach by just memorizing questions you will find both these and the real ones later difficult and frustrating.

The process we suggest is: Learn first from the textbooks and your instructors. When you are comfortable with a subject, are able to see problems from different sides, and when the reasons for each step of a task are obvious; then it is time to prepare for the test. This Test Guide, if properly used, will serve as your proof that you know what you need to know or whether a subject requires further study. If so, the explanation with each question may refresh your understanding. Or the textbook reference will point you to the right place for review.

Where the questions come from:
In 2011, FAA made the decision to stop publishing actual test questions. Previous test guides, where you could memorize each question exactly as it appear on your test, are no more. Instead, questions in this and all other current FAA test guides now contain only examples of the type of question you will see on your actual FAA test.

Questions in this book come from two sources. First are previous FAA written questions which are still relevant to the new curricula covered in the FAA 8083-ATB. Second are new questions written by Aircraft Technical Book Company along with a team of Part 147 A&P instructors to cover topics in the 8083s (the complete FAA required curricula) for which no sample FAA questions exist.

So, should you "make sure" and buy other test guides as well? On one sense it can't hurt. After all, our question on some topics such as cargo bay fire protection may be construed or worded differently than another's. However, all will be different from the actual FAA questions, and different still from those asked by an interviewer, or more important still; by a customer.

So once again, your first job is to study the textbooks and understand the subject. With that, all future questions will be easy and obvious, so making your new career rich and rewarding. Remember, its not the quick way; its the right way.

Aircraft Technical Book Company powerplant peer review team:
We would like to thank the following schools and instructors for their assistance writing and reviewing the sample questions and explanations in this guide.

Robert C Byrd Aerospace Education Ctr - Tom Stosse

Aviation Education Consultants - Harry Whitehead

Fox Valley Technical College - Joe Schmidt

Southern Arkansas Univ. Tech - Bill Archer

Univ. of Alaska, Fairbanks - Kevin Alexander

Sinclair Community College - Don Stark

Introduction to FAA Testing
excerpts from FAA-G-8082-3A

KNOWLEDGE TEST ELIGIBILITY REQUIREMENTS

The general qualifications for an aviation maintenance technician certificate require you to have a combination of experience, knowledge, and skill. If you are pursuing an aviation maintenance technician certificate with airframe and powerplant ratings, you should review the appropriate sections of Title 14 of the Code of Federal Regulations (14 CFR) part 65 for detailed information pertaining to eligibility requirements. Further information may be obtained from the nearest Flight Standards District Office (FSDO). Before taking the certification knowledge and practical tests, you must meet the eligibility requirements. The determination of eligibility of applicants for the general, airframe, and powerplant tests is made on the basis of one of the following options:

1. Civil and/or military experience. (See 14 CFR Part 65, Certification: Airmen Other Than Flight Crewmembers, Subpart A—General and Subpart D— Mechanics.) If you believe you are qualified to exercise this option, you must have your experience evaluated and certified by an FAA aviation safety inspector (airworthiness). If the inspector determines that you have the required experience, two FAA Forms 8610-2, Airman Certificate and/or Rating Application, are completed. These forms are issued, and MUST be presented along with appropriate identification to take the corresponding knowledge tests. Your eligibility to test does not expire.

2. Graduation from an FAA-certificated aviation maintenance technician school (AMTS). Depending upon the testing facility affiliation, a graduation certificate, certificate of completion, or an FAA Form 8610-2, Airman Certificate and/or Rating Application (properly endorsed), is required, along with proper identification.

If you are taking the tests at a computer testing center and the practical testing is administered by a designated mechanic examiner (DME), and *both* are affiliated with the AMTS, a copy of the graduation certificate or certificate of completion (and proper identification) may be all that you are required to present. In this case, the school, the testing center, the DME, and the local FSDO will all be involved and know what authorization is needed. On the other hand, if either or both the testing center and the DME are *not* affiliated with the AMTS, then FAA Form 8610-2 is required.

KNOWLEDGE AREAS ON THE TESTS

Aviation maintenance technician tests are comprehensive because they must test your knowledge in many subject areas. The subject areas for the tests are the same as the required AMTS curriculum subjects listed in 14 CFR part 147, Aviation Maintenance Technician Schools, appendices B, C, and D. However, the subject area titled "Unducted Fans" (in appendix D) is not a tested subject at this time. The terms used in 14 CFR part 147, appendices B, C, and D, are defined in 14 CFR part 147, appendix A.

DESCRIPTIONS OF THE TESTS

All test questions are the objective, multiple-choice type. Each question can be answered by the selection of a single response. Each test question is independent of other questions; therefore, a correct response to one does not depend upon, or influence, the correct response to another.

The Aviation Maintenance Technician—General test contains 60 questions, and you are allowed 2 hours to complete the test.

The Aviation Maintenance Technician—Airframe and Aviation Maintenance Technician— Powerplant tests contain 100 questions each, and you are allowed 2 hours to complete each test.

The minimum passing score is 70 percent.

TEST REGISTRATION

The first step in taking a knowledge test is the registration process. You may either call one of the computer testing designees, or simply use the walk-in basis. If you choose to register by phone, you will need to select a testing center, schedule a test date, and make financial arrangements for test payment. You may register for tests several weeks in advance, and you may cancel your appointment according to the CTD's cancellation policy. If you do not follow the CTD's cancellation policies, you could be subject to a cancellation fee.

The next step in taking a knowledge test is providing proper identification. An acceptable identification document includes a recent photograph, signature, and actual residential address, if different from the mailing address. This information may be presented in more than one form of identification. Acceptable forms of identification include, but are not limited to, drivers' licenses, government identification cards, passports, alien residency (green) cards, and military identification cards. Other forms of identification that meet the requirements of this paragraph are acceptable. Some applicants may not possess the identification documentation described. In any case, you should always check with your local FSDO or IFO if you are unsure of the kind of identification to bring to the interview. You also need to present authorization to test. Acceptable forms of authorization are:
* FAA Form 8610-2.
* A graduation certificate or certificate of completion to an affiliated testing center as previously explained.
* An original (not photocopy) failed Airman Knowledge Test Report, passing Airman Knowledge Test Report, or expired Airman Knowledge Test Report.

Before you take the actual test, you will have the option to take a sample test. The actual test is time limited; however, you should have sufficient time to complete and review your test.

TAKING THE TEST
Communication between individuals through the use of words is a complicated process. In addition to being an exercise in the application and use of aeronautical knowledge, a knowledge test is also an exercise in communication since it involves the use of the written language. Since the tests involve written rather than spoken words, communication between the test writer and the person being tested may become a difficult matter if care is not exercised by both parties. Consequently, considerable effort is expended to write each question in a clear, precise manner. Make sure you read the instructions given with the test, as well as the statements in each test item. When taking a test, keep the following points in mind:
* Answer each question in accordance with the latest regulations and guidance publications.
* Read each question carefully before looking at the answer options. You should clearly understand the problem before attempting to solve it.
* After formulating an answer, determine which answer option corresponds with your answer. The answer you choose should completely resolve the problem.
* From the answer options given, it may appear that there is more than one possible answer; however, there is only one answer that is correct and complete. The other answers are either incomplete, erroneous, or derived from popular misconceptions.
* If a certain question is difficult for you, it is best to mark it for review and proceed to the next question. After you answer the less difficult questions, return to those you marked for review and answer them. The review marking procedure will be explained to you prior to starting the test. Although the computer should alert you to unanswered questions, make sure every question has an answer recorded. This procedure will enable you to use the available time to maximum advantage.
* When solving a calculation problem, select the answer that most nearly matches your solution. The problem has been checked by various individuals and with different types of calculators; therefore, if you have solved it correctly, your answer will be closer to the correct answer than any of the other choices.

USE OF TEST AIDS AND MATERIALS
You may use aids, reference materials, and test materials within the guidelines listed below, if actual test questions or answers are not revealed. All models of aviation oriented calculators may be used, including small electronic calculators that perform only arithmetic functions (add, subtract, multiply, and divide). Simple programmable memories, which allow addition to, subtraction from, or retrieval of one number from the memory, are permissible. Also, simple functions such as square root and percent keys are permissible.

The following guidelines apply:

1. You may use any reference materials provided with the test. In addition, you may use scales, straightedges, protractors, plotters, and electronic or mechanical calculators that are directly related to the test.

2. Manufacturer's permanently inscribed instructions on the front and back of such aids (e.g., formulas, conversions, and weight and balance formulas) are permissible.

3. Testing centers may provide a calculator to you and/or deny use of your personal calculator based on the following limitations:

    a. Prior to and upon completion of the test while in the presence of the proctor, you must actuate the ON/OFF switch and perform any other function that ensures erasure of any data stored in memory circuits.

    b. The use of electronic calculators incorporating permanent or continuous type memory circuits without erasure capability is prohibited. The proctor may refuse the use of your calculator when unable to determine the calculator's erasure capability.

    c. Printouts of data must be surrendered at the completion of the test if the calculator incorporates this design feature.

    d. The use of magnetic cards, magnetic tapes, modules, computer chips, or any other device upon which prewritten programs or information related to the test can be stored and retrieved is prohibited.

    e. You are not permitted to use any booklet or manual containing instructions related to use of test aids.

4. Dictionaries are not allowed in the testing area.

5. The proctor makes the final determination relating to test materials and items you may take into the testing area.

CHEATING OR OTHER UNAUTHORIZED CONDUCT

Computer testing centers are required to follow strict security procedures to avoid test compromise. The FAA has directed testing centers to terminate a test at any time a test proctor suspects a cheating incident has occurred. An FAA investigation will then be conducted. If the investigation determines that unauthorized conduct has occurred, then any airman certificate or rating that you hold may be revoked, and you will be prohibited for 1 year from applying for or taking any test for a certificate or rating.

KNOWLEDGE TEST REPORTS

Upon completion of the knowledge test, you will receive your Airman Knowledge Test Report, which reflects your score.

The Airman Knowledge Test Report lists the learning statement codes for questions answered incorrectly. The total number of learning statement codes shown on the Airman Knowledge Test Report is not necessarily an indication of the total number of questions answered incorrectly.

The Airman Knowledge Test Report must be presented to the examiner prior to taking the practical test. During the oral portion of the practical test, the examiner is required to evaluate the noted areas of deficiency.

Should you require a duplicate Airman Knowledge Test Report due to loss or destruction of the original, send a signed request accompanied by a check or money order for $1 payable to the FAA. Your request should be sent to:

Federal Aviation Administration
Airmen Certification Branch, AFS-760
P.O. Box 25082
Oklahoma City, OK 73125

Airman Knowledge Test Reports are valid for the 24-calendar-month period preceding the month you complete the practical test. If the Airman Knowledge Test Report expires before completion of the practical test, you must retake the knowledge test.

RETESTING PROCEDURES

* You may retake the test after 30 days from the date your last test was taken by presenting your failed Airman Knowledge Test Report.

* You may retest sooner than 30 days if you present your failed Airman Knowledge Test Report and a signed statement from an airman holding the certificate and rating you seek certifying that you have been given additional instruction in each subject failed and that you are now ready for retesting.

If you decide to retake a test you passed in anticipation of a better score, you may retake the test after 30 days from the date your last test was taken. The FAA will not allow you to retake a passed test before the 30-day period has lapsed. Prior to retesting, you must give your current Airman Knowledge Test Report to the test proctor. The score from the last test taken will be the official score.

Knowledge Test Centers

The following is a list of the computer testing designees authorized to give FAA airman knowledge tests. This list should be helpful in case you choose to register for a test or simply want more information.

Computer Assisted Testing Service (CATS)
1801 Murchison Drive, Suite 288
Burlingame, CA 94010
(650) 259-8550

LaserGrade Computer Testing
16821 SE McGillivray Blvd., Suite 201
Vancouver, WA 98683
(360) 896-9111

Learning Statement Codes for A&P Mechanic – Powerplant

Learning statement codes replace the old subject matter codes and are noted on the test report. They refer to measurable statements of knowledge that a student should be able to demonstrate following a defined element of training. The learning statement corresponding to the learning statement code is on the test report.

AMP001	aircraft alternators - components / operating principles / characteristics
AMP002	aircraft batteries - capacity / charging / types / storage / rating / precautions
AMP003	aircraft carburetor - icing / anti-icing
AMP004	aircraft component markings
AMP005	aircraft cooling system - components / operating principles / characteristics
AMP006	aircraft electrical system - install / inspect / repair / service
AMP007	aircraft engine - inspections / cleaning
AMP008	aircraft engines - components / operating principles / characteristics
AMP009	aircraft engines - indicating system
AMP010	aircraft fire classifications
AMP011	aircraft hydraulic systems - components / operating principles / characteristics
AMP012	aircraft instruments - types / components / operating principles / characteristics / markings
AMP013	airflow systems - Bellmouth compressor inlet
AMP014	airframe - inspections
AMP015	altitude compensator / aneroid valve
AMP016	anti-icing / deicing - methods / systems
AMP017	Auxiliary Power Units - components / operating principles / characteristics
AMP018	Auxiliary Power Units - install / inspect / repair / service
AMP019	axial flow compressor - components / operating principles / characteristics

AMP020	basic physics - matter / energy / gas
AMP021	carburetor - effects of carburetor heat / heat control
AMP022	carburetors - components / operating principles / characteristics
AMP023	carburetors - install / inspect / repair / service
AMP024	data - approved
AMP025	DC electric motors - components / operating principles / characteristics
AMP026	electrical system - components / operating principles / characteristics
AMP027	engine cooling system - components / operating principles / characteristics
AMP028	engine cooling system - install / inspect / repair / service
AMP029	engine lubricating oils - function / grades / viscosity / types
AMP030	engine lubricating system - components / operating principles / characteristics
AMP031	engine lubricating system - install / inspect / repair / service
AMP032	engine operations - thrust / thrust reverser
AMP033	engine pressure ratio - EPR
AMP034	fire detection system - types / components / operating principles / characteristics
AMP035	fire detection systems - install / inspect / repair / service
AMP036	fire extinguishing systems - components / operating principles / characteristics
AMP037	float type carburetor - components / operating principles / characteristics
AMP038	float type carburetor - install / inspect / repair / service
AMP039	fuel - types / characteristics / contamination / fueling / defueling / dumping
AMP040	fuel / oil - anti-icing / deicing
AMP041	fuel system - components / operating principles / characteristics
AMP042	fuel system - install / troubleshoot / service / repair
AMP043	fuel system - types
AMP044	generator system - components / operating principles / characteristics
AMP045	information on an Airworthiness Directive
AMP046	magneto - components / operating principles / characteristics
AMP047	magneto - install / inspect / repair / service
AMP048	maintenance publications - service / parts / repair
AMP049	piston assembly - components / operating principles / characteristics
AMP050	powerplant design - structures / components
AMP051	pressure type carburetor - components / operating principles / characteristics
AMP052	propeller system - install / inspect / repair / service
AMP053	propeller system - types/ components / operating principles / characteristics

AMP054	radial engine - components / operating principles / characteristics
AMP055	radial engine - install / inspect / repair / service
AMP056	reciprocating engine - components / operating principles / characteristics
AMP057	reciprocating engine - install / inspect / repair / service
AMP058	regulations - maintenance reports / records / entries
AMP059	regulations - privileges / limitations of maintenance certificates / licenses
AMP060	regulations - privileges of approved maintenance organizations
AMP061	rotor system - components / operating principles / characteristics
AMP062	sea level - standard temperature / pressure
AMP063	starter / ignition system - components / operating principles / characteristics
AMP064	starter / ignition system - install / inspect / repair / service
AMP065	starter system - starting procedures
AMP066	thermocouples - components / operating principles / characteristics
AMP067	thermocouples - install / inspect / repair / service
AMP068	turbine engines - components / operational characteristics / associated instruments
AMP069	turbine engines - install / inspect / repair / service / hazards
AMP070	turbocharger system - components / operating principles / characteristics
AMP071	turbojet - components / operating principles / characteristics
AMP072	type certificate data sheet (TCDS) / supplemental
AMP073	welding types / techniques / equipment

CHAPTER 1

Aircraft Engines

Types of Engines, Connecting Rods, Piston Rings, Firing Order, Valves and Valve Operating Mechanisms, Bearings, Propellers, Efficiencies

1-1) AMP008

The general requirements for an aircraft engine include efficiency, reliability, and a low weight-to-horsepower ratio. It also must

- A. have a short time between overhauls, easy access for maintenance, and a wide range of power output at various speeds and altitudes.
- B. have good fuel economy, high durability, and be capable of sustained high power output.
- C. be compact, efficient, and have a narrow range of power output at a specific speed.

1-2) AMP056

The heat engine used predominantly in aviation is the

- A. Radial engine.
- B. O-type engine.
- C. V-type engine.

1-3) AMP008

The crankcase of an aircraft engine

- A. houses the valve operating mechanism and the engine cylinders.
- B. is lightweight and primarily used as a reservoir for the engine oil.
- C. is the foundation of the engine containing crankshaft bearings and cylinder pads.

1-4) AMP008

The cylinders of an aircraft engine are mounted on cylinder pads that are machined onto the crankcase. The common method of attachment of the cylinders to the crankcase is

- A. by studs mounted in threaded holes in the crankcase.
- B. by bolts into locking helicoils mounted in the crankcase.
- C. by heating the crankcase and cooling the cylinder for an interference fit.

1-5) AMP008

The crankpin is

- A. used to ensure the crankshaft does not shift in the crankcase.
- B. a solid, heavy journal to withstand crankshaft shock loads.
- C. hardened by nitriding and is hollow to reduce weight.

1-6) AMP008

Which statement is correct about radial engine crankshafts?

- A. Moveable counterweights serve to reduce the torsional vibrations in an aircraft reciprocating engine.
- B. Moveable counterweights serve to reduce the dynamic vibrations in an aircraft reciprocating engine.
- C. Moveable counterweights are designed to resonate at the natural frequency of the crankshaft.

1 - Aircraft Engines
Answers

1-1) B.

All of the characteristics listed in the answer choices for this question are general requirements for aircraft engines except for two: In answer A, a long time between overhauls reduces the frequency of maintenance which lowers operating costs, making this preferable to having a short time between overhauls. In answer C, aircraft engines should cover a wide range of power outputs at various speeds and altitudes rather than a narrow range at a specific speed.

[For more detailed information refer to Powerplant Handbook H-8083-32-ATB, Chapter 1 p.2]

1-2) B.

There are many methods of aircraft engine classification, and classification of engines by cylinder arrangement is common. The "O"-type or Opposed engine has cylinders arranged on opposite sides of the crankshaft, 180˚ opposed to each other. This compact shaped, low vibration engine is found on most light aircraft.

[For more detailed information refer to Powerplant Handbook H-8083-32-ATB, Chapter 1 p.4]

1-3) C.

The cast or forged crankcase is the foundation of the aircraft engine. It contains the bearings which support the crankshaft. Cylinders are bolted to the crankcase and the crankcase provides the attach points for the engine to be secured to the airframe. As such it must be very strong to receive the many variations of mechanical loads and forces from these components while keeping the crankshaft stable. The crankcase does act as a reservoir for the engine oil, but with all of its other functions and relatively heavyweight construction, this is not the crankcase's primary function.

[For more detailed information refer to Powerplant Handbook H-8083-32-ATB, Chapter 1 p.5]

1-4) A.

Several studs are installed into the crankcase around the circumference of each machined cylinder pad. These are used to mount the cylinders securely to the crankcase with nuts. The inner portion of a cylinder pad may be chamfered or tapered to permit the installation of a large rubber O-ring around the cylinder skirt. This seals the joint between the cylinder and the crankcase pad against oil leakage.

[For more detailed information refer to Powerplant Handbook H-8083-32-ATB, Chapter 1 p.7]

1-5) C.

Crankpins are the machined journals on the crankshaft to which the piston connecting rods are attached. They are off center from the main journal. The two crank cheeks and the crankpin together make a "throw". When the force of combustion is applied to the crankpin, it causes the crankshaft to rotate. Crankpins are hardened by nitriding to resist wear and are hollow to keep the total weight of the crankshaft as light as possible. The hollow crankpin also permits the passage of oil as it turns in the crankcase.

[For more detailed information refer to Powerplant Handbook H-8083-32-ATB, Chapter 1 p.9]

1-6) B.

Vibration occurs as the crankshaft rotates due to the forces of combustion acting on the pistons, connecting rods, and crankpins. These power impulses cause even a statically balanced crankshaft to vibrate. Moveable counterweights are dynamic dampeners are located in the counterweight lobes of the crankshaft. Using pendulum motion, the dampeners oscillate out of time with the crankshaft vibration thus reducing overall vibration.

[For more detailed information refer to Powerplant Handbook H-8083-32-ATB, Chapter 1 p.10]

1-7) AMP056

Master rod bearings are generally what type of bearing?

- A. Plain.
- B. Roller.
- C. Ball.

1-8) AMP056

Cam ground pistons are installed in some aircraft engines to

- A. provide a better fit at operating temperatures.
- B. act as a compensating feature so that a compensated magneto is not required.
- C. equalize the wear on all pistons.

1-9) AMP056

Full-floating piston pins are those which allow motion between the pin and

- A. the piston
- B. the piston and the large end of the connecting rod.
- C. the piston and the small end of the connecting rod.

1-10) AMP056

How is oil collected by the piston oil ring returned to the crankcase?

- A. Down vertical slots cut in the piston wall between the piston oil ring groove and the piston skirt.
- B. Through holes drilled in the piston oil ring groove.
- C. Through holes drilled in the piston pin recess.

1-11) AMP056

Some cylinder barrels are hardened by

- A. nitriding.
- B. shot peening.
- C. tempering.

1-12) AMP056

The primary concern in establishing the firing order for an opposed engine is to

- A. provide for balance and eliminate vibration to the greatest extent possible.
- B. keep power impulses on adjacent cylinders as far apart as possible in order to obtain the greatest mechanical efficiency.
- C. keep the power impulses on adjacent cylinders as close as possible in order to obtain the greatest mechanical efficiency.

1-7) A.

The master rod bearings refer to the bearing located on the crankpin end and the piston end of the master connecting rod commonly found in radial engines. Whether of solid or split design, plain bearings are used to mate with the crankpin journal of the crankshaft. The piston pin end of the master rod uses a plain bearing usually called a bushing to mate with the piston pin.

[For more detailed information refer to Powerplant Handbook H-8083-32-ATB, Chapter 1 p.23]

1-8) A.

Modern engines use cam ground pistons that have a larger diameter perpendicular to the piston pin. This larger diameter keeps the piston straight in the cylinder as the engine warms up from initial start. As the piston heats up during warm up, the part of the piston in line with the piston pin has more mass. It expands more than the piston area perpendicular to the piston pin making the piston completely round at operating temperature.

[For more detailed information refer to Powerplant Handbook H-8083-32-ATB, Chapter 1 p.13]

1-9) C.

The piston pins used in modern aircraft engines are the full-floating type, so called because the pin is free to rotate in both the piston and in the connecting rod piston pin bearing which is the small end of the connecting rod. As such, full floating piston pins must be held in place to prevent the pin ends from scoring the cylinder walls. This is accomplished with soft aluminum plugs on each end of the piston pin.

[For more detailed information refer to Powerplant Handbook H-8083-32-ATB, Chapter 1 p.14]

1-10) B.

Oil control rings are located just below the compression rings but above the piston pin on the typical aircraft piston. They regulate the thickness of the oil film on the cylinder wall. This keeps excessive oil from entering the combustion chamber past the compression rings. To allow the surplus oil to return to the crankcase, holes are drilled in the bottom of the oil control piston ring grooves or in the lands next to these grooves.

[For more detailed information refer to Powerplant Handbook H-8083-32-ATB, Chapter 1 p.14]

1-11) A.

A cylinder barrel in an aircraft engine is made from a steel alloy forging with the inner surface, hardened to resist wear caused by the piston and piston rings which bear against it. The hardening is usually done by exposing the steel to ammonia or cyanide gas while the steel is very hot. The steel soaks up the nitrogen from the gas, forming iron nitride on the exposed surface of the barrel. Thus, the steel is said to be nitrided. This nitriding only penetrates into the cylinder barrel surface a few thousandths of an inch.

[For more detailed information refer to Powerplant Handbook H-8083-32-ATB, Chapter 1 p.16]

1-12) A.

The firing order of an engine is the sequence in which the power event occurs in the different cylinders. The firing order is designed to provide balance and to eliminate vibration to the greatest extent possible.

[For more detailed information refer to Powerplant Handbook H-8083-32-ATB, Chapter 1 p.17]

1-13) AMP056

What is an advantage of using metallic sodium filled exhaust valves in aircraft reciprocating engines?

A. Increased strength and resistance to cracking.
B. Reduced valve operating temperature.
C. Greater resistance to deterioration at high valve temperature.

1-14) AMP056

What is the purpose of the stem keys installed on the valve stems?

A. To hold the valve guide in position.
B. To hold the valve spring retaining washer in position.
C. To prevent valves from falling into the combustion chamber.

1-15) AMP056

The purpose of two or more valve springs in aircraft engines is to

A. equalize side pressure on the valve stems.
B. eliminate valve spring surge.
C. equalize valve face loading.

1-16) AMP056

The tappet assembly

A. presses against the valve stem tip to open and close the valve.
B. converts rotational movement of the cam lob into reciprocating motion.
C. is located in the cylinder head on an overhead valve engine.

1-17) AMP056

Excessive valve clearance in a piston engine

A. increases valve overlap.
B. increases valve opening time.
C. decreases valve overlap.

1-18) AMP056

Valve clearance changes on opposed-type engines using hydraulic lifters are accomplished by

A. adjusting the rocker arm.
B. replacing the rocker arm.
C. replacing the push rod.

1-13) B.

Some intake and exhaust valves are hollow and partially filled with metallic sodium. This material is used because it is an excellent heat conductor. The sodium melts at 208˚F. The reciprocating motion of the valve circulates the liquid sodium, allowing it to carry heat away from the valve head and into the stem, where the heat is dissipated through the valve guide to the cylinder head and the cooling fins. Operating temperature of a sodium filled valve may be reduced as much as 300˚F to 400˚F.

[For more detailed information refer to Powerplant Handbook H-8083-32-ATB, Chapter 1 p.18]

1-14) B.

The valve stem acts as a pilot for the valve head and rides the valve guide installed in the cylinder head. The stem is surface-hardened to resist wear. A machined groove near the tip of the valve stem opposite the valve head receives the split-ring stem keys. These stem keys form a lock ring to hold the valve spring retaining washer in place.

[For more detailed information refer to Powerplant Handbook H-8083-32-ATB, Chapter 1 p.18]

1-15) B.

Valve springs which slip over the stem of the valves are held in place by the valve spring retaining washer and stem key. The springs hold the valves closed when not forced open via the valve operating mechanism. Any single spring will surge at certain engine speeds, allowing a less that tight seating of the closed valve. By using two or more valve springs on each valve stem, while one spring may be surging at a certain engine RPM, the other(s) will not, due to variation in mass and construction. Thus oscillations are dampened with the added protection of one or more extra springs should one of the springs break.

[For more detailed information refer to Powerplant Handbook H-8083-32-ATB, Chapter 1 p.22]

1-16) B.

The tappet assembly is located in the crankcase and typically contains a cylindrical tappet, a tappet guide, and with some newer engines a tappet roller or face that follows the contour of the cam lobes and a tappet spring. The function of the tappet assembly is to convert the rotational movement of the cam lobe into reciprocating motion and to transmit this motion to the push rod, rocker arm, and then to the valve tip, thus opening the valve at the proper time.

[For more detailed information refer to Powerplant Handbook H-8083-32-ATB, Chapter 1 p.21]

1-17) C.

Reciprocating aircraft engines that use solid lifters or tappets generally require that the clearance between the rocker arm and the valve tip is adjusted to ensure that the valve can fully close. If the clearance is too great, the valve operating mechanism must span this distance which causes the valve timing to be late. The valve will open late and close early. Valve overlap refers to the time period when both the intake and exhaust valve are open. Late opening and early closing of the valves reduces valve overlap.

[For more detailed information refer to Powerplant Handbook H-8083-32-ATB, Chapter 1 p.21]

1-18) C.

Hydraulic lifters are normally adjusted at the time of overhaul. They are assembled dry (no lubrication), clearances checked, and adjustments made by using pushrods of different lengths. A minimum and maximum valve clearance is established in this dry condition. Any measurement between these extremes is acceptable, but a pushrod that creates a clearance halfway between the minimum and maximum extremes is desired. Once assembled with the engine running, the hydraulic lifters are filled with oil; this removes the clearance and provides a quiet, lubricated, low maintenance valve operating mechanism.

[For more detailed information refer to Powerplant Handbook H-8083-32-ATB, Chapter 1 p.22]

1-19) AMP054

Which of the following is a characteristic of a thrust bearing used in most radial engines?

    A. Tapered roller.
    B. Double-row ball.
    C. Deep-grooved ball.

1-20) AMP053

What is the primary advantage of using propeller reduction gears?

    A. To enable the propeller RPM to be increased without an accompanying increase in engine RPM.
    B. To enable the engine RPM to be increased with an accompanying increase in power and allow the propeller shaft to remain at a lower RPM.
    C. To enable the engine RPM to be increased with an accompanying increase in propeller RPM.

1-21) AMP053

Which type of propeller shaft is used on most modern reciprocating and turboprop engines?

    A. Tapered.
    B. Splined.
    C. Flanged.

1-22) AMP056

The five events of a four stroke cycle engine, in the order of their occurrence, are

    A. intake, ignition, compression, power, exhaust.
    B. intake, power, compression, ignition, exhaust.
    C. intake, compression, ignition, power, exhaust.

1 - Aircraft Engines
Answers

1-19) C.
Special deep-grooved ball bearings are used to transmit propeller thrust and radial loads to the engine nose section of radial engines. This type of bearing can accept both radial and thrust loads with minimal friction.
[For more detailed information refer to Powerplant Handbook H-8083-32-ATB, Chapter 1 p.23]

1-20) B.
Increased brake horsepower of an engine results partially from increased crankshaft RPM. However, increasing crankshaft RPM without regard to propeller speed can cause propeller inefficiency--as propeller tip speed approaches the speed of sound, the prop becomes less efficient. Reduction gearing allows the engine RPM to be increased to extract maximum power while rotating the propeller at a slower speed than the crankshaft.
[For more detailed information refer to Powerplant Handbook H-8083-32-ATB, Chapter 1 p.24]

1-21) C.
For A, the propeller shaft of most low power output engines is forged as part of the engine crankshaft--the propeller shaft is a tapered shaft with a milled slot for keying the prop hub to the shaft and the end of the shaft is threaded to accept a nut that secures the prop to the shaft. For B, high output radial engine propeller shafts are generally splined to receive the prop hub, and they also have a threaded end to accept a retaining nut. The answer is C: flanged propeller shafts are used on most modern reciprocating and turboprop engines. One end of the shaft is flanged with drilled holes to accept propeller mounting bolts.
[For more detailed information refer to Powerplant Handbook H-8083-32-ATB, Chapter 1 p.24]

1-22) C.
The four-strokes plus the ignition event are the five events of a four-stroke cycle engine. In order of occurrence, the 5 events are: The Intake Stroke, The Compression Stroke, Ignition, The Power Stroke and The Exhaust Stroke. During the intake stroke, the crankshaft rotates and the piston moves down away from the top of the cylinder. As it does, it draws in a gaseous fuel/air charge through an open intake valve. As the piston nears the bottom of the cylinder, the intake valve closes and the piston reverses direction to begin the compression stroke. The fuel/air charge, trapped between the piston and the cylinder walls, compresses as the piston moves upward toward the cylinder head. Just before top center of the stroke, the spark plug fires which lights off the compressed charge. The energy released by the burning of the fuel air mixture forces the piston down toward the bottom of the cylinder during the power stroke--the heat energy is thus transferred to the crankshaft. The exhaust valve opens and the burnt gases are forced out of the cylinder as the piston returns to the top of the cylinder during the exhaust stroke.
[For more detailed information refer to Powerplant Handbook H-8083-32-ATB, Chapter 1 p.28]

1-23) AMP056

On which stroke are both valves on a four-stroke cycle reciprocating engine open?

    A. Power and exhaust.
    B. Intake and compression.
    C. Intake and exhaust.

1-24) AMP056

If fuel/air ratio is proper and ignition timing is correct, the combustion process should be completed

    A. 20° to 30° before top center at the end of the compression stroke.
    B. when the exhaust valve opens at the end of the power stroke.
    C. just after top center at the beginning of the power stroke.

1-25) AMP056

The actual power delivered to the propeller of an aircraft engine is called

    A. friction horsepower.
    B. brake horsepower.
    C. indicated horsepower.

1-26) AMP056

The compression ratio of an engine is equal to

    A. the volume of the cylinder multiplied by the manifold pressure.
    B. the volume of the combustion chamber multiplied by the manifold pressure.
    C. the volume of the cylinder with the piston at BDC divided by the volume of the cylinder at TDC.

1-27) AMP056

The volume of a cylinder equals 70 cubic inches when the piston is at bottom center. When the piston is at the top of the cylinder, the volume equals 10 cubic inches. What is the compression ratio?

    A. 1:7.
    B. 7:10.
    C. 7:1.

1 - Aircraft Engines

Answers

1-23) C.

The valve timing chart in Figure 1-37 of FAA-H-8083-32 illustrates when the valves open during the four stroke of the engine and upon what strokes both valves are open at the same time, which is known as valve overlap. On a typical reciprocating engine, the intake valve opens just before the piston reaches TDC (Top Dead Center) on the exhaust stroke. The exhaust valve opens just before the exhaust stroke begins and stays open until a little after the exhaust stroke is complete. This means the exhaust valve is open as the intake stroke begins, so both valves are open during a part of the exhaust stroke and a part of the intake stroke.

[For more detailed information refer to Powerplant Handbook H-8083-32-ATB, Chapter 1 p.27]

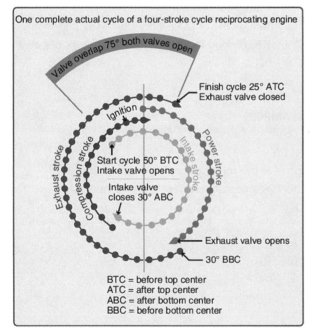

Figure 1-37. Valve timing chart.

1-24) C.

The time of ignition varies from 20° to 30° before TDC (depending upon the requirements of the specific engine) to ensure complete combustion of the charge by the time the piston is slightly past the TDC position.

[For more detailed information refer to Powerplant Handbook H-8083-32-ATB, Chapter 1 p.27]

1-25) B.

Indicated horsepower is the term used to describe the theoretical output of an engine. The total horsepower lost in overcoming friction (friction horsepower) must be subtracted from the indicated horsepower to arrive at the actual horsepower delivered to the propeller by the engine. This is known as brake horsepower.

[For more detailed information refer to Powerplant Handbook H-8083-32-ATB, Chapter 1 p.28]

1-26) C.

All internal combustion engines must compress the fuel/air mixture to receive a reasonable amount of work from each power stroke. The fuel/air charge in the cylinder can be compared to a coil spring. The more it is compressed, the more work it is potentially capable of doing. A comparison of the volume of the cylinder at bottom dead center (BDC) and at top dead center (TDC) of a stroke describes the amount of compression developed. Compression ratio is a controlling factor in the maximum horsepower developed by an engine.

[For more detailed information refer to Powerplant Handbook H-8083-32-ATB, Chapter 1 p.30]

1-27) C.

By definition, compression ratio is expressed as a ratio. The first number in the ratio is the total volume of the cylinder with the piston at BDC – the larger number. The second number is the total volume of the cylinder with the piston at TDC – the smaller number. The small number is divided into the larger number to reduce the ratio into the smallest integers possible.

[For more detailed information refer to Powerplant Handbook H-8083-32-ATB, Chapter 1 p.30]

1-28) AMP056
How many of the following are factors in establishing the maximum compression ratio limitations of an aircraft engine?
1. Detonation characteristics of the fuel used.
2. Design limitations of the engine.
3. Degree of supercharging.
4. Spark plug reach.

    A. 4.
    B. 2.
    C. 3.

1-29) AMP056
The horsepower developed in the cylinders of a reciprocating engine is known as the

    A. shaft horsepower.
    B. indicated horsepower.
    C. brake horsepowe.r

1-30) AMP056
Friction horsepower

    A. is insignificant when considering the actual power output of an engine.
    B. is not included in the calculation of brake horsepower.
    C. may be as high as 10-15% of the indicated horsepower on a modern aircraft engine.

1-31) AMP056
The type of horsepower that determines the performance of the engine – propeller combination is

    A. brake horsepower.
    B. thrust horsepower.
    C. indicated horsepower.

1-32) AMP056
The thermal efficiency of an engine

    A. affects the fuel consumption of an engine.
    B. is a fixed amount directly related to the heat energy of the fuel.
    C. results in less of the heat energy in the fuel being used.

1-33) AMP056
Which of the following will decrease volumetric efficiency in a reciprocating engine?
1. Full throttle operation.
2. Low cylinder head temperature.
3. Improper valve timing.
4. Sharp bends in the induction system.
5. High carburetor air temperatures.

    A. 2, 4, and 5.
    B. 3, 4, and 5.
    C. 1, 2, 3, and 4.

1 - Aircraft Engines
Answers

1-28) C.

Manifold pressure is the average absolute pressure of the air or fuel air charge supplying the engine. Combined with the compression ratio, the total pressure inside the combustion chamber of the engine is determined. Design limitations prevent unlimited pressure inside the engine. Since supercharging affects manifold pressure and fuels have various characteristics which affect their ability to be compressed without exploding, these three factors limit the maximum compression ratio that can be developed by an engine. The reach of the spark plug will affect the ignition of the compressed charge in an engine that has already been designed with the other three factors taken into consideration, however it does not affect maximum compression ratio.

[For more detailed information refer to Powerplant Handbook H-8083-32-ATB, Chapter 1 p.31]

1-29) B.

The indicated horsepower produced by an engine is the horsepower calculated from the indicated mean effective pressure and other factors which affect the power output of an engine. Indicated horsepower is the power developed in the combustion chambers without reference to frictional losses of the engine. This horsepower is calculated as a function of the actual cylinder pressure recorded during engine operation.

[For more detailed information refer to Powerplant Handbook H-8083-32-ATB, Chapter 1 p.31]

1-30) C.

Friction horsepower is the indicated horsepower minus brake horsepower. It is the horsepower used by an engine in overcoming friction of moving parts, drawing in fuel, expelling exhaust, driving oil and fuel pumps, and other engine accessories. On modern engines, this power loss through friction may be as high as 10 to 15 percent of the indicated horsepower.

[For more detailed information refer to Powerplant Handbook H-8083-32-ATB, Chapter 1 p.33]

1-31) B.

Thrust horsepower can be considered the result of the engine and propeller working together. Efficiency of a propeller varies with engine speed, attitude, altitude, temperature, and airspeed. It is not 100 percent and must be applied to the brake horsepower figure to calculate thrust horsepower.

[For more detailed information refer to Powerplant Handbook H-8083-32-ATB, Chapter 1 p.35]

1-32) A.

Each quantity of fuel contains a finite amount of heat energy which can be extracted by the engine for mechanical work. The ratio of useful work done by an engine to the heat energy of the fuel it uses, expressed in work or heat units, is called the thermal efficiency of the engine. High thermal efficiency results in an engine producing the greatest amount of power with minimal excess heat reaching the valves, cylinders, pistons and cooling system of the engine. It also means low specific fuel consumption, therefore less fuel for a flight of a given distance at a given power setting.

[For more detailed information refer to Powerplant Handbook H-8083-32-ATB, Chapter 1 p.35]

1-33) B.

Volumetric efficiency is a ratio expressed in terms of percentages. It is a comparison of the volume of the fuel/air charge inducted into the cylinder to the total piston displacement of the engine. Since piston displacement is unaffected by external factors, volumetric efficiency is a measure of external factors that reduce the total volume of the fuel/air charge inducted into the engine. Some of these factors are: part throttle operation, long intake pipes of narrow diameter, sharp bends in the induction system, high carburetor air temperature, high cylinder head temperature, incomplete scavenging, and improper valve timing. Full throttle operation and low cylinder head temperatures would increase the volume of the induction charge.

[For more detailed information refer to Powerplant Handbook H-8083-32-ATB, Chapter 1 p.36]

1-34) AMP056

Propulsive efficiency

A. can be maximized through the use of a fixed pitched prop.
B. is a ratio of thrust horsepower to the length of the prop.
C. is maximized through the use of a constant-speed prop.

1-35) AMP068

Most modern airliners that fly in the .8 mach speed range are fitted with

A. turbofan engines.
B. turboprop engines.
C. turboshaft engines.

1-36) AMP068

Looking at the diagram below (Figure 1-43 in FAA-H-8083-32), if this engine had 100 pps of airflow through the fan and 20 pps airflow through the core engine, the Bypass Ratio would be

A. 5:1.
B. Low.
C. 10:3.

1-37) AMP068

Accessories such as electric generators and hydraulic pumps on turbine powered aircraft are

A. driven directly off the turbine shaft.
B. driven at the same speed as the engine using a tower shaft.
C. driven at reduced speed from the high pressure compressor via a reduction gear box.

1-38) AMP068

The primary function of the compressor on a gas turbine engine is to

A. cool the engine.
B. supply air in sufficient for combustion.
C. supply the pressure for cabin environmental purposes.

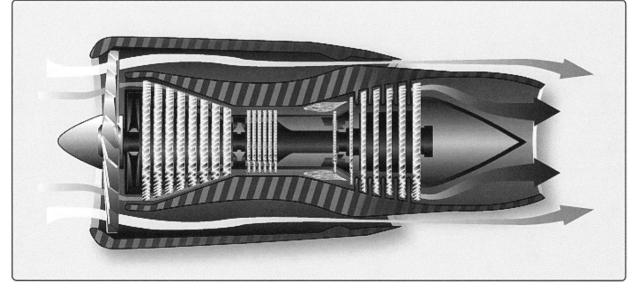

Figure 1-43. Turbofan engine with separate nozzles fan and core.

1 - Aircraft Engines
Answers

1-34) C.
Propeller efficiency affects propulsive efficiency which is defined as the ratio of thrust horsepower to brake horsepower. A constant-speed propeller maximizes propeller efficiency by changing the propeller blade angle to the most efficient angle for the power produced by the engine. This increases thrust horsepower which, by definition, increases propulsive efficiency.
[For more detailed information refer to Powerplant Handbook H-8083-32-ATB, Chapter 1 p.37]

1-35) A.
Differently constructed turbine engines are suited for various aircraft and flying conditions. Most modern airliners use turbofan engines that have at the front of the engine a relatively large diameter fan section. This accounts for the name – turbofan. This type of engine is relatively quiet and has better fuel consumption at the average cruising speed of airline flight. Turboprop engines have greater efficiency at 300-400mph. Turboshaft engine are found on helicopters and auxiliary power units (APUs).
[For more detailed information refer to Powerplant Handbook H-8083-32-ATB, Chapter 1 p.37]

1-36) A.
The bypass ratio of a turbine engine compares the amount of air flow (in pounds per second) from the fan bypass to the amount of air passing through the core of the engine. In the figure, most of the air from the fan passes around the core of the engine making it a high bypass engine. A low bypass engine would send more air through the engine core. A turboprop engine channels all inlet air through the core to develop power to rotate the propeller.
[For more detailed information refer to Powerplant Handbook H-8083-32-ATB, Chapter 1 p.38]

1-37) C.
The accessory section of a gas turbine aircraft has various functions. One of these includes driving accessories concerned with the operation of the aircraft such as electrical generators and hydraulic pumps. The rotational speeds of a turbine engine and its shafts are much greater than the optimum speed for driving rotating accessories. Therefore, turbine engine accessory sections incorporate a series of gears to reduce the speed of the various drives provided for accessories. The gear train is driven by the engine's high pressure compressor through an accessory drive shaft gear coupling.
[For more detailed information refer to Powerplant Handbook H-8083-32-ATB, Chapter 1 p.39]

1-38) B.
The compressor section of a gas turbine engine has many functions. Its primary function is to supply air in sufficient quantities to satisfy the requirements of the combustion burners. Specifically, to fulfill its purpose, the compressor must increase the pressure of the mass of air received from the air inlet duct, and then discharge it to the burner section in the quantities and pressures required. Cooling the engine and supplying air for cabin environmental functions are secondary purposes of the compressor.
[For more detailed information refer to Powerplant Handbook H-8083-32-ATB, Chapter 1 p.39]

1-39) AMP068

What are the two functional elements of the centrifugal flow compressor?

    A. Turbine and Compressor.
    B. Bucket and expander.
    C. Impeller and diffuser.

1-40) AMP068

What is meant by a double entry centrifugal compressor?

    A. A compressor that has two intakes.
    B. A two-stage compressor independently connected to the main shaft.
    C. A compressor with vanes on both sides of the impeller.

1-41) AMP068

Stator blades in the compressor of an axial-flow turbine engine

    A. increase air velocity and prevent swirling.
    B. straighten the airflow and accelerate it.
    C. decrease air velocity and prevent swirling.

1-42) AMP068

What is the function of the inlet guide vane assembly on an axial-flow compressor?

    A. Directs air onto the first stage rotor blades at the proper angle.
    B. Converts velocity energy to pressure energy.
    C. Converts pressure energy to velocity energy.

1-43) AMP068

The non-rotating axial-flow compressor airfoils in an aircraft gas turbine engine, are called

    A. pressurization vanes.
    B. stator vanes.
    C. bleed vanes.

1 - Aircraft Engines

Answers

1-39) C.

A gas turbine engine may use a centrifugal-flow compressor which consists of an impeller (rotor), a diffuser (stator) and a compressor manifold. Although the diffuser is a separate unit from the compressor manifold, it is bolted inside the manifold and the two-piece assembly is referred to as the diffuser (diffuser + manifold). Therefore, the two functional elements are the impeller and the diffuser.

[For more detailed information refer to Powerplant Handbook H-8083-32-ATB, Chapter 1 p.40]

1-40) C.

The impeller in an engine with a centrifugal compressor may be of two types – single entry or double entry. The principal differences between the two types of impellers are size and ducting arrangement. The double entry type has a smaller diameter and is usually operated at higher rotational speed to ensure sufficient airflow. Its impeller has vanes on both sides (i.e. front and back) but requires more complex ducting to have intake air reach both sides. The single entry impeller has simple, conventional inlet ducting but the impeller is of a larger diameter, which increases the overall dimensions of the engine.

[For more detailed information refer to Powerplant Handbook H-8083-32-ATB, Chapter 1 p.40]

1-41) C.

In an axial-flow engine, air flows along an axial path and is compressed at a ratio of approximately 1.25:1 per stage. The action of the rotor increases compression of the air at each stage and accelerates it rearward through several stages. The stator blades act as diffusers at each stage; they partially convert the high velocity to an increase in pressure while ensuring the air is directed smoothly to the next stage without swirling.

[For more detailed information refer to Powerplant Handbook H-8083-32-ATB, Chapter 1 p.41]

1-42) A.

The first stage rotor blades on an axial-flow compressor can be preceded by an inlet guide vane assembly that can be either fixed or variable. The guide vanes help direct the airflow into the first stage rotor blades at the proper angle and establish a swirling motion for the air entering the compressor. This pre-swirl, in the direction of engine rotation, improves the aerodynamic characteristics of the compressor by reducing drag on the first stage rotor blades. The inlet guide vanes are curved steel vanes usually welded to steel inner and outer shrouds.

[For more detailed information refer to Powerplant Handbook H-8083-32-ATB, Chapter 1 p.41]

1-43) B.

The stator has rows of vanes which are attached inside an enclosing case. The stator vanes, which are stationary, project radially toward the rotor axis and fit closely on either side of each stage of the rotor blades.

[For more detailed information refer to Powerplant Handbook H-8083-32-ATB, Chapter 1 p.41]

1-44) AMP019

The compression ratio of an axial flow compressor is a function of the

A. number of compressor stages.
B. rotor diameter.
C. air inlet velocity.

1-45) AMP068

What is the profile of a turbine engine compressor blade?

A. The leading edge of the blade.
B. A cutout that reduces blade tip thickness.
C. The curvature of the blade root.

1-46) AMP068

What is the primary advantage of an axial-flow compressor over a centrifugal flow compressor?

A. High frontal area.
B. Less expensive.
C. Greater pressure ratio.

1-47) AMP068

In the dual axial flow or twin spool compressor system, the first stage turbine drives the

A. N_1 and N_2 compressors.
B. N_2 compressor.
C. N_1 compressor.

1-48) AMP068

What is the purpose of the diffuser section in a turbine engine?

A. To increase pressure and reduce velocity.
B. To convert pressure to velocity.
C. To reduce pressure and increase velocity.

1-49) AMP068

What turbine engine section provides for proper mixing of the fuel and air?

A. Combustion section.
B. Compressor section.
C. Diffuser section.

1 - Aircraft Engines
Answers

1-44) A.

In an axial flow compressor, each consecutive pair of rotor and stator blades constitutes a pressure stage. The number of rows of blades (stages) is determined by the amount of air and total pressure rise required. The compressor pressure ratio increases with the number of compression stages. Most large engines use 16 stages or more.

[For more detailed information refer to Powerplant Handbook H-8083-32-ATB, Chapter 1 p.41]

1-45) B.

Compressor blade tips are reduced in thickness by cutouts, referred to as blade profiles. These profiles prevent serious damage to the blades or housing should the blades contact the compressor housing. Profiling also allows tighter clearances between the blade tips and the compressor case and requires the case interior surface to be lined with a relatively soft material to allow the blades to rub the surface without blade damage.

[For more detailed information refer to Powerplant Handbook H-8083-32-ATB, Chapter 1 p.42]

1-46) C.

In an axial flow engine, at each stage of compression, the air is compressed at a ratio of approximately 1.25 to 1. Each consecutive pair of rotor and stator blades constitutes a pressure stage. The compressor pressure ratio increases with the number of compression stages. Large engines utilize up to 16 stages of compression (or more), and at each stage compression is increased by a ratio of 1.25 to 1 above the previous stage. This gives an axial flow engine the ability to have a much higher overall compression ratio than a centrifugal engine which typically has one stage of compression at approximately an 8 to 1 pressure increase.

[For more detailed information refer to Powerplant Handbook H-8083-32-ATB, Chapter 1 p.43]

1-47) B.

A spool in a split spool or twin spool engine refers to a turbine section, the compressor it drives, and the interconnecting shaft between the two. Each spool is independent of the other. The first stage turbine wheel is located immediately downstream of the combustion section of the engine--it receives the most energy from the combusted gases and, therefore, drives the high pressure compressor which is known as the N_2 compressor. The second stage turbine is behind or downstream of the first stage turbine--it receives less energy from the combusted gases since the gases have already passed through the first stage turbine. The second stage turbine drives the low pressure compressor, which is known as the N_1 compressor.

[For more detailed information refer to Powerplant Handbook H-8083-32-ATB, Chapter 1 p.43]

1-48) A.

The diffuser is the divergent section of the engine after the compressor but before the combustion section. Its function is to increase air pressure at a slower velocity. This prepares the air for the combustion section of the engine where it is mixed with fuel and burned. A continuous burn is desired and the slower velocity air allows the flame to persist without being extinguished and prevents the combustion process from moving forward into the compressor.

[For more detailed information refer to Powerplant Handbook H-8083-32-ATB, Chapter 1 p.44]

1-49) A.

The primary function of the combustion section of a gas turbine engine is to burn the fuel/air mixture, thereby adding heat energy to the air. To do this efficiently, the combustion chamber must provide the means for proper mixing of the fuel and air to ensure good combustion.

[For more detailed information refer to Powerplant Handbook H-8083-32-ATB, Chapter 1 p.44]

1-50) AMP068

The air passing through the combustion chamber of a turbine engine is

A. used to support combustion and to cool the engine.
B. entirely combined with fuel and burned.
C. speeded up and heated by the action of the turbines.

1-51) AMP068

The highest heat to metal contacts in a jet engine are the

A. burner cans.
B. turbine inlet nozzle vanes.
C. turbine blades.

1-52) AMP068

Turbine nozzle diaphrams located on the upstream side of each turbine wheel are used in the gas turbine engine to

A. decrease the velocity of the heated gases flowing past this point.
B. direct the flow of gases parallel to the vertical line of the turbine blades.
C. increase the velocity of the gases flowing past this point.

1-53) AMP068

Reduced blade vibration and improved airflow characteristics in a gas turbine engine are brought about by

A. fir-tree blade attachment.
B. impulse type blades.
C. shrouded turbine rotor blades.

1-54) AMP068

The function of the exhaust cone assembly of a turbine engine is to

A. collect the exhaust gases and act as a noise suppressor.
B. swirl and collect the exhaust gases into a single exhaust jet.
C. straighten and collect the exhaust gases into a solid exhaust jet.

1-55) AMP068

The oil dampened main bearing utilized in some turbine engines is used to

A. provide lubrication of the bearings from the beginning of starting rotation until normal oil pressure is established.
B. provide an oil film between the outer race and the bearing housing in order to reduce vibration tendencies in the rotor system, and to allow for slight misalignment.
C. dampen surges in oil pressure to the bearings.

1-56) AMP068

Main bearing oil seals used in turbine engines are usually what type?

A. Labyrinth and/or carbon rubbing.
B. Teflon and synthetic rubber.
C. Labyrinth and/or silicone rubber.

1 - Aircraft Engines
Answers

1-50) A.
The air entering the combustion chamber is divided into two main streams – the primary and the secondary. The primary or combustion air is directed inside the liner at the front end, where it mixes with the fuel and is burned. Secondary or cooling air passes between the outer casing and the liner and joins the combustion air gases through larger holes toward the rear of the liner, cooling the combustion gases from about 3500°F to below what the turbine section can withstand (near 1500°F on earlier engines).
[For more detailed information refer to Powerplant Handbook H-8083-32-ATB, Chapter 1 p.45]

1-51) B.
The turbine inlet nozzle vanes are located directly aft of the combustion chamber and immediately forward of the turbine wheel. This is the highest or hottest temperature that comes in contact with metal components in the engine. The turbine inlet temperature must be controlled or damage will occur to the turbine inlet nozzle vanes.
[For more detailed information refer to Powerplant Handbook H-8083-32-ATB, Chapter 1 p.47]

1-52) C.
After the combustion chamber has introduced the heat energy into the mass airflow and delivered it evenly to the turbine inlet nozzles, the nozzles must prepare the mass air flow to drive the turbine rotor. The stationary vanes of the turbine inlet nozzles are contoured and set at such an angle that they form a number of small nozzles discharging gas at extremely high speed; thus, the nozzles convert a varying portion of heat and pressure energy into velocity energy that can then be converted into mechanical energy through the rotation of the turbine blades. The second purpose of the turbine inlet nozzle is to direct the gases in the direction of turbine wheel rotation. This would be closer to perpendicular to the vertical line of the turbine blades than parallel to them.
[For more detailed information refer to Powerplant Handbook H-8083-32-ATB, Chapter 1 p.48]

1-53) C.
Most turbines are open at the outer perimeter of the blades. However, a second type, called the shrouded turbine, is sometimes used. The shrouded turbine blades effectively form a band around the outer perimeter of the turbine wheel. This improves efficiency by keeping the air from spilling over the blade tips and reduces vibration by holding the blade tips in place. Lighter turbine stage weights are possible with shrouded turbine rotor blades, but turbine speeds are somewhat limited by their use and more blades are required.
[For more detailed information refer to Powerplant Handbook H-8083-32-ATB, Chapter 1 p.50]

1-54) C.
The exhaust cone collects the exhaust gases discharged from the turbine section and gradually converts them into a solid flow of gases. In performing this, the velocity of the gases is decreased slightly and the pressure is increased.
[For more detailed information refer to Powerplant Handbook H-8083-32-ATB, Chapter 1 p.51]

1-55) B.
The gas turbine rotors are supported by ball and roller bearings, which are antifriction bearings. Many newer engines use hydraulic bearings, in which the outside race is surrounded by a thin film of oil. This reduces vibrations transmitted to the engine and allows for slight misalignment.
[For more detailed information refer to Powerplant Handbook H-8083-32-ATB, Chapter 1 p.52]

1-56) A.
The oil seals for turbine engines are generally labyrinth or carbon rubbing-type seals. Labyrinth type seals are pressurized to minimize oil leakage along the compressor shaft. Carbon seals are usually spring loaded and are similar in material and application to the carbon brushes found in electric motors.
[For more detailed information refer to Powerplant Handbook H-8083-32-ATB, Chapter 1 p.53]

1-57) AMP068

The energy to turn the propeller on a turboprop engine is typically produced by

- A. additional compressor stages.
- B. additional turbine stages.
- C. use of a flow-through combustion chamber.

1-58) AMP068

A turboshaft engine can be defined as:

- A. a gas turbine engine that delivers power through a shaft to operate something other than a propeller.
- B. a free turbine engine.
- C. a full bypass turbofan engine.

1-59) AMP068

Turbofan engines

- A. combine fan airflow with gas generator airflow at the exhaust nozzle (a mixed or common nozzle).
- B. have either a mixed or separate exhaust nozzle.
- C. have separate exhaust nozzle to increase core engine thrust.

1-60) AMP068

Newton`s Third Law of Motion states that:

- A. acceleration is produced when a force acts on a mass. The greater the mass, the greater the amount of force needed.
- B. for every action there is an equal and opposite reaction.
- C. every body persists in its state of rest, or of motion in a straight line, unless acted upon by some outside force.

1-61) AMP068

The Brayton cycle is known as the

- A. constant pressure cycle.
- B. constant temperature cycle.
- C. constant mass cycle.

1-62) AMP068

The most important factors affecting thermal efficiency in a turbine engine are

- A. compressor speed and exhaust gas temperature.
- B. total air temperature and compressor speed.
- C. turbine inlet temperature, compression ratio, and the component efficiencies of the compressor and turbine.

1 - Aircraft Engines
Answers

1-57) B.
Turboprops are, fundamentally, gas turbine engines that have a compressor, combustion section, turbine, and exhaust nozzle (gas generator), all of which operate in the same manner as any other gas engine turbine engine. However, the difference is that the turbine in the turboprop engine usually has extra stages to extract energy to drive the propeller.
[For more detailed information refer to Powerplant Handbook H-8083-32-ATB, Chapter 1 p.54]

1-58) A.
A gas turbine engine that delivers power through a shaft to operate something other than a propeller is referred to as a turboshaft engine. The output shaft may be coupled directly to the engine turbine, or the shaft may be driven by a turbine of its own (free turbine). The turboshaft engine's output is measured in horsepower instead of thrust because the power output is turning a shaft.
[For more detailed information refer to Powerplant Handbook H-8083-32-ATB, Chapter 1 p.55]

1-59) B.
In a turbofan engine, the large, axial flow fan in front of the engine is driven by extra turbine stages similar to a turboprop engine. The fan air can be exhausted through its own nozzle or it can be mixed in a common nozzle with the core engine's exhaust. The large area of the common exhaust nozzle results in the fan producing around ~80% of the total thrust on some engines. Turbofan engines are the most widely used gas turbine engines on transport category aircraft.
[For more detailed information refer to Powerplant Handbook H-8083-32-ATB, Chapter 1 p.56]

1-60) B.
The principle used by a gas turbine engine as it provides force to move an airplane is based on Newton's law of reaction. The law states that for every action, there is an equal and opposite reaction. Therefore, if the engine accelerates a mass of air (action) it applies a force on the aircraft (reaction) which moves the aircraft in the direction opposite to the accelerated mass of air.
[For more detailed information refer to Powerplant Handbook H-8083-32-ATB, Chapter 1 p.57]

1-61) A.
The Brayton cycle is the name given to the thermodynamic cycle of a gas turbine engine to produce thrust. This is a variable-volume, constant-pressure cycle of events and is commonly called the constant pressure cycle. A more recent term is continuous combustion cycle. The four continuous and constant events are: intake, compression, expansion (which includes power) and exhaust.
[For more detailed information refer to Powerplant Handbook H-8083-32-ATB, Chapter 1 p.58]

1-62) C.
Thermal efficiency is a prime factor in gas turbine performance; it's the ratio of net work produced by the engine to the chemical energy supplied in the form of fuel. The three most important factors affecting the thermal efficiency are turbine inlet temperature, compression ratio, and the component efficiencies of the compressor and turbine. Other factors that affect thermal efficiency are compressor inlet temperature and combustion efficiency.
[For more detailed information refer to Powerplant Handbook H-8083-32-ATB, Chapter 1 p.59]

1-63) AMP068
An engine's thrust output temporarily decreases as aircraft speed increases from static. This is overcome at higher speeds by

    A.   turbine efficiency.
    B.   ram air effect.
    C.   exhaust nozzle pressure.

1-63) B.

A rise in pressure above ambient pressure at the engine inlet as a result of forward velocity of an aircraft is referred to as ram pressure. Since any ram effect causes an increase in compressor entrance pressure over atmospheric, the resulting pressure rise causes an increase in the mass airflow and gas velocity, both of which tend to increase thrust. An engine's thrust output temporarily deceases as aircraft speed increases from static, but soon ceases to decrease. Moving toward higher speeds, thrust output increases again due to the increases pressure of ram recovery.

[For more detailed information refer to Powerplant Handbook H-8083-32-ATB, Chapter 1 p.60]

Applicants for powerplant certification are required to answer oral examination questions before, after, or in conjunction with the practical examination portion of the airman certification process. The oral examination is used to establish knowledge. The practical examination is used to establish skill, which is the application of knowledge. Use the following questions to prepare for the oral examination. The questions are examples aligned with Practical Test Standards subject matter from which the examiner will choose topics for oral examination.

1-1(O). What is the reciprocating engine theory of operation?

1-2(O). What is the basic radial engine design and how does it operate?

1-3(O). What is firing order and how is it determined?

1-4(O). Why are valves adjusted on a radial engine?

1-5(O). What is the purpose of a master rod and articulating rods?

1-6(O). What is the purpose, function, and operation of multiple springs on a valve?

1-7(O). What is propeller reduction gearing and why is it used?

1-8(O). What is the basic theory of operation of a gas turbine engine?

1-9(O). What are some causes for turbine engine performance losses?

1-10(O). What is the purpose of a turbine engine diffuser?

1-11(O). What type of engine is a typical APU (auxiliary power unit)? What is its function and how does it operate?

1 - Aircraft Engines
Oral Answers

1-1(O). A reciprocating engine is an internal combustion device that converts the energy in fuel into mechanical energy. A compressed fuel/air charge is burned in each cylinder of the engine. The energy released pushes the piston down in successive cylinders so that the crankshaft, which is attached to the pistons via connecting rods, develops a rotational motion (force). This force is transferred to a propeller geared off of the end of the crankshaft to produce thrust. A camshaft is geared to the crankshaft to enable valves to open and close at precise times. The valves let the fuel/air mixture into each cylinder and, after the charge is burned, the valves let the exhaust gases out. Magnetos develop a high-tension current that is distributed to successive cylinders at the precise time it is advantageous to ignite the fuel air mixture. Most reciprocating aircraft engines are 4-stroke cycle engines. A stroke is the movement of the piston in the cylinder from top to bottom or from bottom to top. The 4 strokes are labeled to indicate their function in the cycle. They are in order of occurrence: the intake, compression, power, and exhaust strokes. Ignition of the fuel/air mixture via spark plugs in each cylinder occurs just before the piston reaches the top of the compression stroke. The force created by burning the fuel is then transmitted by the piston to the crankshaft on the power stroke.
Reference: FAA-H-8083-32-ATB Page 1-24 to 1-28

1-2(O). Radial engines are simply reciprocating engines with the cylinders arranged radially around a central crankcase and crankshaft. It operates like any other 4-stroke cycle reciprocating engine.
Reference: FAA-H-8083-32-ATB Page 1-5

1-3(O). The firing order of an engine is the sequence in which the power event occurs in the different cylinders. Firing order is designed to provide for balance and to eliminate vibration. It is set by the engineers of the engine. Cylinder firing order in opposed reciprocating aircraft engines is usually listed in pairs of cylinders as each pair fires across the center main bearing. On single row radial engines, the firing order is the sequential odd numbered cylinders followed by the sequential even numbered cylinders (from low number to high number each). Double row radials can be calculated by using a pair of firing order numbers that are either added or subtracted to the number of the cylinder previously fired as is possible.
Reference: FAA-H-8083-32-ATB Page 1-17

1-4(O). Reciprocating engines with solid lifters or cam followers generally require the valve clearance to be adjusted manually by adjusting a screw and locknut. Valve clearance is needed to assure that the valve has enough clearance in the valve train to close completely. This adjustment (or inspection thereof) is a continuous maintenance item except on engines with hydraulic lifters. Hydraulic lifters automatically keep the valve clearance at zero.
Reference: FAA-H-8083-32-ATB Page 1-21

1-5(O). The master rod serves as the connecting link between the piston pin and the crankpin. The crankpin end contains the master rod bearing. Flanges around the large end of the master rod provide for the attachment of articulating rods. They are attached to the master rod with knuckle pins which are pressed into the holes in the master rod flanges. The master and articulating rod assembly is commonly used on radial engines. In radial engines, the piston in one cylinder in each row is connected to the crankshaft by the master rod. All other pistons in the row are connected to the crankshaft through the master rod via the articulating rods.
Reference: FAA-H-8083-32-ATB Page 1-11

1-6(O). The function of the valve springs is to close the valve and to hold the valve securely on the valve seat. The purpose of having two or more valve springs on each valve is to prevent vibration and valve surging at certain speeds. The springs are arranged one inside the other and vibrate at different engine speeds. The result is rapid damping of all spring-surge vibrations. Two or more springs also reduce the danger of weakness and possible failure by breakage due to heat and metal fatigue.
Reference: FAA-H-8083-32-ATB Page 1-19 to 1-22

1-7(O). For an engine to develop high power, an increase in crankshaft rotational speed is required. However as propeller tip speed approaches the speed of sound, efficiency is greatly reduced. Propeller reduction gearing is used to allow the engine to turn at a high RPM while keeping the propeller speed lower and efficient. The propeller is geared to the engine crankshaft in such a way as to make the propeller not turn as fast as the engine. There are three common types of reduction gearing: spur planetary, bevel planetary, and spur and pinion.
Reference: FAA-H-8083-32-ATB Page 1-24

1-8(O). A gas turbine engine is an internal combustion engine. Like a reciprocating engine, the functions of intake, compression, combustion, and exhaust are all required. The difference is that, in a turbine engine, these functions happen in dedicated sections of the engine and they happen continuously. Air is taken in at the front of the engine and is compressed in the compressor section, either axially or centrifugally. From there it is sent through a diffuser to the combustion section where fuel is discharged and combustion takes place. The energy in the fuel is released and is directed into the turbine section. Turbine wheel(s) extract the energy in the burning fuel. Depending on the engine type, the energy is converted into rotational mechanical energy to operate the engine and create thrust by turning a fan, propeller, or rotor. In turbojet engines, just enough energy is extracted to operate the engine and the remainder is directed out of the exhaust of the engine to be used as thrust.
Reference: FAA-H-8083-32-ATB Page 1-37 to 1-57

1-9(O). The thermal efficiency of a gas turbine engine is a prime factor in performance. This is the ratio of the net work produced by the engine to the chemical energy supplied in the fuel. The turbine inlet temperature, compression ratio, and component efficiencies are the three most important factors affecting thermal efficiency. Other factors are compressor inlet temperature and combustion efficiency. A high turbine inlet temperature will result in higher efficiency and more power. However, temperature limits must be adhered to or the turbine section can be overheated and destroyed. If the efficiency of the engine components is reduced, then engine performance will reduce. So, damaged or worn components will produce performance losses. Also, if the stagnation density (a combination of airspeed, altitude, and ambient temperature) is reduced, the performance is reduced. This results from the reduced mass of air flowing through the engine.
Reference: FAA-H-8083-32-ATB Page 1-58 to 1-59

1-10(O). The diffuser is the divergent section of the engine after the compressor and before the combustion section. It functions to reduce the velocity of the compressor discharge air and increase its pressure so that it can be combined with fuel and burned in the combustion section. The lower velocity of the gases aids in the continuous burning process. If the gases pass through the combustion section at too high of a velocity, the flame could extinguish.
Reference: FAA-H-8083-32-ATB Page 1-44

1-11(O). A typical APU is a turboshaft gas turbine engine that is made to transfer horsepower to a shaft. The shaft turns the engine compressor from which bleed air for the aircraft is obtained. It also drives an accessory gearbox that rotates a generator. The generator supplies the aircraft with electrical power on the ground and in the air. The APU is often operated with no personnel on the flight deck.
Reference: FAA-H-8083-32-ATB Page 10-58, 9-19 and 1-38

1 - Aircraft Engines
Practical

Applicants for powerplant certification are required to demonstrate the ability to apply knowledge by performing maintenance related tasks for the examiner. The Practical Test Standards (PTS) list the subject areas from which the skill elements to be performed by the applicant are chosen. The following examples resemble tasks an examiner may ask an applicant to perform. The Performance Level required to be demonstrated for each skill element is listed. Consult the PTS for Level descriptions.

1-1(P). Given an actual aircraft reciprocating engine or mockup, measure the valve clearance with the lifters deflated and record your findings. [Level 2]

1-2(P). Given an actual aircraft reciprocating engine or mockup, accomplish a compression test, and record all findings. [Level 3]

1-3(P). Given an actual aircraft reciprocating engine or mockup, inspect engine control cables for proper rigging and record your findings. [Level 3]

1-4(P). Given an actual aircraft reciprocating engine or mockup, inspect engine push-pull tubes for proper rigging and record your findings. [Level 3]

1-5(P). Given an actual aircraft reciprocating engine or mockup, inspect ring gap and record your findings. [Level 3]

1-6(P). Given an actual aircraft reciprocating engine or mockup, install piston rings on a piston and record maintenance. [Level 3]

1-7(P). Given an actual aircraft reciprocating engine or mockup, install an aircraft engine cylinder and record maintenance. [Level 3]

1-8(P). Given an aircraft engine component and appropriate publications, inspect dimensionally and record your findings. [Level 3]

1-9(P). Given an actual aircraft reciprocating engine or mockup, component, and appropriate publications, install the component and record the maintenance. [Level 3]

1-10(P). Given a turbine engine compressor blade and appropriate publications, complete a repair by blending and record maintenance. [Level 3]

1-11(P). Given an actual aircraft turbine engine or mockup, component, and appropriate publications, install the component and record the maintenance. [Level 3]

1-12(P). Given the required information, calculate the cycle life remaining between overhaul of a turbine engine life limited component. [Level 2]

1-13(P). Given an actual aircraft turbine engine or mockup and appropriate publications, check the rigging of a turbine engine inlet guide vane system and record your findings. [Level 3]

1-14(P). Given an actual aircraft turbine engine or mockup and appropriate publications, measure a compressor or turbine blade clearance and record your findings. [Level 3]

1-15(P). Given an actual aircraft turbine engine or mockup, appropriate publications, and an unknown discrepancy, troubleshoot a turbine engine and record your findings. [Level 3]

1-16(P). Given an actual aircraft turbine engine or mockup, locate and identify various turbine engine components. [Level 2]

1-17(P). Given an aircraft turbine component and appropriate publications, inspect turbine engine component and record your findings. [Level 3]

NOTE: AUXILIARY POWER UNITS may be tested at the same time as TURBINE ENGINES. No further testing of auxiliary power units is required.

Fuel and Fuel Metering

CHAPTER 2

Basic Fuel Systems, Fuel Metering Devices, Carburetor Fuel Systems,
Fuel System Maintenance, Turbine Engine Fuel Systems

2-1) AMP041
Fuel lines kept away from sources of heat, sharp bends, and steep rises are avoided to reduce the possibility of

A. liquid lock.
B. vapor lock.
C. positive lock.

2-2) AMP042
Where should the main fuel strainer be located in the aircraft fuel system?

A. Downstream from the wobble pump check valve.
B. At the lowest point in the fuel system.
C. At any point in the system lower than the carburetor strainer.

2-3) AMP022
On a carburetor without an automatic mixture control, as you ascend to altitude, the mixture will

A. be enriched.
B. be leaned.
C. not be affected.

2-4) AMP041
1. The mixture used at rated power in air cooled reciprocating engines is richer than the mixture used through the normal cruising range.
2. The mixture used at idle in air cooled reciprocating engines is richer than the mixture used at rated power.

Regarding the above statements,

A. only No. 1 is true.
B. only No. 2 is true.
C. both No. 1 and No. 2 are true.

2 - Fuel and Fuel Metering
Answers

2-1) B.
The three general causes of vapor lock are the lowering of the pressure on the fuel, high fuel temperatures and excessive fuel turbulence. Vapor in the fuel lines leading to engine fuel metering devices can cause an interruption in fuel flow and potentially cause the engine to stop running. To reduce the possibility of vapor lock, fuel lines are kept away from sources of heat to avoid high fuel temperature. Also, sharp bends and steep rises are avoided to aid in keeping sufficient pressure on the fuel to avoid vaporization.
[For more detailed information refer to Powerplant Handbook H-8083-32-ATB, Chapter 2 p.2]

2-2) B.
From each fuel tank on the aircraft, a line leads to the selector valve. This valve is set from the flight deck to select the tank from which fuel is to be delivered to the engine. A boost pump forces the fuel through the selector valve to the main fuel strainer. This filtering unit, located in the lowest part of the fuel system, removes water and dirt from the fuel.
[For more detailed information refer to Powerplant Handbook H-8083-32-ATB, Chapter 2 p.3]

2-3) A.
Typically, air density decreases as altitude increases. A normally aspirated engine has a fixed volume of air that it can draw in during the intake stroke. Therefore, less air is drawn into the engine as altitude increases because of the lower air density. Less air results in the fuel air mixture being more rich as you ascend in altitude. A mixture control is provided on some aircraft to lean the mixture during climbs. On some aircraft this is done manually. On other, it is automatic.
[For more detailed information refer to Powerplant Handbook H-8083-32-ATB, Chapter 2 p.3]

2-4) C.
The graphic below displays the fuel air mixtures for a typical air cooled reciprocating engine. Notice that the mixture is most rich at idle. At rated power during climb and takeoff, the mixture is higher than at minimum and maximum cruise. The mixture must be enriched more than the stoichiometric mixture at high power setting to lower the temperature of combustion and keep cylinder head temperature within limits. At idling speed, some air or exhaust gas is drawn into the cylinder through the exhaust port during valve overlap. The mixture that enters the cylinder through the intake port must be must be rich enough to compensate for this gas or additional air.
[For more detailed information refer to Powerplant Handbook H-8083-32-ATB, Chapter 2 p.2-5] Figure 2-1 in FAA-H-8083-32

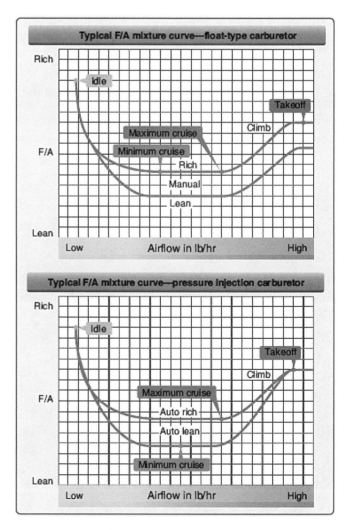

Figure 2-1. Fuel/air mixture curves.

2-5) AMP022
What carburetor component measures the amount of air delivered to the engine?

    A.   Economizer valve.
    B.   Automatic mixture control.
    C.   Venturi.

2-6) AMP037
The throttle valve of float-type carburetors is located

    A.   ahead of the venture and main discharge nozzle.
    B.   after the main discharge nozzle and ahead of the venture.
    C.   between the venture and the engine.

2-7) AMP037
The fuel metering force of a conventional float-type carburetor in its normal operating range is the difference between the pressure acting on the discharge nozzle located within the venturi and the pressure

    A.   acting on the fuel in the float chamber.
    B.   of the fuel as it enters the carburetor.
    C.   air as it enters the venturi (impact pressure).

2-8) AMP056
Which of the following best describes the function of an altitude mixture control?

    A.   Regulates the richness of the fuel/air charge entering the engine.
    B.   Regulates air pressure above the fuel in the float chamber.
    C.   Regulates the air pressure in the venturi.

2-9) AMP037
What component is used to ensure fuel delivery during periods of rapid engine acceleration?

    A.   Acceleration pump.
    B.   Water injection pump.
    C.   Power enrichment unit.

2 - Fuel and Fuel Metering
Answers

2-5) C.
As the velocity of air increases to get through the narrow portion of the venture, pressure drops. This pressure drop is proportional to the velocity and is therefore a measure of the airflow. The basic operating principle of most carburetors depends on the differential pressure between the inlet and the venture throat.
[For more detailed information refer to Powerplant Handbook H-8083-32-ATB, Chapter 2 p.6]

2-6) C.
The throttle valve is located between the venture and the engine. Mechanical linkage connects this valve with the throttle lever in the cockpit. By means of the throttle, airflow to the cylinders is regulated and controls the power output of the engine. As the throttle is opened, more air is admitted to the carburetor which automatically supplies enough additional fuel to maintain the correct fuel air ratios. As the volume of airflow increases, the velocity in the venturi increases, lowering the pressure and allowing more fuel to be forced into the airstream.
[For more detailed information refer to Powerplant Handbook H-8083-32-ATB, Chapter 2 p.6]

2-7) A.
The discharge nozzle is located in the throat of the venturi at the point where the lowest drop in pressure occurs as air passes through the carburetor to the engine cylinders. There are two different pressures acting on the fuel in the carburetor – the low pressure at the discharge nozzle and a higher pressure at the float chamber. The higher pressure in the float chamber forces the fuel through the discharge nozzle into the airstream in the venturi.
[For more detailed information refer to Powerplant Handbook H-8083-32-ATB, Chapter 2 p.7]

2-8) A.
The mixture control system determines the ratio of fuel to air in the mixture. This can be done manually with a cockpit control, or, an automatic mixture control can be built into the carburetor. As an aircraft climbs, the atmospheric pressure decreases. There is also a corresponding decrease in the weight of the air passing through the induction system. The volume, however, remains constant. It is the volume of air that determines the pressure drop across the venturi. Therefore, regardless of altitude, the same amount of fuel is metered into the engine from the discharge nozzle. Thus, with less air weight due to lower air density at altitude, the mixture tends to become too rich. The automatic or manual mixture control decreases the rate of fuel discharge to compensate for the decrease in air density.
[For more detailed information refer to Powerplant Handbook H-8083-32-ATB, Chapter 2 p.8]

2-9) A.
The acceleration pump supplies extra fuel during sudden increases in engine power. When the throttle is opened, the airflow through the carburetor increases to obtain more power from the engine. The main metering system then increases the fuel discharged. However, the increase in airflow can be so rapid that there is a slight time lag before the increase in fuel discharged is sufficient to provide the correct mixture ratio with the new airflow. By supplying extra fuel during this period, the acceleration system prevents the temporary leaning out of the mixture and gives smooth acceleration.
[For more detailed information refer to Powerplant Handbook H-8083-32-ATB, Chapter 2 p.8]

2-10) AMP037

The economizer system in a float-type carburetor

    A.   keeps the fuel/air ratio constant.
    B.   functions only at cruise and idle speeds.
    C.   increases the fuel air ratio at high power settings.

2-11) AMP003

Carburetor icing is most severe at

    A.   air temperatures between 30 and 40°F.
    B.   at high altitudes.
    C.   low engine temperatures.

2-12) AMP037

The fuel level within the float chamber of a properly adjusted float-type carburetor will be

    A.   slightly higher than the discharge nozzle outlet.
    B.   slightly lower than the discharge nozzle outlet.
    C.   at the same level as the discharge nozzle outlet.

2-13) AMP037

One purpose of an air bleed in a float-type carburetor is _____

    A.   increase fuel flow at altitude.
    B.   meter air to adjust the mixture.
    C.   decrease fuel density and destroy surface tension.

2-14) AMP037

Fuel is discharged for idling speeds on a float-type carburetor

    A.   from the idle discharge nozzle.
    B.   in the venturi.
    C.   through the idle discharge air bleed.

2 - Fuel and Fuel Metering
Answers

2-10) C.

The economizer system in a float-type carburetor is also known as the power enrichment system. It increases the richness of the mixture during high power operation. At cruising speeds, a lean mixture is desirable for economy reasons, while at high power output, the mixture must be rich to obtain maximum power and to aid in cooling the engine cylinders. Essentially, the economizer is a valve that is closed at cruising speed and opened to supply extra fuel to the mixture during high power operation.

[For more detailed information refer to Powerplant Handbook H-8083-32-ATB, Chapter 2 p.9]

2-11) A.

There are three general types of icing: fuel evaporation ice, throttle ice, and impact ice. All three can form at temperatures between 30 and 40°F, however, fuel evaporation ice can form during ambient air temperature of up to 100°F. When fuel evaporates in the venturi of a float-type carburetor, temperature decreases. Any water vapor present can freeze onto the fuel discharge nozzle, throttle valve, or inside the venturi if the temperature drops below 32°F. Throttle ice is formed typically when air makes its way around a partially closed throttle valve. A pressure differential is formed around the obstruction and ice can form on the back side of the throttle when moisture is present. This condition is usually limited to temperature below 38°F. Impact ice occurs when water, snow, ice, etc. is present in the atmosphere and it contacts a cold surface of the aircraft. The carburetor screen is an especially susceptible and dangerous area for impact ice to form but it can also form inside the carburetor. This type of ice forms when temperature of the aircraft structure is below 32°F.

[For more detailed information refer to Powerplant Handbook H-8083-32-ATB, Chapter 2 p.9-10]

2-12) B.

A float chamber is provided between the fuel supply and the main metering system of the carburetor. This chamber provides a nearly constant level of fuel to the main discharge nozzle which is usually about 1/8" below the holes in the main discharge nozzle. The fuel level must be maintained slightly below the discharge nozzle outlet holes to provide the correct amount of fuel flow and to prevent leakage from the nozzle when the engine is not operating.

[For more detailed information refer to Powerplant Handbook H-8083-32-ATB, Chapter 2 p.10-11]

2-13) C.

Air bleed into the main metering fuel system decreases the fuel density and destroys surface tension. This results in better vaporization and control of fuel discharge, especially at lower engine speeds. See figures 2-13 in FAA-H-8083-32 and associated description in paragraph of same page.

[For more detailed information refer to Powerplant Handbook H-8083-32-ATB, Chapter 2 p.12]

2-14) A.

With the throttle valve closed at idling speeds, air velocity through the venturi is so low that it cannot draw enough fuel from the main discharge nozzle. However, low pressure that exists on the engine side of the throttle valve. To allow the engine to idle, a fuel passageway is incorporated to discharge fuel from an opening in this low pressure area near the edge of the throttle valve. This is called the idling jet or idle discharge nozzle. With the throttle open enough so that the main discharge nozzle is operating, fuel does not flow out of the idling jet. As soon as the throttle is closed far enough to stop the spray from the main discharge nozzle, fuel flows out of the idle discharge nozzle.

[For more detailed information refer to Powerplant Handbook H-8083-32-ATB, Chapter 2 p.12]

2-15) AMP056

Which of the following best describes the function of an altitude mixture control?

    A.   Regulates the richness of the fuel/air charge entering the engine.

    B.   Regulates the air pressure above the fuel in the float chamber.

    C.   Regulates the air pressure in the venturi.

2-16) AMP041

An aircraft carburetor is equipped with a mixture control in order to prevent the mixture from becoming too _____.

    A.   lean at high altitudes.

    B.   rich at high altitudes.

    C.   rich at high speeds.

2-17) AMP041

Manual mixture control systems in float-type carburetors

    A.   can use a needle-type system or a back-suction type arrangement.

    B.   are connected to the throttle lever.

    C.   are independent of the idle system.

2-18) AMP037

Float-type economizers which are equipped with economizers are normally set for

    A.   their richest mixture delivery and leaned by means of the economizer system.

    B.   the economizer system to supplement the main system supply at all engine speeds above idling.

    C.   their leanest practical mixture delivery at cruising speeds and enriched by means of the economizer system at high power settings.

2-19) AMP051

In a pressure injection carburetor, there is no float chamber. Fuel to the discharge nozzle is controlled by a diaphragm that uses a comparison of

    A.   venturi air pressure and throttle body air pressure.

    B.   fuel pump pressure and venturi air pressure.

    C.   venturi air pressure and carburetor inlet air pressure.

2-20) AMP051

On an engine equipped with a pressure type carburetor, fuel supply in the idling range is ensured by the inclusion in the carburetor of

    A.   a spring in the unmetered fuel chamber to supplement the action of the normal metering forces.

    B.   an idle metering jet that bypasses the carburetor in the idle range.

    C.   a separate boost venturi that is sensitive to the reduced airflow at start and idle speeds.

2-15) A.

As altitude increases, the air becomes less dense. Because the same volume of fuel is discharged through fuel nozzle regardless of altitude, the less dense air at altitude results in a rich mixture being delivered to the engine at higher altitudes. It is the function of the altitude mixture control to reduce the richness of the fuel/air charge entering the engine at altitude. This provides the correct amount of fuel for air of varying densities.
[For more detailed information refer to Powerplant Handbook H-8083-32-ATB, Chapter 2 p.12-13]

2-16) B.

The action of the venturi draws the same volume of fuel through the discharge nozzle at high altitudes as it does at low altitudes. Therefore, the fuel mixture becomes richer as altitude increases due to the low air density. This can be overcome by either a manual or an automatic mixture control.
[For more detailed information refer to Powerplant Handbook H-8083-32-ATB, Chapter 2 p.13]

2-17) A.

On float-type carburetors, two types of purely manual or cockpit controllable devices are in general use for controlling fuel air mixtures. They are the needle-type and the back-suction type. Both types are operated in the cockpit by an independent mixture control lever. On the needle type, pulling the lever full aft into the idle cutoff position seats a needle in the float chamber and all fuel is cut off. On the back-suction type, the idle cutoff position of the lever connects the air in the float chamber to the extreme low pressure of the piston suction side of the throttle valve which causes fuel flow to stop.
[For more detailed information refer to Powerplant Handbook H-8083-32-ATB, Chapter 2 p.14]

2-18) C.

For an engine to develop maximum power at full throttle, the fuel mixture must be richer than for cruise. An economizer is essentially a valve that is closed at throttle settings below approximately 60-70 percent of rated power. This system is operated by the throttle control. At cruise speed, the economizer valve is closed. Through linkages, as the throttle is advanced, the valve opens and supplies more fuel at higher power settings.
[For more detailed information refer to Powerplant Handbook H-8083-32-ATB, Chapter 2 p.14-15]

2-19) C.

In a pressure injected carburetor, venturi air pressure is used on one side of a diaphragm in the pressure regulator unit. This venturi pressure drop is compared to air pressure at the carburetor inlet which is ported to the other side of the diaphragm. As the throttle valve is opened, the corresponding pressure drop through the venturi as the volume of air increases causes the diaphragm move. It is connected to a valve that controls the amount of fuel supplied to the discharge nozzle from the fuel pump. Thus, the difference in pressure proportional to the airflow through the carburetor is met with the proper fuel flow.
[For more detailed information refer to Powerplant Handbook H-8083-32-ATB, Chapter 2 p.16]

2-20) A.

Under low power settings (low airflows), the difference in pressure created by the boost venturi is not sufficient to accomplish consistent regulation of the fuel. Therefore, an idle spring is incorporated in the regulator unit. As the poppet valve moves toward the closed position, it contacts the idle spring. The spring holds the poppet valve off its seat far enough to supply more fuel than is needed for idling. This potentially over rich mixture is regulated by the idle valve. At idling speeds, the idle valve restricts the fuel flow to the proper amount. At higher speeds, it is withdrawn from the fuel passage and has no metering effect.
[For more detailed information refer to Powerplant Handbook H-8083-32-ATB, Chapter 2 p.17]

2-21) AMP051
What will occur if the vapor vent float in a pressure carburetor losses its buoyancy?

  A. The amount of fuel returning to the fuel tank from the carburetor will be increased.
  B. The engine will continue to run after the mixture control is placed in IDLE CUTOFF.
  C. A rich mixture will occur at all engine speeds.

2-22) AMP051
What is the relationship between the accelerating pump and the enrichment valve in a pressure injection carburetor?

  A. no relationship since they operate independently.
  B. Unmetered fuel pressure affects both units.
  C. The accelerating pump actuates the enrichment valve.

2-23) AMP051
The function of the automatic mixture control on a pressure injection carburetor is

  A. to increase the amount of fuel delivered to the discharge nozzle at high power settings.
  B. to compensate for changes in air density due to temperature and altitude changes.
  C. to provide the correct fuel/air ratio during idle and slow engine speeds.

2-24) AMP051
Which of the following causes a single diaphragm acceleration pump to discharge fuel?

  A. An increase in venturi suction when the throttle is open.
  B. An increase in manifold pressure that occurs when the throttle is open.
  C. A decrease in manifold pressure that occurs when the throttle is opened.

2-25) AMP041
The purpose of the fuel metering section of the Bendix/Percision fuel injection system is to

  A. regulate the flow of fuel into the airflow section.
  B. meter and control the fuel flow to the flow divider.
  C. return excess fuel to the tank.

2-26) AMP041
The primary purpose of the air bleed openings used with continuous flow fuel injector nozzles is to

  A. provide for automatic mixture control.
  B. lean out the mixture.
  C. aid in proper fuel vaporization.

2-27) AMP042
An aircraft engine continuous cylinder fuel injection system normally discharged fuel during which strokes?

  A. Intake.
  B. Intake and compression.
  C. All (continuously).

2-21) A.
If the vapor vent valve sticks open or the vapor vent float becomes filled with fuel and sinks, a continuous flow of fuel and vapor occurs through the vent line. It is important to detect this condition, as the fuel flow from the carburetor to the fuel tank may cause an overflowing tank with resultant increased fuel consumption.
[For more detailed information refer to Powerplant Handbook H-8083-32-ATB, Chapter 2 p.17]

2-22) A.
The power enrichment valve in a pressure injected carburetor is completely independent of the acceleration pump. The power enrichment valve is the poppet-type which begins to open at the beginning of the power range. It is opened by the unmetered fuel pressure overcoming metered fuel pressure and spring tension. The power enrichment valve continues to open wider during the power range until the combined flow through the valve and auto-rich jet exceeds that of the power enrichment jet. At this point, the power enrichment jet takes over and meters fuel throughout the power range. This action occurs in the fuel control unit and is independent of any accelerating pump.
[For more detailed information refer to Powerplant Handbook H-8083-32-ATB, Chapter 2 p.18-19]

2-23) B.
The purpose of the automatic mixture control is to compensate for changes in air density due to temperature and altitude changes. The automatic mixture control unit consists of a bellows assembly, calibrated needle, and seat located at the carburetor inlet. The expansion and contraction of the bellows in response to pressure changes moves the tapered needle in the atmospheric line which controls pressure in the "A" chamber of the pressure regulator and the small bleed holes in the diaphragm therein. The result is that fuel mixture is automatically adjust as the aircraft experiences pressure changes associated with altitude and/or temperature changes.
[For more detailed information refer to Powerplant Handbook H-8083-32-ATB, Chapter 2 p.19]

2-24) B.
A single diaphragm accelerator pump such as one in a Stromberg PS carburetor, is a spring loaded diaphragm assembly located in the metered fuel channel. The opposite side of the diaphragm is vented to the engine side of the throttle valve. With this arrangement, opening the throttle results in a rapid decrease in suction (increase in manifold pressure). This permits the spring to extend and move the acceleration pump diaphragm which displaces the fuel in the acceleration pump and forces it into the discharge nozzle.
[For more detailed information refer to Powerplant Handbook H-8083-32-ATB, Chapter 2 p.21]

2-25) B.
The fuel metering section is attached to the air metering section and contains an inlet fuel strainer, a manual mixture control valve, an idle valve and the main metering jet. The purpose of the fuel metering section is to meter and control fuel flow to the flow divider where it is kept under pressure and divided for delivery to the various cylinders at all engine speeds.
[For more detailed information refer to Powerplant Handbook H-8083-32-ATB, Chapter 2 p.21-24]

2-26) C.
The fuel discharge nozzles are of the air bleed configuration. Each nozzle incorporates a calibrated jet. The fuel is discharged through this jet into an ambient air pressure chamber within the nozzle assembly. Before entering the individual intake valve chambers, the fuel is mixed with air to aid in the atomizing of the fuel.
[For more detailed information refer to Powerplant Handbook H-8083-32-ATB, Chapter 2 p.24]

2-27) C.
The continuous fuel injection system injects fuel into the intake valve port in each cylinder head. The fuel system consists of a fuel injector pump, a control unit, a fuel manifold, and a fuel discharge nozzle. It is a continuous-flow type which controls fuel flow to match engine airflow. This permits the use of a rotary vane pump which does not require timing to the engine.
[For more detailed information refer to Powerplant Handbook H-8083-32-ATB, Chapter 2 p.25]

2-28) AMP041
How are discharge nozzles in a fuel injected reciprocating engine identified to indicate the flow range?

    A. By an identification letter stamped on one of the hexes of the nozzle body.
    B. By an identification metal tag attached to the nozzle body.
    C. By color codes on the nozzle body.

2-29) AMP023
Which statement is true regarding proper throttle rigging of an airplane?

    A. The throttle stop on the carburetor must be contacted before the stop in the cockpit.
    B. The stop in the cockpit must be contacted before the stop on the carburetor.
    C. The throttle control is properly adjusted when neither stop makes contact.

2-30) AMP023
When a new carburetor is installed on an engine,

    A. warm up the engine and adjust the float level.
    B. do not adjust the idle mixture setting; this was accomplished on the flow bench.
    C. and the engine is warmed up to normal operating temperature, adjust the idle mixture and then the idle speed.

2-31) AMP042
Fuel system inspection and maintenance

    A. does not include operation of the boost pumps to prevent flooding of the carburetor.
    B. includes the complete system except for the fuel tanks which are considered airframe components.
    C. consists of an examination of the system for conformity to design requirements and functional tests to prove correct operation.

2-32) AMP068
It is necessary to control acceleration and deceleration rates in turbine engines in order to

    A. prevent blowout or die-out.
    B. prevent over-temperature.
    C. prevent friction between turbine wheels and the case due to expansion and contraction.

2-33) AMP041
Which type of fuel control is used on most of today's turbine engines?

    A. Electromechanical.
    B. Mechanical.
    C. Hydromechanical or electronic.

2 - Fuel and Fuel Metering
Answers

2-28) A.
On Continental/TCM fuel injection systems, the fuel discharge nozzles are located in the cylinder heads with the outlets directed into the intake port. The nozzle body contains a drilled central passage with a counterbore at each end. The lower end is used as a chamber for fuel air mixture before the spray leaves the nozzles. The upper bore contains a removable orifice for calibrating the nozzles. Nozzles are calibrated in several flow ranges, and all nozzles furnished for one engine are of the same range. They are identified by a stamped letter on the hex of the nozzle body.
[For more detailed information refer to Powerplant Handbook H-8083-32-ATB, Chapter 2 p.28]

2-29) A.
Connect and adjust carburetor or fuel metering equipment throttle controls so that full movement of the throttle is obtained from the corresponding full movement of the control in the cockpit. Also, check and adjust the throttle control linkages so that springback on the throttle quadrant in the aircraft is equal in both the full-open and full-closed positions. Correct any excess play or looseness of control linkages or cables. Controls should be checked so that they go stop-to-stop on the carburetor. Check for complete and full travel of each control.
[For more detailed information refer to Powerplant Handbook H-8083-32-ATB, Chapter 2 p.30]

2-30) C.
Before checking the idle mixture on any engine, warm up the engine until oil and cylinder head temperatures are normal. The idle mixture adjustment is made on the idle mixture fuel control valve. It should not be confused with the adjustment of the idle speed. Excessively rich idle mixture results in incomplete combustion and spark plug fouling. Excessively lean idle mixture results in faulty acceleration. After adjusting idle mixture, reset the idle stop to the idle RPM specified in the aircraft maintenance manual.
[For more detailed information refer to Powerplant Handbook H-8083-32-ATB, Chapter 2 p.31]

2-31) C.
The inspection of a fuel system installation consists basically of an examination of the system for conformity to design requirements together with functional tests to prove correct operation. It is important that the manufacturer's instructions for the aircraft concerned be followed when performing inspection and maintenance functions. Boost pumps and fuel tanks are part of the aircraft fuel system and should be fully inspected and tested for operation when performing system inspection and maintenance.
[For more detailed information refer to Powerplant Handbook H-8083-32-ATB, Chapter 2 p.32]

2-32) A.
If the quantity of fuel becomes excessive in relation to mass airflow through the engine, it could produce compressor stall and a condition referred to as rich blowout. If there is not enough fuel for the mass airflow, a lean flame-out or die-out can occur. Thus, a balanced amount of fuel and air must occur in the engine for combustion to be sustained. Rapid acceleration of deceleration are instances where fuel adjustments must be made by the fuel control to match the extreme airflow changes to prevent blowout or die-out.
[For more detailed information refer to Powerplant Handbook H-8083-32-ATB, Chapter 2 p.34]

2-33) C.
There are 3 basic types of fuel controls used on turbine engines: Hydromechanical, Hydromechanical/Electronic, and Full Authority Digital Electronic Control (FADEC). Hydromechanical controls are the original type of fuel control. An improvement over the standard Hydromechanical fuel control occurred when electronic sensing was added. FADEC fuel controls are a further improvement with electronic inputs and outputs governing the system. So, regardless of how advanced the turbine engine fuel control in question, it will be Hydromechanical, Electronic, or a combination of both.
[For more detailed information refer to Powerplant Handbook H-8083-32-ATB, Chapter 2 p.34]

2-34) AMP068

Which of the following influences the operation of an automatic fuel control on a turbojet engine?

    A.   Burner pressure.
    B.   Mixture control position.
    C.   Exhaust gas temperature.

2-35) AMP068

In a supervisory electronic engine control EEC, any fault in the EEC that adversely affects engine operation

    A.   causes redundant back-up systems to take over and continue normal operation.
    B.   usually degrades performance to the extent that continued operation can cause damage to the engine.
    C.   causes an immediate reversion to control by the hydromechanical fuel control unit.

2-36) AMP041

Which pressure is input into the EFCU to control fuel metering to the engine?

    A.   Compressor inlet pressure.
    B.   Compressor discharge pressure.
    C.   Fuel pump outlet pressure.

2-37) AMP041

A full authority digital electronic control (FADEC)

    A.   uses the hydromechanical fuel control as a back-up.
    B.   combines electronic inputs with mechanical input for full control of fuel delivery.
    C.   has no hydromechanical fuel control back-up.

2-38) AMP041

A significant pilot controlled input into the EFCU for controlling fuel metering is the

    A.   power lever angle through a pedestal mounted potentiometer.
    B.   indicated airspeed control interconnect.
    C.   fuel/air sensor throughput.

2-39) AMP068

An EEC (Electronic Engine Control) in a FADEC (Full Authority Digital Engine Control) aircraft

    A.   requires a second computer as back-up should the EEC fail.
    B.   relies on crosstalk between channels for the best engine control output.
    C.   eliminates the need for a fuel metering unit.

2 - Fuel and Fuel Metering

Answers

2-34) A.
Regardless of the type, all fuel controls schedule the fuel flow to match the power required by the pilot. Some sense more engine variables than others. Fuel controls can sense many different inputs, such as power lever position, engine RPM for each spool, compressor inlet pressure and temperature, burner pressure, compressor discharge pressure and more. There is no mixture control selector in the cockpit of aircraft powered by turbine engines as the fuel control automatically schedules the correct furl flow given input parameters. Exhaust gas temperature is monitored on most turbine engines but more as feedback to ensure proper operation than as an input for fuel scheduling.
[For more detailed information refer to Powerplant Handbook H-8083-32-ATB, Chapter 2 p.35]

2-35) C.
A supervisory EEC uses electronic control to adjust fuel flow through a hydromechanical fuel control unit. It uses numerous inputs of engine parameters to issue commands. An EEC can be thought of as the computer which calculates the correct fuel metering for the engine and then issues outputs for the Hydromechanical fuel control to follow. If the EEC fails, the hydromechanical portion of the fuel control will take over.
[For more detailed information refer to Powerplant Handbook H-8083-32-ATB, Chapter 2 p.35]

2-36) B.
Fuel is supplied to the fuel control through a 200-micron inlet filter screen and is metered to the engine by the servo-operated metering valve. It is a fuel flow/compressor discharge pressure (Wf/P3) ratio device that positions the metering valve in response to engine compressor discharge pressure (P3). Fuel pressure differential across the servo valve is maintained by a servo-operated bypass valve in response to commands from the EFCU.
[For more detailed information refer to Powerplant Handbook H-8083-32-ATB, Chapter 2 p.36]

2-37) C.
A full authority digital electronic control controls (FADEC) fuel flow on most new turbine engine models. A true FADEC system has no hydromechanical fuel control back-up. The system uses electronic sensors that feed engine parameter information into the Electronic Engine Control unit. The EEC is a computer that gathers the needed information to determine fuel flow. The fuel metering valve simply reacts to the commands from the EEC.
[For more detailed information refer to Powerplant Handbook H-8083-32-ATB, Chapter 2 p.37]

2-38) A.
Much of the operation of the EFCU is automatic guided by parameters automatically sensed and input into the EFCU. The pilot does need to request a power setting which is accomplished by positioning the throttle lever on the flight deck. The power lever angle (PLA) is converted to an electronic input by a potentiometer mounted in the throttle quadrant. The transmitted signal to the EFCU represents engine thrust demand in relation to the throttle position.
[For more detailed information refer to Powerplant Handbook H-8083-32-ATB, Chapter 2 p.36-38 Figure 2-51]

2-39) B.
The EEC is a two channel computer that controls every aspect of engine operation. Each channel, which is an independent computer, can completely control the operation of the engine. The processor(s) do all of the control calculations and supply all the data for the control signals to torque motors and solenoids. Cross-talk logic compares data from channels A and B and uses the cross-talk to find which EEC channel is best to control the output driver for a torque motor or solenoid bank. The EEC controls the metering valve in the FMU (fuel metering unit) to supply fuel flow for combustion.
[For more detailed information refer to Powerplant Handbook H-8083-32-ATB, Chapter 2 p.39]

2-40) AMP068

After control signals are sent from the EEC to regulate fuel flow to the engine,

   A.   feedback from several systems in the engine is sent back to the EE.
   B.   the fuel pump output is increased or decreased as instructed.
   C.   rotary differential transformers position the metering devices as directed.

2-41) AMP068

On a FADEC system aircraft, the EEC

   A.   manages only engine parameters and fuel flow.
   B.   lacks the mechanical outputs to control the variable stator vanes.
   C.   controls many engine subsystems as well as the FMU.

2-42) AMP069

When trimming a turbine engine, the fuel control is adjusted to

   A.   produce as much power as the engine is capable of producing.
   B.   set idle RPM and maximum speed or EPR.
   C.   allow the engine to produce maximum RPM without regard to power output.

2-43) AMP069

Generally, the practice when trimming an engine is to

   A.   turn all accessory bleed air off.
   B.   turn all accessory bleed air on.
   C.   make adjustments (as necessary) for all engines on the same aircraft with accessory bleed air settings the same – either on or off.

2-40) A.

The EEC controls the metering valve in the fuel metering unit to supply fuel flow for combustion. The EEC also sends a signal to the minimum pressure and shutoff valve in the fuel metering unit to start or stop fuel flow. The EEC receives position feedback for several engine components by using rotary differential transformers and linear variable differential transformers. It also receives thermocouple signal inputs. These sensors feed engine parameters information from several sources back to the EEC.

[For more detailed information refer to Powerplant Handbook H-8083-32-ATB, Chapter 2 p.39-40]

2-41) C.

The EEC uses a torque motor driver to control the position of the metering valve in the fuel metering unit. The EEC uses solenoid drivers to control the other functions of the FMU. The EEC also controls several other subsystems of the engine through torque motors and solenoids as shown in Figure 2-56 on page 2-41 of FAA-H-8083-32. Some of these subsystems are: fuel and air oil coolers, bleed valves, variable stator vanes, turbine cooling air valves, and the turbine case cooling system.

[For more detailed information refer to Powerplant Handbook H-8083-32-ATB, Chapter 2 p.40-42] Figure 2-56]

2-42) B.

During engine trimming, the fuel control is checked for idle RPM, maximum RPM, acceleration and deceleration. In general, the procedure consists of obtaining the ambient air temperature and the field barometric pressure immediately preceding the trimming of the engine. Using these readings, the desired turbine discharge pressure or EPR reading, computed from charts published in the maintenance manual, should be attained.

[For more detailed information refer to Powerplant Handbook H-8083-32-ATB, Chapter 2 p.42]

2-43) A.

After the engine has started and run until stabilized, a check should be made to ensure that the compressor air bleed valves have fully closed. All accessory drive air bleed for which the trim curve has not been corrected must be turned off. Then, a comparison can be made of the observed and computed turbine discharge pressure Pt7 (or EPR) to trim as necessary. The engine fuel control is then adjusted to obtain the target turbine discharge pressure Pt7 or EPR.

[For more detailed information refer to Powerplant Handbook H-8083-32-ATB, Chapter 2 p.42]

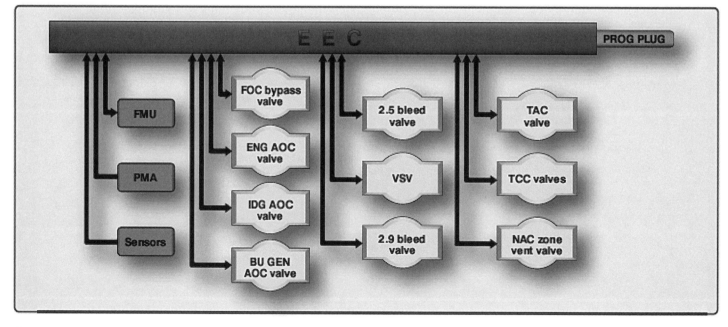

Figure 2-56. *Systems controlled by EEC.*

2-44) AMP068

The main engine-driven fuel pump on a turbine engine

    A.   is a variable displacement pump.
    B.   produces adequate capacity at all operating conditions and has excess capacity over most of the range of operation.
    C.   is a single stage pump.

2-45) AMP068

The temperature of turbine engine fuel is often kept above 32˚F

    A.   by fuel heaters located in the wing and main fuselage tanks.
    B.   to ensure rapid combustion in the engine.
    C.   so that ice crystals do not form in the filter and block fuel flow.

2-46) AMP042

Hot spots can burn a hole in the combustion section liner on a turbine engine. This is caused by

    A.   a misaligned fuel nozzle resulting in a flame that is not centered in the flame area.
    B.   insufficient fuel flow to the fuel nozzles.
    C.   excessive fuel flow to the fuel nozzle which cannot be fully combusted.

2-47) AMP068

What is the purpose of the flow divider in a turbine engine duplex fuel nozzle system?

    A.   Allows an alternative flow of fuel if the primary flow clogs or is restricted.
    B.   Creates the primary and secondary fuel supplies.
    C.   Provides a flow path for bleed air which aids in the atomization of fuel.

2-48) AMP068

What is the purpose of a dump valve as used with fuel on a gas turbine engine?

    A.   It cuts off the fuel flow to the engine fuel manifold and dumps the manifold fuel into the combustor to burn just before the engine shuts down.
    B.   It drains the engine manifold lines to prevent fuel boiling and subsequent deposits in the lines as a result of residual engine heat (at engine shutdown).
    C.   It dumps extra fuel into the engine in order to provide for quick acceleration during rapid throttle advancement.

2 - Fuel and Fuel Metering

Answers

2-44) B.
Main fuel pumps deliver a continuous supply of fuel at the proper pressure and at all times during operation of the aircraft engine. They are positive displacement pumps so, often, when fuel requirements are low during a flight segment, a pressure relief valve bypasses excess fuel back to the pump inlet. A centrifugal, variable displacement pump often discharges into the inlet of the positive-displacement second stage pump which produces the pump outlet fuel flow.
[For more detailed information refer to Powerplant Handbook H-8083-32-ATB, Chapter 2 p.43]

2-45) C.
Gas turbine engine fuel systems are every susceptible to the formation of ice in the fuel filters. When fuel inside the aircraft fuel tanks cools to 32°F or below, residual water in the fuel tends to freeze, forming ice crystals. These ice crystals can become trapped in the fuel filter and block fuel flow to the engine.
[For more detailed information refer to Powerplant Handbook H-8083-32-ATB, Chapter 2 p.43]

2-46) A.
The fuel nozzles inject fuel into the combustion area in a highly atomized, precisely patterned spray so that burning is completely even, in the shortest possible time, and in the smallest possible space. It is very important that the fuel be evenly distributed and well centered in the flame area within the liners. This is to preclude the formation of any hot spots in the combustion chambers and to prevent the flame burning through the liner.
[For more detailed information refer to Powerplant Handbook H-8083-32-ATB, Chapter 2 p.45]

2-47) B.
Fuel nozzle types vary considerably between engines, although for the most part, fuel is sprayed into the combustion area under pressure through small orifices in the nozzles. The two types of fuel nozzles generally used are the simplex and the duplex configuration. The duplex nozzle usually requires a dual manifold and a pressurizing valve or a flow divider for dividing primary and secondary (main) fuel flow. A flow divider creates primary and secondary fuel supplies that are discharged through separate manifolds, providing two separate fuel flows.
[For more detailed information refer to Powerplant Handbook H-8083-32-ATB, Chapter 2 p.45-46]

2-48) B.
Drain valves are units used for draining fuel from the various components of the engine where accumulated fuel is most likely to present operating problems. The possibility of combustion chamber accumulations with the resultant fire hazard is one problem. A residual problem is the deposit of lead and/or gum, after evaporation, in such places as fuel manifolds and nozzles. In some instances, fuel manifolds are drained by an individual unit known as a drip or dump valve. This type of valve may be operated by pressure differential or it may be solenoid operated.
[For more detailed information refer to Powerplant Handbook H-8083-32-ATB, Chapter 2 p.47]

Applicants for powerplant certification are required to answer oral examination questions before, after, or in conjunction with the practical examination portion of the airman certification process. The oral examination is used to establish knowledge. The practical examination is used to establish skill, which is the application of knowledge. Use the following questions to prepare for the oral examination. The questions are examples aligned with Practical Test Standards subject matter from which the examiner will choose topics for oral examination.

2-1(O). Name two maintenance or inspection tasks performed during routine fuel system inspection and maintenance.

2-2(O). What checks of a fuel system can be made to verify proper operation?

2-3(O). What is the function and operation of a fuel boost (booster) pump?

2-4(O). What is the function of a fuel selector valve?

2-5(O). What is done to inspect an engine driven pump for leaks and security?

2-6(O). What is the function and operation of engine fuel filters on a turbine engine fuel system?

2-7(O). What is vapor lock and how can it be avoided or remedied?

2-8(O). What is a possible reason for fuel running out of a carburetor throttle body?

2-9(O). What are some indications that the mixture is improperly adjusted?

2-10(O). What is the procedure for checking idle mixture adjustment on a reciprocating engine?

2-11(O). What are possible causes of poor engine acceleration, engine backfiring or missing when the throttle is advanced?

2-12(O). What are three types of fuel metering systems used on reciprocating engine and how do they operate?

2-13(O). Name the fuel metering system components in a float type carburetor.

2-14(O). What is the purpose of the part power stop on some engines when accomplishing engine trim procedure?

2-15(O). Explain the operation of a fuel flow indicating system and where it is connected into the engine.

2-16(O). What is the operation of a manifold pressure gauge?

2-1(O). Drain sumps, change or clean filters, check linkages for smooth stop-to-stop operation, check fuel lines for cracks and hoses for deterioration, leak check, check pump operation and motor brush wear, check selector valve for wear, check fuel tanks for corrosion and leaks, check fuel quantity and pressure gauges for proper operation, check vents for obstruction, check function of warning system.
Reference: FAA-H-8083-30-ATB page 2-32, 2-33, and 2-34

2-2(O). A fuel system should have no external leaks. Make sure all units are securely attached. Drain plugs and valves should be opened to clear any water or sediment. The same is true for the filter, screen, and sump. Filter screens and auxiliary pumps must be clean and free from corrosion. Fuel system controls should move freely, lock securely, and should not rub or chafe. Fuel vents must be in the correct position and free from obstruction. Overall engine performance checks give insight into proper fuel system operation. If engine input (manifold pressure) results in the correct power output (engine RPM), the engine performance is acceptable and it is likely the fuel system is operating properly. Check all fuel system related gauges for indications of fuel system operation. Carburetor air temperature, fuel flow, fuel pressure, and cylinder head temperature indications can all indicate potential fuel system problems. An idle mixture check can also be performed.
Reference: FAA-H-8083-30-ATB page 2-31, 2-32, 10-22, 10-23, 10-24, and 10-39

2-3(O). A fuel boost pump is designed to provide positive fuel pressure to the engine fuel system. The boost pump forces fuel through the selector valve to the main line strainer. During starting, the boost pump forces fuel through a bypass in the engine-driven fuel pump to the carburetor or fuel injection system. Once the engine driven pump is up to speed, it takes over and delivers the fuel to the metering device.
Reference: FAA-H-8083-30-ATB page 2-3

2-4(O). A fuel selector valve is controlled on the flight deck to select the tank from which tank fuel will be delivered to the engine.
Reference: FAA-H-8083-30-ATB page 2-3

2-5(O). If booster pumps are installed, they should be energized to check the fuel system for leaks. (During this check, an ammeter can be used to insure all boost pumps pull roughly the same amperage.) The drain lines of the engine drive pump should be free of traps, bends, or restrictions. Check for leaks and the security of the engine driven pump mounting bolts. Check the vent and drain lines for obstructions.
Reference: FAA-H-8083-30-ATB page 2-32

2-6(O). The function of the engine fuel filters is to remove micronic particles that may be in the fuel so they do not damage the fuel pump or the fuel control unit. Typically, a low-pressure filter is installed between the supply tanks and the engine fuel system. An additional high-pressure fuel filter is installed between the fuel pump and the fuel control. Three kinds of filters are used: micron, wafer screen, and screen mesh. The micron has the smallest particle filtering capability. It requires a bypass valve because it could be easily clogged. Many filters have a bypass indicator. Periodic servicing and replacement of filter elements is imperative. Daily draining of fuel tank sumps and low pressure filters eliminates much filter trouble and undue maintenance of fuel pumps and fuel control units.
Reference: FAA-H-8083-30-ATB page 2-44 and 2-45

2-7(O). Fuel should be in the liquid state until it is discharged in the intake air stream for combustion. Under certain conditions, the fuel may vaporize in the lines, pumps, or other units. The vapor pockets formed restrict fuel flow through the units to the fuel-metering device. The partial or complete interruption of fuel flow is called vapor lock. The three general causes of vapor lock are low pressure on the fuel, high fuel temperatures, and excessive fuel turbulence. Fuel systems are designed to avoid vapor lock. The most significant remedy for vapor lock is the use of boost pumps which pump the fuel from the storage tank to the metering devise under pressure so it cannot vaporize prematurely.
Reference: FAA-H-8083-30-ATB page 2-2

2-8(O). The float level and fuel level in the float chamber of the carburetor must be below the level of the discharge nozzle or fuel will leak from the nozzle when the engine is not operating.
Reference: FAA-H-8083-30-ATB page 2-7, 2-10 and 2-11

2-9(O). Carbon deposits on the spark plugs and spark plug fouling are signs that the ide mixture is not properly set. Also, faulty acceleration may be an indication of an excessively lean mixture.
Reference: FAA-H-8083-30-ATB page 2-30 to 2-31

2-10(O). To check the idle mixture on a warmed up engine, move the mixture control slowly toward the idle cutoff position. Observe the tachometer for a slight RPM rise (10 – 50 RPM) before the engine cuts out. If this does not occur, adjust the idle mixture until it does.
Reference: FAA-H-8083-30-ATB page 2-30 to 2-31

2-11(O). A lean mixture is the most like likely cause. A cracked distributor block or high-tension leak between two ignition leads can also cause these symptoms and backfiring.
Reference: FAA-H-8083-30-ATB page 2-31, 10-37, and 10-39

2-12(O). Float-type carburetors, pressure carburetors, and fuel injection systems are all used on reciprocating aircraft engines. A float type carburetor uses the volume of air moving through a venturi to cause a suction that meters the fuel. A pressure carburetor uses a closed, pressurized fuel system. The venturi serves only to create pressure differentials that control the quantity of fuel to the metering jet in proportion to the airflow to the engine. The fuel is discharged under positive pressure. A fuel injection system is a continuous flow system that measures engine air consumption and uses airflow forces to control the fuel flow to the engine. Fuel is injected into the airstream on a float type carburetor just before the throttle valve, just after the throttle valve on a pressure carburetor and directly into the cylinder head on a fuel injection system.
Reference: FAA-H-8083-30-ATB page 2-10 through 2-15, 2-22

2-13(O). The main metering system components include the throttle, the venturi, the discharge nozzle, and the float and float valve in the float chamber. The idling system components include the idling jet and the idle mixture adjustment. The mixture control system includes either a needle valve or a back-suction line, the acceleration system including a piston/pump and the economizer system including the economizer needle valve.
Reference: FAA-H-8083-30-ATB page 2-11 to 2-15

2-14(O). The engine is operated at full power or at the part power control trim stop for a sufficient amount of time to ensure it has completely stabilized. This is usually at least 5 minutes. Follow all manufacturer's instructions.
Reference: FAA-H-8083-30-ATB page 2-42

2-15(O). A fuel pressure gauge, calibrated in pounds per hour fuel flow, is used as a fuel flow meter with the Bendix RSA fuel injection system for reciprocating aircraft engines. This gauge is connected to the flow divider and senses the pressure being applied to the discharge nozzles. This pressure is in direct proportion to the fuel flow and indicates engine power output and fuel consumption.
Reference: FAA-H-8083-30-ATB page 2-24

2-16(O). The manifold pressure gauge indicates the pressure in the induction system of a reciprocating aircraft engine. The pressure is measured in the intake manifold downstream of the throttle valve. It is displayed on the flight deck in inches of mercury (Hg) and is directly proportional to the power output of the engine.
Reference: FAA-H-8083-30-ATB page 2-1, 10-39

Applicants for powerplant certification are required to demonstrate the ability to apply knowledge by performing maintenance related tasks for the examiner. The Practical Test Standards (PTS) list the subject areas from which the skill elements to be performed by the applicant are chosen. The following examples resemble tasks an examiner may ask an applicant to perform. The Performance Level required to be demonstrated for each skill element is listed. Consult the PTS for Level descriptions.

2-1(P). Given an actual aircraft engine or mockup, complete an operational check of a fuel selector valve and record your findings. [Level 3]

2-2(P). Given an actual aircraft engine or mockup, inspect an engine fuel filter assembly for leaks and record your findings. [Level 3]

2-3(P). Given an actual aircraft engine or mockup, inspect a repair to an engine fuel system and record your findings. [Level 3]

2-4(P). Given an actual aircraft engine or mockup, complete an operational check of a fuel boost pump and record your findings. [Level 3]

2-5(P). Given an actual aircraft engine or mockup, appropriate publications, and tooling, repair a fuel selector valve and record maintenance. [Level 3]

2-6(P). Given an actual aircraft engine or mockup, inspect a main fuel filter assembly for leaks and record your findings. [Level 3]

2-7(P). Given an actual aircraft engine or mockup, complete an operational check of a remotely located fuel valve and record your findings. [Level 3]

2-8(P). Given an actual aircraft engine or mockup, locate and identify a turbine engine fuel heater. [Level 2]

2-9(P). Given an actual aircraft engine or mockup, appropriate publications, equipment, and materials service an engine fuel strainer and record maintenance. [Level 3]

2-10(P). Given an actual aircraft engine or mockup, inspect an engine driven fuel pump for leaks and security and record your findings. [Level 3]

2-11(P). Given an actual aircraft engine or mockup and appropriate publication, complete an operational check of the engine fuel pressure and record your findings. [Level 3]

2-12(P). Given an actual aircraft engine or mockup, appropriate publications, equipment and tooling repair an engine fuel system. [Level 3]

2-13(P). Given an actual aircraft engine or mockup, appropriate publications, equipment and tooling repair an engine fuel system component. [Level 3]

2-14(P). Given an actual aircraft engine or mockup, appropriate publications, appropriate testing equipment, if necessary and an unknown discrepancy, troubleshoot a fuel pressure system and record your findings. [Level 3]

2-15(P). Given an actual aircraft engine or mockup, appropriate publications, equipment and tooling remove and install the accelerating pump in a float-type carburetor and record maintenance. [Level 3]

2-16(P). Given an actual aircraft engine or mockup, appropriate publications, equipment and tooling remove and install the accelerating pump in a float-type carburetor and record maintenance. [Level 3]

2-17(P). Given an actual aircraft engine or mockup, appropriate publications, equipment and tooling check and adjust the float level of a float-type carburetor and record maintenance. [Level 3]

2-18(P). Given an actual aircraft engine or mockup, appropriate publications, equipment and tooling check the needle and seat in a float-type carburetor for proper operation and record your findings. [Level 2]

2-19(P). Given an actual aircraft engine or mockup, appropriate publications, equipment and tooling check a fuel injection nozzle for proper spray pattern and record your findings. [Level 2]

2-20(P). Given an actual aircraft engine or mockup, appropriate publications, equipment and tooling install a fuel injector nozzle and record maintenance.
[Level 3]

2-21(P). Given an actual aircraft engine or mockup, appropriate publications, equipment and tooling check and adjust the idle mixture and record maintenance. [Level 3]

2-22(P). Given an actual aircraft engine or mockup, appropriate publications, equipment and tooling install a turbine engine fuel nozzle and record maintenance. [Level 3]

2-23(P). Given an actual aircraft engine or mockup, locate and identify various fuel metering system components. [Level 2]

2-24(P). Given an actual aircraft engine or mockup, appropriate publications, equipment, and tooling service a carburetor fuel screen and record maintenance. [Level 3]

Induction and Exhaust Systems

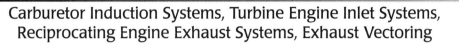

CHAPTER 3

Carburetor Induction Systems, Turbine Engine Inlet Systems,
Reciprocating Engine Exhaust Systems, Exhaust Vectoring

3-1) AMP003
A method commonly used to prevent carburetor icing is to

    A. preheat the intake air.
    B. mix alcohol with the fuel.
    C. electrically heat the venturi and throttle valve.

3-2) AMP070
One source commonly used for carburetor air heat is

    A. turbocharger heated air.
    B. alternate air heat.
    C. exhaust gases.

3-3) AMP056
On an airplane equipped with an alternate air door in the carburetor air box, when the main air duct air filter becomes blocked or clogged, the

    A. system will automatically allow warm, unfiltered air to be drawn into the engine through a spring loaded air valve.
    B. the carburetor heat door will automatically open to supply the engine.
    C. alternate air must be selected in the cockpit to continue induction into the engine.

3-4) AMP056
The action of a carburetor air scoop is to supply air to the carburetor, but it may also

    A. cool the engine.
    B. keep fuel lines cool and prevent vapor lock.
    C. increase the pressure of the incoming air by ram effect.

3-5) AMP003
During engine operation, if carburetor heat is applied, it will

    A. increase air to fuel ratio.
    B. increase engine RPM.
    C. decrease air density to the carburetor.

3-6) AMP003
The use of carburetor heat when it is not needed causes

    A. a very lean mixture.
    B. excessive increase in manifold pressure.
    C. a decrease in power and possible detonation.

3 - Induction and Exhaust Systems
Answers

3-1) A.

A simple way to prevent carburetor icing is to heat the air entering the carburetor so that components remain above freezing temperature and water in the air cannot freeze. When selected, warm air is ducted from around the exhaust system and directed into the carburetor to be mixed with the fuel for combustion in the engine. This raises the intake air temperature and essentially acts as a preheat of the intake air.
[For more detailed information refer to General Handbook H-8083-30-ATB, Chapter 5 p.16]

3-2) C.

The carburetor heat valve admits air from the outside air scoop for normal operation and it admits warm air from the engine compartment for operation during icing conditions. The carburetor heat is operated by a push- pull control in the cockpit. When selected, warm ducted air from around the exhaust system is directed into the carburetor. This raises the intake air temperature.
[For more detailed information refer to General Handbook H-8083-30-ATB, Chapter 5 p.16]

3-3) A.

On a basic carburetor induction system found on a light aircraft with reciprocating engine, an induction air box allows air to be drawn from a scoop mounted in the nose cowling or, when selected, from inside the cowling for the purpose of warming the carburetor by ducting air past the exhaust system. However, an alternate air door can be opened by engine suction if the normal route of airflow should be blocked by something. The valve is spring loaded closed and is sucked open by the engine if needed.
[For more detailed information refer to General Handbook H-8083-30-ATB, Chapter 5 p.16]

3-4) C.

The carburetor air filter is installed in the air scoop in front of the carburetor air duct. The air duct provides passage for outside air to the carburetor. Air enters the duct through the scoop. The intake opening is located in the slipstream so air is forced into the induction system giving ram air effect to the incoming airflow (raises pressure).
[For more detailed information refer to General Handbook H-8083-30-ATB, Chapter 5 p.16]

3-5) C.

Improper or careless use of carburetor heat can be just as dangerous as the most advanced stage of induction system ice. Increasing the temperature of the air causes it to expand and decrease in density. This action reduces the weight of the charge delivered to the cylinder and causes a noticeable loss in power because of decreased volumetric efficiency.
[For more detailed information refer to General Handbook H-8083-30-ATB, Chapter 5 p.16]

3-6) C.

Improper or careless use of carburetor heat can be just as dangerous as the most advanced stage of induction system ice. Increasing the temperature of the air causes it to expand and decrease in density. This action reduces the weight of the charge delivered to the cylinder and causes a noticeable loss in power because of decreased volumetric efficiency. Also, high intake air temperature may cause detonation as cylinder head temperature increases and engine failure is possible especially during takeoff and high power operation.
[For more detailed information refer to General Handbook H-8083-30-ATB, Chapter 5 p.16]

3-7) AMP003

When starting an engine equipped with a carburetor air heater, in what position should the heater control be placed?

  A. Hot.
  B. Cold.
  C. Neutral.

3-8) AMP070

Boost manifold pressure is generally considered to be any manifold pressure above

  A. 14.7 inches Hg.
  B. 50 inches Hg.
  C. 30 inches Hg.

3-9) AMP056

What is used to drive a supercharger?

  A. Exhaust gasses.
  B. Gear train from the crankshaft.
  C. Belt drive through a pulley arrangement.

3-10) AMP070

An external supercharger or turbosupercharger, also known as a turbocharger is composed of three main parts. They are

  A. the compressor assembly, the turbine wheel assembly and a full floating shaft bearing assembly.
  B. the turbine, the diffuser, and the waste gate.
  C. the turbine, the compressor, and the carburetor.

3-11) AMP070

What directly regulates the speed of a turbocharger?

  A. Turbine.
  B. Waste gate.
  C. Throttle.

3-12) AMP070

If the turbocharger waste gate is completely closed,

  A. none of the exhaust gases are directed through the turbine.
  B. the turbocharger is in the OFF position.
  C. all the exhaust gases are directed through the turbine.

3 - Induction and Exhaust Systems
Answers

3-7) B.
When there is no danger of icing, the carburetor heat control is normally kept in the COLD position. To prevent damage to the heater valve in the case of backfire, carburetor heat should not be used while starting the engine. Also during ground operation, only enough carburetor heat should be used to give smooth engine performance.
[For more detailed information refer to General Handbook H-8083-30-ATB, Chapter 5 p.16]

3-8) C.
A true supercharged engine, called a ground boosted engine, can boost the manifold pressure above 30 inches Hg. In other words, a true supercharger boosts manifold pressure above ambient pressure which is 29.92 inches Hg. So in general, boost manifold pressure or "boost pressure" when discussing manifold pressure is manifold pressure above 30 inches Hg.
[For more detailed information refer to General Handbook H-8083-30-ATB, Chapter 5 p.16]

3-9) B.
A fuel distribution impeller is connected directly to the crankshaft to aid in even fuel distribution. Since it operates at the same speed as the crankshaft, this is accomplished without materially increasing boost or increasing the pressure on the fuel/air mixture flowing into the cylinders. A supercharger, or blower impeller, is designed to increase the pressure on the charge delivered to the cylinders. It is driven through a gear train from the crankshaft so that it can rotate at a higher speed than the crankshaft to compress the charge.
[For more detailed information refer to General Handbook H-8083-30-ATB, Chapter 5 p.16]

3-10) A.
Externally driven superchargers or turbochargers derive their power from the energy of the engine exhaust gases directed against a turbine which drives an impeller that compresses the air used for combustion in the engine. The typical turbocharger, shown in Figure 3-12 on page 3-9 of FAA-H-8083-32, is comprised of three main parts. The turbine wheel assembly, the compressor wheel assembly, and the full floating shaft bearing assembly that supports the rotating shaft that connects the two.
[For more detailed information refer to General Handbook H-8083-30-ATB, Chapter 5 p.16]

3-11) B.
The turbine wheel, driven by exhaust gasses, drives the compressor impeller. The turbocharger housing collects and directs the exhaust gases onto the turbine wheel. The waste gate regulates the amount of exhaust gases directed to the turbine. As such, it regulates the speed of the rotor (the turbine and impeller on the common shaft). By regulating the speed of the turbocharger rotor, the amount of compression applied to the engine induction air is controlled.
[For more detailed information refer to General Handbook H-8083-30-ATB, Chapter 5 p.16]

3-12) C.
If the waste gate is completely closed, all the exhaust gases are "backed up" and forced through the turbine wheel. If the waste gate is partially closed, a corresponding amount of exhaust gas is directed to the turbine. When the waste gate is fully open, nearly all of the exhaust gases pass overboard providing little or no boost.
[For more detailed information refer to General Handbook H-8083-30-ATB, Chapter 5 p.16]

3-13) AMP056

What is the purpose of a normalized turbocharger system used on a small reciprocating aircraft engine?

    A. Compresses the air to hold the cabin pressure constant after the aircraft has reached its critical altitude.

    B. Maintains constant air velocity in the intake manifold.

    C. Compresses air to maintain manifold pressure constant from sea level to the critical altitude of the engine.

3-14) AMP070

What are the three basic regulating components of a sea-level boosted turbocharger system?

1. Exhaust bypass assembly.
2. Compressor assembly.
3. Pump and bearing casing.
4. Density controller.
5. Differential pressure controller.

    A. 2, 3, and 4.

    B. 1, 4, and 5.

    C. 1, 2, and 3.

3-15) AMP070

The absolute pressure controller (APC) on some small engines is designed to regulate oil pressure which flows through the waste gate actuator and then through the controllers on the turbocharger system; the pressure between the turbocharger and the throttle valve is called

    A. turbocharger boost pressure.

    B. induction manifold pressure.

    C. upper deck pressure.

3-16) AMP070

To what altitude will a turbocharger maintain sea level pressure?

    A. Critical altitude.

    B. Service ceiling.

    C. Pressure altitude.

3-17) AMP070

What is the purpose of the density controller in a turbocharger system?

    A. Limits the maximum manifold pressure that can be produced at other than full throttle conditions.

    B. Limits the maximum manifold pressure that can be produced at full throttle.

    C. Maintains constant air velocity at the carburetor inlet.

3-18) AMP070

An indication of unregulated power changes that result in continuous drift of manifold pressure indication on a turbocharged aircraft engine is known as

    A. overshoot.

    B. waste gate fluctuation.

    C. bootstrapping.

3-13) C.
A normalizing turbocharger system found on a small aircraft engine compensates for the power lost due to pressure drop resulting from increased altitude. It is designed to operate only above the altitude at which the engine can no longer develop full power. As such, it not a true "supercharger" because it does not provide a pressure boost of the induction air above 30 inches Hg.
[For more detailed information refer to General Handbook H-8083-30-ATB, Chapter 5 p.16]

3-14) B.
A sea level boosted turbocharger system is regulated by the position of the oil controlled exhaust bypass assembly. The density controller which is designed to limit the manifold pressure below the turbocharger's critical altitude, repositions the oil bleed valve that sends the controlling oil to exhaust gas bypass assembly. The differential pressure controller functions during all positions of the exhaust bypass valve except the fully open position. It compares pressure on both sides of the throttle valve and adjusts oil bleed return to the crankcase which affects the position of the exhaust bypass valve.
[For more detailed information refer to General Handbook H-8083-30-ATB, Chapter 5 p.16]

3-15) C.
The pressure from the outlet of the compressor of the turbocharger to the throttle is referred to as deck pressure or upper deck pressure. Induction manifold pressure is the pressure between the throttle and the intake valve. Turbocharger boost pressure is manifold pressure greater than ambient air pressure (above 30 inches Hg). The APC senses upper deck pressure and regulates waste gate pressure, thereby positioning the waste gate valve to regulate maximum upper deck pressure.
[For more detailed information refer to General Handbook H-8083-30-ATB, Chapter 5 p.16]

3-16) A.
When the waste gate of a turbocharger system is fully closed, the maximum volume of exhaust gases flow into the turbocharger turbine. This provides the maximum pressurization of the induction air. Critical altitude is the altitude above which, even with the waste gate fully closed, maximum power (manifold pressure) cannot be maintained. Since air is most dense at sea level, power developed at sea level is the same as that developed at the critical altitude. Above critical altitude, only power less than that which can be developed at sea level can be achieved.
[For more detailed information refer to General Handbook H-8083-30-ATB, Chapter 5 p.16]

3-17) B.
The density controller is designed to limit the manifold pressure below the turbocharger's critical altitude. A nitrogen-filled bellows reacts to temperature and density changes. It repositions the oil bleed valve which changes the pressure sent to the exhaust vent valve to move it to the correct position at full throttle. In this way, the density controller prevents overboost of the engine.
[For more detailed information refer to General Handbook H-8083-30-ATB, Chapter 5 p.16]

3-18) C.
Bootstrapping is the undesirable cycle of turbocharging events which causes the manifold pressure to drift in an attempt to reach a state of equilibrium. It is caused by slight changes in power due to temperature or RPM drift which is then magnified by the turbocharger. The differential pressure controller reduces the transient increases in power when the throttle is partially open.
[For more detailed information refer to General Handbook H-8083-30-ATB, Chapter 5 p.16]

3-19) AMP070

The purpose of an aftercooler when used with a turbocharged engine is to cool the

A. exhaust gases before they come in contact with the turbo drive.
B. turbocharger bearings.
C. air entering the induction system from the turbocharger.

3-20) AMP068

The purpose of the engine inlet on a turbine engine is to

A. provide a well-mixed volume of air to the inlet of the compressor.
B. provide a uniform and steady airflow to avoid compressor stall.
C. reduce the speed of the incoming air and direct it at the correct angle toward the compressor blades.

3-21) AMP008

Ram recovery refers to

A. increasing pressure and airflow to make up for thrust loss at high speeds.
B. conversion of drag to useful air velocity.
C. the use of inlet air doors to guide the air into the inlet.

3-22) AMP008

A divided-entrance inlet air duct on a turbine powered aircraft

A. is found on newer designs because it reduces the frontal area of the inlet duct.
B. has better flow characteristics than a single opening.
C. presents difficulty to designers due to the amount of drag produced.

3-23) AMP013

The purpose of a bellmouth compressor inlet is to

A. provide an increase in ram air effect at low airspeeds.
B. maximize aerodynamic efficiency of the inlet.
C. provide an increased pressure drop in the inlet.

3-24) AMP008

Which statement is true concerning inlet icing of turbine engines?

A. Turboprops rely on propeller anti-icing to keep the inlet(s) free from ice.
B. Most turbofan inlets use AC powered electric anti-icing.
C. Electric anti-icing is found more commonly on turboprop engines than turbofan engines.

3-19) C.

When the turbocharger compresses air for induction, the temperature of the air increases. If the air is too hot, it can exceed maximum throttle inlet temperature which can lead to detonation of the fuel air charge in the combustion chamber. The aftercooler cools the compressed air from the turbocharger compressor which increases the charge air density resulting in better engine performance.

[For more detailed information refer to General Handbook H-8083-30-ATB, Chapter 5 p.16]

3-20) B.

The engine inlet of a turbine engine is designed to provide a relatively distortion-free flow of air in the required quantity to the inlet of the compressor. Many engines use inlet guide vanes to help straighten the airflow and direct it into the first stages of the compressor. A uniform steady airflow is necessary to avoid compressor stall and excessive internal temperatures in the turbine section.

[For more detailed information refer to General Handbook H-8083-30-ATB, Chapter 5 p.16]

3-21) A.

As aircraft speed increases, thrust tends to decrease somewhat. As the aircraft speed reaches a certain point, ram recovery compensates for the losses caused by the increases in speed. The inlet must be able to recover as much of the total pressure of the free airstream as possible. As air molecules are trapped and begin to be compressed in the inlet, much of the pressure loss is recovered. This added pressure at the inlet of the engine increases the pressure and airflow to the engine. This is known as ram recovery or total pressure recovery.

[For more detailed information refer to General Handbook H-8083-30-ATB, Chapter 5 p.16]

3-22) C.

The divided air duct can be either a wing-root inlet or a scoop at each side of the fuselage. The inlet scoops are generally placed as far forward as possible to permit a gradual bend toward the compressor inlet for smoother air flow. Two entrances present more problems to the aircraft designer than a single-entrance duct because of the difficulty of obtaining sufficient air scoop area without imposing prohibitive amounts of drag. The divided-entrance turbine engine inlet duct is found primarily on military aircraft.

[For more detailed information refer to General Handbook H-8083-30-ATB, Chapter 5 p.16]

3-23) B.

A bellmouth inlet is usually installed on a turbine engine undergoing testing in a test cell. The bellmouth is designed with the single objective of obtaining very high aerodynamic efficiency. Essentially, the inlet is a bell-shaped funnel having carefully rounded shoulders which offer practically no air resistance. Duct loss is so slight that it is considered to be zero.

[For more detailed information refer to General Handbook H-8083-30-ATB, Chapter 5 p.16]

3-24) C.

The inlet for many types of turboprop engines are anti-iced by using electrical elements in the lip opening of the air intake area. Deflector doors are sometimes used to deflect ice or dirt away from the intake as well. Warm bleed air is drawn from the compressor and circulated on the inside of the inlet lip for anti-icing on turbofan engines.

[For more detailed information refer to General Handbook H-8083-30-ATB, Chapter 5 p.16]

3-25) AMP068

Turbofan engine inlets

   A. divert air away from the center of the fan blades.
   B. contain sound absorbing materials.
   C. have unconventional air inlets to eliminate FOD (foreign object damage).

3-26) AMP056

What type of nuts are used to hold an exhaust system to the cylinders?

   A. Brass or heat–resistant high temperature locknuts.
   B. High temperature fiber self-locking nuts.
   C. High temperature aluminum self-locking nuts.

3-27) AMP056

All of the following are recommended markers for reciprocating engine exhaust systems except

   A. Indian ink.
   B. lead pencil.
   C. white chalk.

3-28) AMP057

How may reciprocating engine exhaust leaks be detected?

   A. An exhaust trail of of the tailpipe on the airplane exterior.
   B. Fluctuating manifold pressure indication.
   C. Signs of exhaust soot inside the cowling and on adjacent components.

3-29) AMP057

Repair of exhaust system components

   A. is impossible because the material cannot be identified.
   B. must be accomplished by the component manufacturer.
   C. is not recommended to be accomplished in the field.

3-30) AMP057

Reciprocating engine exhaust systems that have repairs or sloppy weld beads which protrude internally are unacceptable because they cause

   A. base metal fatigue.
   B. localized cracks.
   C. local hot spots.

3-31) AMP068

The exhaust section of a turbine engine is designed to

   A. impart a high exit velocity to the exhaust gases.
   B. increase temperature, therefore increase velocity.
   C. decrease temperature, therefore decreasing the pressure.

3-25) B.
Inside the inlet of a turbofan engine, sound reducing materials lower the noise generated by the large diameter fan. The fan permits the use of a conventional air inlet duct, resulting in low inlet duct loss. The fan also reduces engine damage from the ingestion of foreign material because much of any material that may be ingested is thrown radially outward and passes through the fan discharge rather than through the core of the engine.
[For more detailed information refer to General Handbook H-8083-30-ATB, Chapter 5 p.16]

3-26) A.
The down-stacks of the exhaust on a horizontally opposed reciprocating engine are connected to the cylinders with high temperature locknuts and are secured to the collector tube by ring clamps. Fiber self-locking nuts and aluminum nuts cannot withstand the high temperatures encountered on exhaust systems.
[For more detailed information refer to General Handbook H-8083-30-ATB, Chapter 5 p.16]

3-27) B.
Exhaust system parts should never be marked with lead pencil. The lead is absorbed by the metal of the exhaust system when heated creating a distinct change in its molecular structure. This change softens the metal in the area of the mark causing cracks and eventual failure.
[For more detailed information refer to General Handbook H-8083-30-ATB, Chapter 5 p.16]

3-28) C.
An exhaust leak is indicated by a flat gray or a sooty black streak on the pipes, on the cowling in the area of the leak, or on adjacent components.
[For more detailed information refer to General Handbook H-8083-30-ATB, Chapter 5 p.16]

3-29) C.
It is generally recommended that exhaust stacks, mufflers, tailpipes, etc., be replaced with new or reconditioned components rather than repaired. Welded repairs to exhaust systems are complicated by the difficulty of accurately identifying the base metal so that the proper repair materials can be selected. Changes in composition and grain structures of the original base metal further complicate the repair.
[For more detailed information refer to General Handbook H-8083-30-ATB, Chapter 5 p.16]

3-30) C.
When welded repairs are necessary, the original contours should be retained. The exhaust system alignment must not be warped or otherwise affected. Repairs or sloppy weld beads that protrude internally are not acceptable as they cause local hot spots and may restrict exhaust gas flow.
[For more detailed information refer to General Handbook H-8083-30-ATB, Chapter 5 p.16]

3-31) A.
On turbine engines, through the use of a convergent exhaust nozzle, the exhaust gases increase in velocity before they are discharged from the exhaust nozzle. Increasing the velocity of the gases increases their momentum and increases the thrust produced (15-20 percent of total engine thrust is typical on a turbofan engine). The exception to this is the turboshaft engine in which all possible energy produced by the engine is designated for rotating the shaft and a divergent duct may be used.
[For more detailed information refer to General Handbook H-8083-30-ATB, Chapter 5 p.16]

3-32) AMP068

In a convergent exhaust nozzle, the diameter of the outlet

A. doesn't affect exhaust gas velocity.
B. must not be too large or energy will be wasted.
C. is as small as possible without stalling the engine.

3-33) AMP032

Engines using cold stream or cold and hot stream reversing include

A. high bypass turbofan engines.
B. turbojets.
C. turbojets with afterburners.

3-34) AMP032

The purpose of cascade vanes in a thrust reversing system is to

A. form a solid blocking door in the jet exhaust path.
B. turn the exhaust gases forward just after exiting the exhaust nozzle.
C. turn to a forward direction the fan airstream.

3-35) AMP032

Turbojet and turbofan thrust reverser systems are generally powered by

A. electricity or exhaust gases.
B. hydraulics or pneumatics.
C. hydraulics only.

3-36) AMP008

Turbine engines produce noise primarily from engine air intake, vibration, and engine exhaust. Which of these is of the greatest concern?

A. vibration from high speed rotation of the turbine blades.
B. engine intake noise from air being drawn into the engine at high velocity.
C. engine exhaust noise from the high velocity jet stream moving through a relatively quiet atmosphere.

3-37) AMP068

Turbine engine emissions

A. are caused by high combustion temperatures.
B. are caused by low combustion temperatures.
C. account for so little of all emissions into the atmosphere that they are of little concern.

3-32) B.

The restriction of the opening of the outlet of the exhaust nozzle is limited by two factors. If the nozzle opening is too big, thrust is being wasted. If it is too little, the flow is choked in the other components of the engine. In other words, the exhaust nozzle acts as an orifice the size of which determines the density and velocity of the gases as they emerge from the engine. This is critical to thrust performance.

[For more detailed information refer to General Handbook H-8083-30-ATB, Chapter 5 p.16]

3-33) A.

Mechanical blockage thrust reversing is accomplished by placing a removable obstruction in the exhaust gas stream rear of the exhaust nozzle. This type is generally used with ducted turbofan engines where the fan and core flow mix in a common nozzle before exiting the engine. In the aerodynamic blockage type of thrust reverser, used mainly with un-ducted turbofan engines, only fan air is used to slow the aircraft. Therefore, turbofan engines may use cold stream or cold and hot stream obstruction for thrust reversing. Note: turbojets do not have cold stream airflow. All air passes through the core of the engine (hot stream).

[For more detailed information refer to General Handbook H-8083-30-ATB, Chapter 5 p.16]

3-34) C.

In the aerodynamic blockage type of thrust reverser, used mainly with un-ducted turbofan engines, only fan air is used to slow the aircraft. A modern aerodynamic thrust reverser system consists of a translating cowl, blocker doors, and cascade vanes that redirect the fan airflow to slow the aircraft. If the thrust levers are at idle position and the aircraft has weight on wheels, moving the thrust levers aft activates the translating cowl to open. This closes the blocker doors and stops the fan airflow from going aft. It redirects the air through the cascade vanes which direct airflow forward to slow the aircraft.

[For more detailed information refer to General Handbook H-8083-30-ATB, Chapter 5 p.16]

3-35) B.

A thrust reverser systems consist of several components that move either the clam shell doors or the blocker doors and translating cowl. Actuating power is generally pneumatic or hydraulic and uses gearboxes, flex-drives, jackscrews, control valves, and air or hydraulic motors to deploy or stow the thrust reverser systems.

[For more detailed information refer to General Handbook H-8083-30-ATB, Chapter 5 p.16]

3-36) C.

There are three sources of noise involved in operation of a gas turbine engine. The engine air intake and vibration from the engine housing are sources of some noise, but the noise generated by these does not compare in magnitude with that produced by the engine exhaust. The noise produced by the engine exhaust is caused by the high degree of turbulence of a high velocity jet stream moving through a relatively quiet atmosphere. Turbulence within the high speed jet stream is very fine grain turbulence and produces relatively high frequency noise. As the velocity of the jet stream slows down, the jet stream mixes with the atmosphere and turbulence of a courser type is generated creating a lower frequency noise.

[For more detailed information refer to General Handbook H-8083-30-ATB, Chapter 5 p.16]

3-37) A.

Lowering exhaust emission from gas turbine engines, especially oxides of nitrogen (NO_x), continues to require improvement. Most advanced designs rely on a method of pre-mixing the fuel/air before it enters the combustion burner area. High energy swirlers adjacent to the fuel nozzles create a more thorough and leaner mix of fuel which burns at lower temperatures than in previous gas turbine engines. The NO_x levels are higher if the burning fuel/air mixture stays at high temperatures for a longer time.

[For more detailed information refer to General Handbook H-8083-30-ATB, Chapter 5 p.16]

Applicants for powerplant certification are required to answer oral examination questions before, after, or in conjunction with the practical examination portion of the airman certification process. The oral examination is used to establish knowledge. The practical examination is used to establish skill, which is the application of knowledge. Use the following questions to prepare for the oral examination. The questions are examples aligned with Practical Test Standards subject matter from which the examiner will choose topics for oral examination.

3-1(O). What are some indications of a leak in the induction system?

3-2(O). What are some inspection procedures for ice control systems?

3-3(O). Describe the automatic and manual operation of the alternate air valve.

3-4(O). What can be done to troubleshoot ice control systems?

3-5(O). Explain how a carburetor heat system operates and the procedure to verify proper operation.

3-6(O). What is the cause and effect of one kind of induction system ice?

3-7(O). Explain the function and operation of one type of supercharging.

3-8(O). Name some indicators of an exhaust leak or methods of detecting exhaust leaks.

3-9(O). Explain thrust reverser system operation and some of the main components.

3-10(O). Explain the differences between a cascade and a mechanical blockage door thrust reverser.

3-11(O). What are the hazards of exhaust system failure?

3-12(O). What are the effects of using improper materials to mark on exhaust system components?

3-13(O). What is the function and operation of a turbine engine exhaust nozzle?

3-1(O). Leaks in the induction system can cause an engine to idle improperly, run rough, or overheat. In severe cases, the engine may not start or may cut out. It also could fail to develop full power. A visual inspection for cracks and leaks should occur during all regularly scheduled engine inspections including ensuring the security of mounting of all components.
Reference: FAA- H-8083-32-ATB Pages 3-5, 10-34 to 10-38

3-2(O). Controlling ice in the induction system of a reciprocating aircraft engine is primarily accomplished by raising the temperature of the induction air. This is done with what is known as carburetor heat. The air intake ducting is equipped with a valve controlled from the flight deck. When opened, warm air that has been circulated around the exhaust system is diverted into carburetor. Carburetor heat should only be used when needed. An excessively hot fuel air charge can result in a loss of power, detonation, and engine failure. Therefore, inspection procedures for this ice control system must include the integrity and free motion of this valve and its control cable. It must fully open and fully close to ensure safe operation. Follow the manufacturer's instruction for lubricating the cable and valve hinge.
Reference: FAA- H-8083-32-ATB Page 3-4

3-3(O). An engine may be fitted with an alternate induction system air inlet that incorporates a dust filter. This type of air filter system normally consists of a filter element and a door that is electrically operated from the flight deck. The pilot opens the door manually with the electric actuator when operating in dusty conditions. Some installations have a spring loaded filter door that automatically opens when the filter is excessively restricted. This prevents the air from being cut off when the filter is clogged with dirt or ice.
Reference: FAA- H-8083-32-ATB Page 3-5

3-4(O). An ice control system like carburetor heat is very simple and relatively trouble free. Regular inspection of the ducting, valve, and operating mechanism should reveal any operational problems. When the carburetor heat valve is fully opened, it should only be a matter of a few minutes until the ice is cleared. If this is reported as not being the case, then, if application of the heat was timely, it is likely that the valve is not opening all the way. Check the cable and the valve itself for unrestricted movement and full travel. Any report of low power could be the result of the carburetor heat valve not closing fully. Again, inspect the cable and the valve for proper operation.
Reference: FAA- H-8083-32-ATB Page 3-4

3-5(O). Eliminating ice in the induction system of a reciprocating engine is primarily accomplished by raising the temperature of the induction air. This is done with a carburetor heat system. The air intake ducting is equipped with a valve controlled from the flight deck. When opened, warm air that has been circulated around the exhaust system is diverted into the carburetor. This carburetor heat should only be used when needed. An excessively hot fuel air charge can result in a loss of power, detonation, and engine failure. Therefore inspection procedure for this ice control system must include the integrity and free motion of this valve and its control cable. It must fully open and fully close to ensure safe operation. Follow the manufacturer's instruction for lubricating the cable and valve hinge. If running up the engine on the ground, application of full carburetor heat should be accompanied by a reduction in manifold pressure because the intake air becomes less dense.
Reference: FAA- H-8083-32-ATB Page 3-4

3-6(O). Fuel evaporation ice is formed because of the decrease in temperature resulting from the evaporation of fuel when it is introduced into the intake airstream at the fuel discharge nozzle. The temperature of the air and components around the evaporating fuel reduces to below freezing and any moisture present becomes ice that settles on the discharge nozzle and nearby structure. This ice builds up and can interfere with fuel flow, affect mixture distribution and lower manifold pressure.
Reference: FAA- H-8083-32-ATB Page 3-9

3-7(O). A turbosupercharger or turbocharger system functions to increase manifold pressure on a reciprocating engine. It is an externally driven supercharger that compresses the intake air before it is delivered to the fuel metering device. Engine exhaust gases are directed against a turbine that drives an independent impeller mounted on the same shaft. The impeller compresses the intake air and sends it to the fuel metering device. A controller modulates a wastegate valve in the exhaust stream. The amount of gases directed against the turbine is varied by the position of the wastegate. Thus, the amount of intake air compression is controlled which directly affects the power output of the engine.
Reference: FAA-H-8083-32-ATB Pages 3-8 to 3-17

3-8(O). An exhaust leak is indicated by a flat grey or sooty black streak on the pipes near the leak. Misaligned exhaust system pipes or components are an indicator that a leak may exist.
Reference: FAA- H-8083-32-ATB Page 3-25

3-9(O). Without any adverse effect of the engine, a thrust reverser system prevents continued forward thrust of the engine by not allowing the engine fan and/or exhaust airflow to flow aft. Typically, a mechanical blockage or redirection of the air occurs through the use of hydraulic or pneumatic power. When the thrust lever on the flight deck is moved aft of idle, and the aircraft has weight on wheels, a control valve diverts the power to a motor. Through the use of jackscrews, flex-drives, and gear boxes, the reverser mechanism unlocks and deploys to change the direction of the engine outflow. When the aircraft has slowed, the power lever is moved forward and the thrust reverser mechanism stows.
Reference: FAA-H-8083-32-ATB Page 3-29

3-10(O). The two types of thrust reverser systems are the mechanical blockage and the aerodynamic blockage systems. The mechanical blockage system places a removable obstruction in the exhaust gas stream. This is usually done rear of the exhaust nozzle. The exhaust gases therefore are mechanically blocked and diverted at a suitable angle in the reverse direction. The obstruction can be cone-shaped, clamshell-like in appearance or a half-sphere. Since it is directly in the path of the hot exhaust gases, the mechanical blockage type thrust reverser must be able to withstand high temperatures. The aerodynamic blockage type of thrust reverser is used on turbofan engines. Since 80 percent of the forward thrust comes from the fan of a turbofan engine, the aerodynamic thrust reverser redirects the fan air to slow the aircraft. Typically, a translating cowl slides aft and as it does so, blocking panels are deployed into the fan airstream. These redirect the air through cascade vanes that further direct the air forward to slow the aircraft. Since the aerodynamic thrust reverser system deflects fan air, it does not have to be particularly resistant to heat.
Reference: FAA- H-8083-32-ATB Page 3-29

3-11(O). Any exhaust system failure should be regarded as a severe hazard. Depending on the location and type of failure, it can result in carbon monoxide poisoning of crew and passengers, partial or complete loss of engine power, or an aircraft fire.
Reference: FAA- H-8083-32-ATB Page 3-24

3-12(O). Exhaust systems marked with a lead pencils as well as the use of galvanized or zinc-plated tools must be avoided. The lead, zinc, or galvanized mark is absorbed by the metal of the exhaust system when heated. This creates a distinct change in the molecular structure of the metal. This change softens the metal in the area of the mark causing cracks and eventual failure.
Reference: FAA- H-8083-32-ATB Page 3-24

3-13(O). A turbine engine exhaust nozzle directs the exhaust gases. While doing so, it aids in the extraction of power from the engine. A converging nozzle will speed up the gases and extract more thrust. A divergent nozzle will slow the gases and reduce thrust. A nozzle can also help straighten the gases when they exit the turbine or reduce turbulence. A turboprop or turboshaft engine extracts most of the energy for rotating a propeller, rotor blades, or driving accessories such as in an APU. The exhaust nozzle on these engines does little more than direct the gases clear of the aircraft structure since no directional thrust is required. They typically use divergent nozzles or tailpipes. Turbofan engines gain 15 to 20 percent of thrust from the exhaust gases. Therefore convergent exhaust nozzles are common on turbofan engines. Un-ducted turbofans use two nozzles – one for the fan air and one for the engine core exhaust gases. The fan air exhaust nozzle and the engine core cowling combine to direct fan air aft with as little disturbance as possible using a convergent nozzle shape. The engine core exhaust gases also use a convergent nozzle to extract as much thrust from these gases as possible. Note that the length and opening size of an exhaust nozzle are calculated to ensure the correct gas volume, velocity, and pressure at the rear of the engine.
Reference: FAA- H-8083-32-ATB Pages 3-26 to 3-28

Applicants for powerplant certification are required to demonstrate the ability to apply knowledge by performing maintenance related tasks for the examiner. The Practical Test Standards (PTS) list the subject areas from which the skill elements to be performed by the applicant are chosen. The following examples resemble tasks an examiner may ask an applicant to perform. The Performance Level required to be demonstrated for each skill element is listed. Consult the PTS for Level descriptions.

3-1(P). Given an actual aircraft engine or mockup, inspect an engine ice control system and record your findings. [Level 3]

3-2(P). Given an actual aircraft engine or mockup, inspect the induction manifolds and record your findings. [Level 3]

3-3(P). Given an actual aircraft engine or mockup, appropriate publications, and tooling, repair a defective condition in a carburetor heat box and record maintenance. [Level 3]

3-4(P). Given an actual aircraft engine or mockup, complete an operational check of an engine anti-ice system and record your findings. [Level 3]

3-5(P). Given an actual aircraft engine or mockup, appropriate publications, and tooling, rig a carburetor heat box and record maintenance. [Level 3]

3-6(P). Given an actual aircraft engine or mockup, inspect an induction system and record your findings. [Level 3]

3-7(P). Given an actual aircraft engine or mockup, appropriate publications, and tooling, replace an induction system manifold gasket and record maintenance. [Level 3]

3-8(P). Given an actual aircraft engine or mockup, appropriate publications, and tooling, replace an induction tube and record maintenance. [Level 3]

3-9(P). Given an actual aircraft engine or mockup, appropriate publications, equipment, and supplies service an induction system air filter and record maintenance. [Level 3]

3-10(P). Given an actual aircraft engine or mockup, appropriate publications, required tooling, equipment, and an unknown discrepancy troubleshoot an engine malfunction resulting from a defective induction system and record your findings. [Level 3]

3-11(P). Given an actual aircraft engine or mockup, appropriate publications, required tooling, equipment, and an unknown discrepancy troubleshoot an engine malfunction resulting from a supercharging system and record your findings. [Level 3]

3-12(P). Given an actual aircraft engine or mockup, inspect an exhaust system and record your findings. [Level 3]

3-13(P). Given an actual aircraft engine or mockup, inspect a turbocharger system and record your findings. [Level 3]

3-14(P). Given an actual aircraft engine or mockup, determine if components of the exhaust system are serviceable and record your findings. [Level 2]

3-15(P). Given an actual aircraft engine or mockup and the appropriate publications demonstrate the procedures to accomplish a pressurization check of an exhaust system. [Level 2]

3-16(P). Given an actual aircraft engine or mockup, appropriate publications, and tooling, repair an exhaust system component and record maintenance. [Level 3]

3-17(P). Given an actual aircraft engine or mockup, complete an operational check of an engine exhaust system and record your findings. [Level 3]

3-18(P). Given an actual aircraft engine or mockup, appropriate publications, and tooling, replace an exhaust gasket and record maintenance. [Level 3]

3-19(P). Given an actual aircraft engine or mockup, appropriate publications, and tooling, install an engine exhaust and record maintenance. [Level 3]

3-20(P). Given an actual aircraft engine or mockup, complete an operational check of a turbocharger and waste gate system and record your findings. [Level 3]

3-21(P). Given an actual aircraft engine or mockup, appropriate publications, appropriate testing equipment, if necessary and an unknown discrepancy, troubleshoot a turbine engine thrust reverser system and record your findings. [Level 3]

3-22(P). Given an actual aircraft engine or mockup, appropriate publications, appropriate testing equipment, if necessary and an unknown discrepancy, troubleshoot a turbine engine thrust reverser component and record your findings. [Level 3]

3-23(P). Given an actual aircraft engine or mockup, appropriate publications, and tooling, repair a turbine engine thrust reverser and record maintenance. [Level 3]

3-24(P). Given an actual aircraft engine or mockup, appropriate publications, and tooling, repair a turbine engine thrust reverser component and record maintenance. [Level 3]

Engine Ignition and Electrical Systems

CHAPTER 4

Magneto-Ignition Systems, FADEC Systems, Spark Plugs,
Timing Devices, Powerplant Electrical Systems, Cable Stripping

4-1) AMP063
In a four-stroke cycle aircraft engine, when does the ignition event take place?

A. Before the piston reaches TDC on compression stroke.
B. After the piston reaches TDC on the power stroke.
C. After the piston reaches TDC on the compression stroke.

4-2) AMP063
Which of the following are distinct circuits on a high-tension magneto?
1. Magnetic.
2. Primary.
3. E-gap.
4. P-lead.
5. Secondary.

A. 1, 2, and 5.
B. 1, 3, and 4.
C. 2, 4, and 5.

4-3) AMP063
Which components make up the magnetic system of a magneto?

A. Pole shoes, the pole shoe extensions, and the primary coil.
B. Primary and Secondary coils.
C. Rotating magnet, the pole shoes, the pole shoe extensions, and the coil core.

4-4) AMP046
What is the radial location of the two North poles of a four-pole rotating magnet in a high tension magneto?

A. 180° apart.
B. 270° apart.
C. 90° apart.

4-5) AMP046
The greatest density of flux lines in the magnetic circuit of a rotating magnet-type magneto occurs when the magnet is in what position?

A. Full alignment with the field shoe faces.
B. A certain angular displacement beyond the neutral position referred to as E-gap angle or position.
C. The position where the contact points are open.

4 - Engine Ignition and Electrical Systems
Answers

4-1) A.
All ignition systems must deliver a high-tension spark across the electrodes of each spark plug in each cylinder of the engine in the correct firing order. At a predetermined number of degrees ahead of top dead center position of the piston as measured by crankshaft travel in degrees of rotation, the spark occurs inside the cylinder.
[For more detailed information refer to Powerplant Handbook H-8083-32-ATB, Chapter 4 p.1]

4-2) A.
The high-tension magneto system can be divided for purposes of discussion into three distinct circuits: magnetic, primary electrical, and secondary electrical circuits. The magnetic circuit consists of a permanent multi-pole rotating magnet, a soft iron core, and pole shoes. The primary electrical circuit consists of a set of breaker contact points, a condenser, and the primary windings of the coil. The secondary circuit contains the secondary windings of the coil, distributor rotor, distributor cap or block, ignition leads and spark plugs.
[For more detailed information refer to Powerplant Handbook H-8083-32-ATB, Chapter 4 p.2]

4-3) C.
The magnetic circuit consists of a permanent multi-pole rotating magnet, a soft iron core which is called the coil core, and pole shoes which are shaped with extension that protrude to the area when the rotating magnet passes. The primary and secondary coils are separate systems of the magneto which make the other answers incorrect.
[For more detailed information refer to Powerplant Handbook H-8083-32-ATB, Chapter 4 p.2-3]

4-4) A.
The poles of the magnet are arranged in alternate polarity so the flux can pass out of the north pole through the coil core and back to the south pole of the magnet. On a 4-pole magnet, this results in the north poles being opposite each other, and the south poles being opposite each other, or radially 180° apart. See figure 4-3 of Chapter 4 of FAA-H-8083-32.
[For more detailed information refer to Powerplant Handbook H-8083-32-ATB, Chapter 4 p.2-3]

4-5) A.
When the north pole is aligned with one of the coil core pole shoes and the south pole is aligned with the other coil core pole shoe, the number of magnetic lines of flux through the coil is maximum because the two magnetically opposite poles are perfectly aligned with the pole shoes. This position of the magnet is called the full register position. When the magnet is moved away from the full register position, the amount of flux passing through the coil core begins to decrease because some lines of flux take a shorter route from pole to pole through the pole shoe extensions.
[For more detailed information refer to Powerplant Handbook H-8083-32-ATB, Chapter 4 p.2-3]

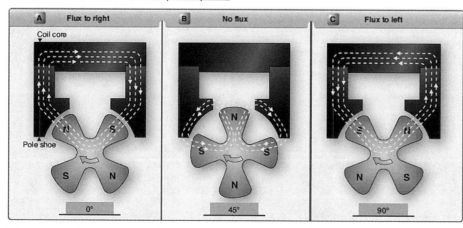

Figure 4-3. Magnetic flux at three positions of the rotating magnet.

4-6) AMP063

What is the electrical location of the primary capacitor in a high tension magneto?

- A. In parallel with the breaker points.
- B. In series with the breaker points.
- C. In series with the primary and secondary windings.

4-7) AMP064

What is the approximate position of the rotating magnet in a high-tension magneto when the points first close?

- A. Full register.
- B. Neutral.
- C. A few degrees after neutral.

4-8) AMP063

The E-gap angle is usually defined as the number of degrees between the neutral position of the rotating magnet and the position

- A. where the contact points close.
- B. where the contact points open.
- C. of greatest magneto flux density.

4-9) AMP063

Magneto breaker points must be timed to open when the

- A. rotating magnet is positioned a few degrees before neutral.
- B. greatest magnetic field stress exists in the magneto circuit.
- C. rotating magnet is in the full register position.

4-10) AMP063

The secondary coil of a magneto is grounded through the

- A. ignition switch.
- B. primary coil.
- C. grounded side of the breaker points.

4-11) AMP063

What is the relationship between the distributor and crankshaft speed of aircraft reciprocating engines?

- A. The distributor turns at one-half crankshaft speed.
- B. The distributor turns at one and one half crankshaft speed.
- C. The crankshaft turns at one-half distributor speed.

4-6) A.

The primary electrical circuit consists of a set of breaker contact points, a condenser (capacitor), and an insulated coil. The capacitor is wired in parallel with the breaker points. The capacitor prevents arcing at the points when the circuit is opened and hastens the collapse of the magnetic field about the primary coil.

[For more detailed information refer to Powerplant Handbook H-8083-32-ATB, Chapter 4 p.4]

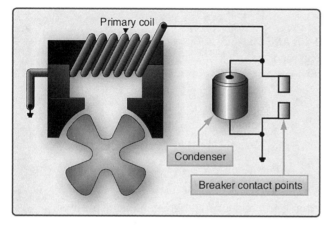

Figure 4-5. Primary electrical circuit of a high-tension magneto.

4-7) A.

The primary breaker points close at approximately full register position. When the breaker points are closed, the primary electrical circuit is completed and the rotating magnet induces current flow in the primary circuit. This is current flow generates its own magnetic field which is in a direction that opposes any change in the magnetic flux of the permanent magnet's circuit.

[For more detailed information refer to Powerplant Handbook H-8083-32-ATB, Chapter 4 p.4]

4-8) B.

The current flowing in the primary circuit holds the flux in the core at a high value in one direction until the rotating magnet has time to rotate through the neutral position to a point a few degrees beyond neutral. This position is called the E-gap position (E stands for efficiency). A very high rate of flux change can be obtained by opening the primary breaker points in this position.

[For more detailed information refer to Powerplant Handbook H-8083-32-ATB, Chapter 4 p.4]

4-9) B.

Without current flowing through the primary coil, the flux in the coil core gradually decreases to zero as the magnet rotor turns to neutral and flux starts to increase in the opposite direction. However, it is the rate of change of the flux lines that controls the magnitude of the current flow induced in the coil(s). When the primary coil is added to the magnet and coil core, the electromagnetic action of the primary coil prevents the gradual change in flux in the coil core. It temporarily holds the field in place even though the magnet has rotated past the pole shoe. The breaker points are timed to open when the magnetic field stress is the greatest because it causes the flux field to rapidly collapse thus inducing the greatest amount of voltage in the coils.

[For more detailed information refer to Powerplant Handbook H-8083-32-ATB, Chapter 4 p.5]

4-10) B.

The secondary coil is made up of windings containing 13,000 turns of fine, insulated wire. One end of the coil wire is grounded to the primary coil or to the coil core. The other end of the secondary coil wire is connected to the distributor rotor.

[For more detailed information refer to Powerplant Handbook H-8083-32-ATB, Chapter 4 p.6]

4-11) A.

It is the function of the distributor to send a spark to each cylinder in the engine. Therefore it contains the same number of contacts as there are cylinders in the engine. The engine crankshaft, however, must rotate twice to have all of the cylinders travel to TDC on the compression stroke in order to combust the fuel air mixture. Therefore, the distributor rotates at one-half of the crankshaft speed so that each cylinder receives a spark in one revolution of the distributor during two revolutions of the crankshaft.

[For more detailed information refer to Powerplant Handbook H-8083-32-ATB, Chapter 4 p.7]

4-12) AMP064

What are the parts of a distributor in an aircraft engine ignition system?

1. Coil
2. Block.
3. Stator.
4. Rotor.
5. Transformer.

    D.   2 and 4.
    E.   3 and 4.
    F.   2 and 5.

4-13) AMP064

What is a result of "flashover" in a distributor?

    A.   Intense voltage at the spark.
    B.   Reversal of current flow.
    C.   Conductive carbon trail.

4-14) AMP046

Aircraft magneto housings are usually ventilated in order to

    A.   prevent the entrance of outside air which may contain moisture.
    B.   allow heated air from the accessory compartment to keep the internal parts of the magneto dry.
    C.   provide cooling and remove corrosive gases produced by normal arcing.

4-15) AMP063

Shielding is used on spark plug and ignition wires to

    A.   protect the wires from short circuits as a result of chafing and rubbing.
    B.   prevent outside electromagnetic emissions from disrupting the operation of the ignition system.
    C.   prevent interference with radio reception.

4-16) AMP064

How does the high tension ignition shielding tend to reduce radio interference?

    A.   Prevents ignition flashover at high altitudes.
    B.   Reduces voltage drop in the transmission of high-tension current.
    C.   Receives and grounds high frequency waves coming from the magneto and high-tension ignition leads.

4-17) AMP046

When the switch is off in a magneto ignition system, the primary circuit is

    A.   grounded.
    B.   opened.
    C.   shorted.

4-12) A.
The high-voltage induced in the secondary coil is directed to the distributor which consists of two parts; revolving and stationary. The revolving part is called the distributor rotor and the stationary part is called a distributor block.
[For more detailed information refer to Powerplant Handbook H-8083-32-ATB, Chapter 4 p.7]

4-13) C.
The high-voltage current that normally arcs across the air gaps of the distributor can flash across a wet insulating surface to ground, or the high-voltage current can be misdirected to some spark plug other than the one that should be fired. This condition is known as flashover and usually results in cylinder misfiring. Flashover can lead to carbon tracking. The carbon trail results from the electric spark burning dirt particles that contain hydrocarbon materials. The water in the hydrocarbon material is evaporated during flashover leaving carbon to form a conductive path for current.
[For more detailed information refer to Powerplant Handbook H-8083-32-ATB, Chapter 4 p.7-8]

4-14) C.
Magnetos cannot be hermetically sealed to prevent moisture from entering a unit because the magneto is subject to pressure and temperature changes in altitude. Adequate drains and proper ventilation reduce the tendency of flashover and carbon tracking. Good magneto circulation also ensures that corrosive gases produced by normal arcing across the distributor gap, such as ozone, are carried away.
[For more detailed information refer to Powerplant Handbook H-8083-32-ATB, Chapter 4 p.8]

4-15) C.
The ignition harness leads serve a dual purpose. It provides the conductor path for the high-tension voltage to the spark plug. It also serves as a shield for stray magnetic fields that surround the wires as they momentarily carry high-voltage current. By conducting these magnetic lines of force to ground, the ignition harness cuts down electrical interference with the aircraft radio and other electrically sensitive equipment.
[For more detailed information refer to Powerplant Handbook H-8083-32-ATB, Chapter 4 p.8]

4-16) C.
A magneto is a high frequency radiation emanating (radio wave) device during its operation. If the magneto and ignition leads are not shielded, they would form antennas and transmit the random frequencies from the ignition system. By conducting the magnetic lines of flux associated with the high frequencies to ground, ignition harness and magneto radio interference are reduced.
[For more detailed information refer to Powerplant Handbook H-8083-32-ATB, Chapter 4 p.8]

4-17) A.
The type of ignition switch used varies with the number of engines on the aircraft and the type of magnetos used. All switches, however, turn the system ON and OFF in much the same manner. The ignition switch is different in at least one respect from all other type of switches: when the ignition switch is in the OFF position, a circuit is completed through the switch to ground. In other switches, the OFF position normally breaks or opens the circuit.
[For more detailed information refer to Powerplant Handbook H-8083-32-ATB, Chapter 4 p.9]

4-18) AMP064

What component of a dual magneto is shared by both ignition systems?

    A. High tension coil.
    B. Rotating magnet.
    C. Capacitor.

4-19) AMP063

An advantage of a low-tension ignition system use on aircraft reciprocating engines is

    A. a coil for each cylinder.
    B. elimination of high-tension ignition wires.
    C. elimination of high voltage used in the distributor.

4-20) AMP063

FADEC:

    A. is a solid state ignition and fuel control system on reciprocating engines.
    B. is only applied to the ignition system on a reciprocating engine.
    C. is only used for turbine engine fuel control.

4-21) AMP063

The coil packs of a FADEC ignition system for a reciprocating engine are

    A. low voltage units mounted above the ECU.
    B. high voltage units that fire according to crankshaft position.
    C. located on each cylinder head for which it provides a spark.

4-22) AMP063

A booster coil on a radial engine

    A. uses battery power to boost the magnet in the magneto during starting.
    B. uses three coils windings to achieve a hotter spark for starting than the magneto.
    C. operates off of battery power and a trailing finger in the distributor.

4-23) AMP046

What is the purpose of an impulse coupling with a magneto?

    A. To absorb impulse vibrations between the magneto and the engine.
    B. To compensate for backlash in the magneto and the engine gears.
    C. To produce a momentary high rotational speed of the magneto.

4-24) AMP063

In reference to a shower of sparks ignition system:
1. the retard breaker points are designed to keep the affected ignition system operating if the advance breaker points should fail during normal engine operation (after start).
2. the timed opening of the retard breaker points is designed to prevent engine "kickback" during start.
    Regarding the above statements,

    A. only No. 1 is true.
    B. only No. 2 is true.
    C. both No. 1 and No. 2 are true.

4 - Engine Ignition and Electrical Systems
Answers

4-18) B.
High-tension system magnetos used on aircraft engines are either single or dual type magnetos. The dual magneto incorporates two magnetos contained in a single housing. One rotating magnet and a cam are common to two sets of breaker points and coils. Two distributor units are mounted in the magneto.
[For more detailed information refer to Powerplant Handbook H-8083-32-ATB, Chapter 4 p.10]

4-19) C.
The low-tension ignition system virtually eliminates flashover in both the distributor and the harness because the air gaps within the distributor have been eliminated by the use of a brush-type distributor. High voltage is present only in the short leads between each transformer and the spark plugs.
[For more detailed information refer to Powerplant Handbook H-8083-32-ATB, Chapter 4 p.12]

4-20) A.
A FADEC is a modern solid state digital electronic ignition and electronic, sequential, port fuel injection system with only one moving part that consists of the opening and closing of the fuel injector. FADEC continually monitors and controls ignition, timing, and fuel mixture/delivery/injection, and spark ignition as an integrated control system.
[For more detailed information refer to Powerplant Handbook H-8083-32-ATB, Chapter 4 p.12]

4-21) B.
The PowerLink ignition system of a reciprocating engine FADEC unit consists of the high voltage coils atop of the ECU, the high voltage harness, and spark plugs. One end of each ignition lead on the high voltage harness attaches to a spark plug and the other end of the lead wire attaches to the spark plug towers on each ECU. Each coil pack generates a high-voltage pulse for two spark plug towers. The ignition spark is timed to the engine's crankshaft position. The timing is variable throughout the engine's operating range.
[For more detailed information refer to Powerplant Handbook H-8083-32-ATB, Chapter 4 p.14-15]

4-22) C.
The booster coil is separate from the magneto and can generate a series of sparks on its own. During the start cycle, these sparks are routed to the trailing finger on the distributor rotor and then to the appropriate cylinder ignition lead. The primary winding has one end grounded at the internal grounding strip and its other end connected to the moving contact point. The stationary contact is fitted with a terminal to which battery voltage is applied when the magneto switch is placed in the start position, or automatically applied when the starter is engaged.
[For more detailed information refer to Powerplant Handbook H-8083-32-ATB, Chapter 4 p.16]

4-23) C.
Many opposed engines are equipped with an impulse coupling as the auxiliary starting system. An impulse coupling gives one of the magnetos attached to the engine, generally the left, a brief acceleration that produces a more intense spark for engine starting. Without an impulse coupling or other starting aid, the intensity of magneto spark magneto sparks produced during start is low because of the slow rotation speed of the engine and, therefore, the magneto.
[For more detailed information refer to Powerplant Handbook H-8083-32-ATB, Chapter 4 p.17]

4-24) B.
During the starting cycle, the engine is turning very slowly compared to normal operating speed. The ignition must be retarded or moved back to prevent kickback of the piston trying to rotate opposite normal rotation. Each starting system has a method of retarding the spark during starting of the engine. After the engine begins to accelerate, the manual starter switch is released causing the vibrator coils to become deenergized and the vibrator and retard breaker circuits to become inoperative.
[For more detailed information refer to Powerplant Handbook H-8083-32-ATB, Chapter 4 p.16-20]

4-25) AMP063

Iridium and platinum fine wire electrode spark plugs

    A. produce a hot spark but are not as durable as massive electrodes.
    B. are gapped with a smaller gap due to the reduced amount of electrode material.
    C. provide a more intense spark but cost more than massive electrode plugs.

4-26) AMP063

A spark plug's heat range is the result of

    A. the area of the plug exposed to the cooling airstream.
    B. its ability to transfer heat from the firing end of the spark plug to the cylinder head.
    C. the heat intensity of the spark.

4-27) AMP064

The term reach as applied to spark plug design and/or type indicates the

    A. linear distance from the shell gasket seat to the end of the threads on the shell skirt.
    B. length of the center electrode exposed to the flame of combustion.
    C. length of the shielded barrel.

4-28) AMP064

When installing a magneto on an engine, the

    A. piston in the No. 1 cylinder must be a prescribed number of degrees before top center on the compression stroke.
    B. magneto breaker points must be just closing.
    C. piston in the No. 1 cylinder must be a prescribed number of degrees after top center on the intake stroke.

4-29) AMP057

What tool is generally used to measure the crankshaft rotation in degrees?

    A. Dial Indicator.
    B. Timing disk.
    C. Prop protractor.

4-30) AMP047

When internally timing a magneto, the breaker points begin to open when

    A. the piston has just past TDC at the end of the compression stroke.
    B. the magnet poles are a few degrees beyond the neutral position.
    C. the magnet poles are fully aligned with the pole shoes.

4-25) C.
Fine wire iridium and platinum spark plug electrodes have a very high melting point and are considered precious metals. Therefore, the cost of this type of plug is higher than massive electrode spark plugs but they have a longer service life. The iridium electrode allows for a larger spark gap which creates a more intense spark that increases performance.
[For more detailed information refer to Powerplant Handbook H-8083-32-ATB, Chapter 4 p.21, 4-22]

4-26) B.
The heat range of a spark plug is a measure of its ability to transfer the heat of combustion to the cylinder head. The length of the nose core is the principle factor in establishing the plug's heat range. Hot plugs have a long insulator nose that creates a long heat transfer path; cold plugs have a relatively short insulator to provide a rapid transfer of heat to the cylinder head.
[For more detailed information refer to Powerplant Handbook H-8083-32-ATB, Chapter 4 p.22]

4-27) A.
A spark plug with the proper reach ensures that the electrode end inside the cylinder is in the best position to achieve ignition. The spark plug reach is the length of the threaded portion that is inserted in the spark plug bushing of the cylinder.
[For more detailed information refer to Powerplant Handbook H-8083-32-ATB, Chapter 4 p.22]

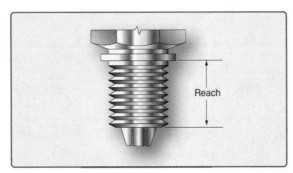

Figure 4-36. Spark plug reach.

4-28) A.
The ignition timing requires precise adjustment and painstaking care so that the following four conditions occur at the same instant: 1. The piston in the No. 1 cylinder must be in a position a prescribed number of degrees before top dead center on the compression stroke. 2. The rotating magnet of the magneto must be in the E-gap position. 3. The beaker points must be just opening on the No. 1 cam lobe. and, 4. The distributor finger must be aligned with the electrode serving the No. 1 cylinder.
[For more detailed information refer to Powerplant Handbook H-8083-32-ATB, Chapter 4 p.22-23]

4-29) B.
Most timing disk devices are mounted to the crankshaft flange and use a timing plate. The markings vary according to the specifications of the engine. This plate is temporarily installed on the crankshaft flange with a scale numbered in crankshaft degrees and the pointer attached to the timing disk.
[For more detailed information refer to Powerplant Handbook H-8083-32-ATB, Chapter 4 p.24]

4-30) B.
When replacing or preparing a magneto for installation, the first concern is with the internal timing of the magneto. For each magneto model, the manufacturer determines how many degrees beyond the neutral position a pole of the rotor magnet should be to obtain the strongest spark at the instant of breaker point separation. This angular displacement from the neutral position, known as the E-gap angle, varies with different magneto models.
[For more detailed information refer to Powerplant Handbook H-8083-32-ATB, Chapter 4 p.25]

4-31) AMP046

In what position should the ignition switch be placed when attempting to use a timing light to time the magneto to the engine?

    A. OFF.
    B. LEFT.
    C. BOTH.

4-32) AMP063

If the ignition switch is moved from BOTH to either LEFT or RIGHT during an engine ground check, normal operation is usually indicated by a

    A. large drop in RPM.
    B. momentary interruption of both ignition systems.
    C. slight drop in RPM.

4-33) AMP063

In the aircraft magneto system, if the P-lead is disconnected, the magneto will be

    A. on regardless of ignition switch position.
    B. grounded regardless of ignition switch position.
    C. open regardless of ignition switch position.

4-34) AMP064

A spark plug is fouled when

    A. its spark grounds by jumping electrodes.
    B. it causes pre-ignition.
    C. its spark grounds without jumping electrodes.

4-35) AMP007

Upon inspection of the spark plugs in an aircraft engine, the plugs were found caked with a heavy black soot. This indicates

    A. worn oil seal rings.
    B. a rich mixture.
    C. a lean mixture.

4-36) AMP063

Spark plug fouling caused by lead deposits occurs most often

    A. during cruise with rich mixtures.
    B. when cylinder head temperatures are relatively low.
    C. when cylinder head temperature are relatively high.

4-31) C.

When using a timing light to check a magneto in a complete ignition system installed on the aircraft, the ignition switch for the engine must be turned to BOTH. Otherwise, the lights do not indicate when the breaker points will open. In the OFF position, the primary circuit will be grounded so current will flow to ground not through the points or to the timing light. In the LEFT or RIGHT position of the ignition switch, one or the other of the left or right breaker points will be grounded so only one light will illuminate when the breaker points open.
[For more detailed information refer to Powerplant Handbook H-8083-32-ATB, Chapter 4 p.27]

4-32) C.

The ignition system has checks performed on it during the aircraft engine run-up before flight. At a manufacturer specified RPM, the ignition switch is moved from the BOTH position to the LEFT position. The drop in RPM is noted and the switch is returned to the BOTH position. After the engine RPM stabilizes, the switch is moved to the RIGHT position and the RPM drop is noted. The magneto drop should be even for both magnetos and is generally slight, in the area of 25-75 RPM for each magneto. This RPM drop is because operation on one magneto is not as efficient as it is with two magnetos providing sparks in the cylinder.
[For more detailed information refer to Powerplant Handbook H-8083-32-ATB, Chapter 4 p.27-28]

4-33) A.

If the engine does not cease firing with the ignition switch in the OFF position, the magneto ground lead, more commonly known as the P-lead, is open and the trouble must be corrected. This means that one or more of the magnetos are not being shut off so the magneto is on regardless of the ignition switch position.
[For more detailed information refer to Powerplant Handbook H-8083-32-ATB, Chapter 4 p.28]

4-34) C.

Spark plug operation can often be a major source of engine malfunctions. Many spark plug failures can be minimized by good operational and maintenance practices. A spark plug is considered to be "fouled" if it has stopped allowing the spark to bridge the electrode gap either completely or intermittently.
[For more detailed information refer to Powerplant Handbook H-8083-32-ATB, Chapter 4 p.30]

4-35) B.

A rich fuel/air mixture is detected by soot or black smoke coming from the exhaust and by an increase in RPM when idling fuel/air mixture is leaned to best power. The soot that forms as a result of overly rich idle fuel/air mixture settles on the inside of the combustion chamber because the heat of the engine and turbulence in the combustion chamber are slight. The heavy black soot on the spark plug is known as carbon fouling.
[For more detailed information refer to Powerplant Handbook H-8083-32-ATB, Chapter 4 p.30]

4-36) B.

Lead fouling may occur at any power setting but perhaps the power setting most conducive to lead fouling is cruising with lean mixtures. At this power, the cylinder head temperature is relatively low and there is more oxygen than needed to consume all the fuel in the fuel air mixture. When all of the fuel is consumed, some of the excess oxygen unites with some of the lead in the fuel and forms lead/oxygen compounds that solidify and build up in layers as they contact the relatively cool cylinder walls and the spark plugs.
[For more detailed information refer to Powerplant Handbook H-8083-32-ATB, Chapter 4 p.31]

4-37) AMP064

What will be the effect of a spark plug that is gapped too wide?

    A.   Insulation failure.
    B.   Hard starting.
    C.   Lead damage.

4-38) AMP064

When spark plugs are removed from an aircraft engine,

    A.   if one is dropped, it must be inspected before being returned to service.
    B.   they must be replaced with new plugs.
    C.   a replacement plug must be used if a spark plug is dropped.

4-39) AMP064

To obtain the correct gap setting on a spark plug before it is installed in an aircraft engine

    A.   a feeler gauge must be used.
    B.   a wire thickness gauge should be used.
    C.   a sight gauge is recommended.

4-40) AMP064

Aircraft engine spark plugs should be installed

    A.   in the exact same position as they were in the engine when removed.
    B.   finger tight and torqued with a torque wrench.
    C.   be installed finger tight and then ¼ rotation farther to crush the copper shoulder gasket for a gas tight fit.

4-41) AMP063

What would be the result if a magneto breaker point mainspring did not have sufficient tension?

    A.   The points will stick.
    B.   The points will not open to the specified gap.
    C.   The points will float or bounce.

4-42) AMP064

Which of the following breaker points characteristics is associated with a faulty capacitor?

    A.   Crowned.
    B.   Fine grained.
    C.   Coarse grained.

4-37) B.

As the air gap of a spark plug increases, the resistance that the spark plug must overcome in jumping the gap also increases. This means that the magneto must produce a higher voltage to overcome the higher resistance. Wide spark plug gap settings raise the coming in speed of the magneto and therefore cause hard starting.
[For more detailed information refer to Powerplant Handbook H-8083-32-ATB, Chapter 4 p.32]

4-38) C.

Since spark plugs can be easily damaged, the importance of careful handling cannot be over emphasized. To prevent damage, spark plugs should be handled individually. If a plug is dropped on the floor or a hard surface, it should not be installed in an engine since the shock of impact usually causes small, invisible cracks in the insulators. A dropped spark plug should be discarded.
[For more detailed information refer to Powerplant Handbook H-8083-32-ATB, Chapter 4 p.32]

4-39) B.

Spark plug electrode gap setting should be checked with a round wire-thickness gauge. A flat type gauge gives an incorrect clearance indication because the massive ground electrodes are contoured to the shape of the round center electrode. When using a wire-thickness gauge, insert the gauge in each gap parallel to the centerline of the center electrode. If the gauge is tilted slightly, the indication is incorrect. Do not install a plug that does not have an air gap within the specified clearance range.
[For more detailed information refer to Powerplant Handbook H-8083-32-ATB, Chapter 4 p.34]

4-40) B.

To install a spark plug, start it into the cylinder without using a wrench of any kind and turn it until the spark plug is seated on the gasket. If high torque is needed to install the plug, dirty or damaged threads on either the plug or plug bushing is indicated. This should be remedied before installing the plug. After a spark plug has been seated with the fingers, use a torque wrench and tighten to the specified torque.
[For more detailed information refer to Powerplant Handbook H-8083-32-ATB, Chapter 4 p.35]

4-41) C.

If the breaker contact points are spread wider than recommended, the mainspring (the spring carrying the movable contact point) is likely to take a permanent set. If the mainspring takes a permanent set, the moveable contact point loses some of its closing tension and the points then either bounce or float, preventing the normal induction buildup of the magneto.
[For more detailed information refer to Powerplant Handbook H-8083-32-ATB, Chapter 4 p.36]

4-42) C.

The condition caused by a faulty capacitor or an opened circuit capacitor is easily recognized by the coarse, crystalline surface and the black "sooty" appearance of the sides of the points. The lack of effective condenser action results in an arc of intense heat being formed each time the points open. This, together with the oxygen in the air, rapidly oxidizes and erodes the platinum surface of the points, producing a coarse, crystalline, or frosted appearance.
[For more detailed information refer to Powerplant Handbook H-8083-32-ATB, Chapter 4 p.37]

4-43) AMP064
What is commonly used to clean accessible condensers and coil cases in a magneto?

A. Acetone.
B. MEK.
C. Mineral Spirits.

4-44) AMP063
Which statement is correct regarding the ignition system of a turbine engine?

A. The system is normally de-energized as soon as the engine starts.
B. It is energized during starting and warm-up periods only.
C. The system generally includes a polar inductor-type magneto.

4-45) AMP068
The capacitor type ignition system is used almost universally on turbine engines primarily because of its high voltage and

A. low amperage.
B. long life.
C. high heat intensity.

4-46) AMP068
The type of ignition system used on most turbine aircraft engines is

A. high resistance.
B. low tension.
C. capacitor discharge.

4-47) AMP063
Why are turbine engine igniters less susceptible to fouling than reciprocating engine spark plugs?

A. The high intensity spark cleans the igniter.
B. The frequency of the spark is less for igniters.
C. Turbine igniters operate at cooler temperatures.

4-48) AMP063
Which of the following are included in a turbine engine exciter unit?
1. Two igniter plugs.
2. Two transformers.
3. Two storage capacitors.

A. 1, 2, and 3.
B. 2, and 3 only.
C. 3, only.

4-49) AMP069
Generally, when removing a turbine engine igniter plug, in order to eliminate the possibility of the technician receiving a lethal shock, the ignition switch is turned off and

A. disconnected from the power supply circuit.
B. the transformer-exciter input lead is disconnected and a prescribed amount of time is waited before the igniter lead is disconnected from the plug.
C. the igniter lead is disconnected and a prescribed amount of time is waited before the igniter is removed from the engine.

4-43) A.

A phase of magneto inspection is the dielectric inspection. This inspection is a visual check for cleanliness and cracks. If the inspection reveals that the coil cases, condensers, distributor rotor, or blocks are oily or dirty or have any trace of carbon tracking, they require cleaning and possibly waxing to restore their dielectric qualities. Clean all accessible condensers and coil cases by wiping them with a lint-free cloth moistened with acetone. Do not dip, submerge, or saturate the parts in any solution because the solution used may seep inside the condenser and short out the plates.

[For more detailed information refer to Powerplant Handbook H-8083-32-ATB, Chapter 4 p.38]

4-44) A.

Since turbine engine ignition systems are operated mostly for a brief period during the engine starting cycle, they are, as a rule, more trouble free than the typical reciprocating engine ignition system. The turbine engine ignition system does not need to be timed to spark during an exact point in the operational cycle. It is used to ignite the fuel in the combustor and then it is switched off.

[For more detailed information refer to Powerplant Handbook H-8083-32-ATB, Chapter 4 p.39]

4-45) C.

The fuel in turbine engines can be ignited readily in ideal atmospheric conditions but, since they often operate in the low temperature of high altitudes, it is imperative that the system be capable of supplying a high heat intensity spark.

[For more detailed information refer to Powerplant Handbook H-8083-32-ATB, Chapter 4 p.40]

4-46) C.

Most gas turbine engines are equipped with a high energy, capacitor-type ignition system and are cooled by fan airflow. Some gas turbine engines may be equipped with an electronic-type ignition system, which is a variation of the simpler capacitor type system.

[For more detailed information refer to Powerplant Handbook H-8083-32-ATB, Chapter 4 p.40]

4-47) A.

The employment of a high-frequency triggering transformer, with a low-reactance secondary winding, holds the time duration of the discharge for the igniter spark to a minimum. The concentration of maximum energy in minimum time achieves an optimum spark across the igniter electrodes capable of blasting carbon deposits. The spark is of great heat intensity which burns away any foreign deposits on the electrodes. Thus, electrode fouling is minimized by the heat of the high intensity spark.

[For more detailed information refer to Powerplant Handbook H-8083-32-ATB, Chapter 4 p.40-42]

4-48) B.

Typical turbine engine ignition systems vary in construction but most include a dual ignition exciter unit which prepares electricity for the igniter plug. The energy is stored in the capacitors inside the unit. Each discharge circuit incorporates two storage capacitors. The voltage across the capacitors is stepped up by transformer units. The exciter is a dual unit that produces sparks at each of the two igniter plugs. The igniter plugs are located in the combustion section of the engine.

[For more detailed information refer to Powerplant Handbook H-8083-32-ATB, Chapter 4 p.40]

4-49) B.

A good procedure to perform before disconnecting the ignition lead from an igniter plug is to disconnect the low-voltage primary lead to the ignition exciter unit. Wait at least one minute (or the manufacturer's prescribed amount of time) to permit the stored energy to dissipate before disconnecting the high-voltage cable from the igniter.

[For more detailed information refer to Powerplant Handbook H-8083-32-ATB, Chapter 4 p.44]

4-50) AMP026

Aircraft electrical wire size is measured according to the

    A.   Military Specifications system.
    B.   American Wire Gauge system.
    C.   Technical Standard Order system.

4-51) AMP026

Of the following, which are factors in the selection of the size of wire used in a particular application?
1. Voltage drop.
2. Current loss.
3. Heat gain.
4. Allowable power loss.
5. Current carrying capability.

    A.   1, 4, and 5.
    B.   1, 2, and 3.
    C.   2, and 4.

4-52) AMP026

In general, the two most common materials for conductors in aircraft applications are:

    A.   copper and silver.
    B.   nickel and aluminum.
    C.   copper and aluminum.

4-53) AMP026

The resistance of the current return path through the aircraft is always considered negligible, provided the

    A.   voltage drop across the circuit is checked.
    B.   generator is properly grounded.
    C.   structure is adequately bonded.

4-54) AMP026

Refer to the graph in Figure 4-79, FAA-H-8083-32-ATB page 4-49. In a 28 volt system, what is the maximum continuous current that can be carried by a single No. 10 copper wire 25 feet long, routed in free air?

    A.   20 amperes.
    B.   30 amperes.
    C.   40 amperes.

4-55) AMP004

The wire identification code of aircraft wire is

    A.   the choice of the manufacturer.
    B.   standardized throughout the industry.
    C.   labeled only at each end of the wire near the terminal.

4-56) AMP006

It is recommended that wire bundles contain no more than

    A.   75 wires.
    B.   50 wires.
    C.   25 wires.

4-50) B.
Wire is manufactured in sizes to a standard known as the American wire gauge (AWG). The wire diameters become smaller as the gauge numbers become larger.
[For more detailed information refer to Powerplant Handbook H-8083-32-ATB, Chapter 4 p.45]

4-51) A.
Several factors must be considered in selecting the size of the wire for transmitting and distributing electrical power. One factor is the allowable power lost (PR) in the line. This loss represents electrical energy converted to heat. A second factor is the permissible voltage drop (IR drop) in the line. This is affected by the load in the circuit. A third factor is the current carrying ability of the conductor. The temperature of the operating environment as well as current carried must be considered as this factor considers the heat carrying capability of the selected wire.
[For more detailed information refer to Powerplant Handbook H-8083-32-ATB, Chapter 4 p.45-46]

4-52) C.
Although silver is the best conductor, its cost limits its use to special circuits where a substance with high conductivity is required. The two most generally used conductors are copper and aluminum. Each has advantages and disadvantages. Copper has higher conductivity per cross sectional area, is more ductile, can be drawn out, has relatively high tensile strength, can be easily soldered, and has fewer issues with corrosion. However, it is more expensive than aluminum. Pound for pound, aluminum is a better conductor and its use can save weight on an aircraft. larger diameters used to match conductivity also reduce corona. However, aluminum is prone to high resistance connections due to its natural tendency to form a protective oxide coating which requires more attention to details when crimping or bonding.
[For more detailed information refer to Powerplant Handbook H-8083-32-ATB, Chapter 4 p.48]

4-53) C.
The resistance of the current path through the aircraft may not be negligible if the aircraft is not properly bonded. A resistance measurement of 0.005 ohms from ground point of the generator or battery to ground terminal of any electrical device is considered acceptable.
[For more detailed information refer to Powerplant Handbook H-8083-32-ATB, Chapter 4 p.48]

4-54) B.
In the table on the left side of the illustration, find the column that represents 28 volts. This becomes the vertical scale for the graph on the right side of the illustration. The vertical scale is the length of the wire to be used so locate 25 on the vertical scale and follow that across the graph until it intersects with the vertical line drawn upward from wire size No. 10 found on the horizontal scale of the graph. The two intersect on a diagonal red line which represents the amount of amps able to be carried with a 1 volt drop (30 amps). Note: be sure you are referencing the correct chart for continuous versus intermittent current flow when making calculations using this kind of graph.
[For more detailed information refer to Powerplant Handbook H-8083-32-ATB, Chapter 4 p.48-49]

4-55) A.
There is no standard procedure for marking and identifying wiring; each manufacturer develops its own identification code. Most manufacturers mark the wires at intervals not more than 15 inches lengthwise and within 3 inches of each junction or terminating point.
[For more detailed information refer to Powerplant Handbook H-8083-32-ATB, Chapter 4 p.50]

4-56) A.
Grouping or bundling certain wires such as electrically unprotected power wiring and wiring to duplicate vital equipment should be avoided. Wire bundles should generally be limited in size to 75 wires, or approximately 2" in diameter where practicable.
[For more detailed information refer to Powerplant Handbook H-8083-32-ATB, Chapter 4 p.51]

4-57) AMP006

When installing electrical wiring parallel to a fuel line, the wiring should be

A. in metal conduit.
B. in a non-conductive fire-resistant sleeve.
C. above the fuel line.

4-58) AMP006

Aircraft wire groups or bundles should be tied where supports are more than 12 inches apart using

A. nylon tie-wraps.
B. Teflon tie-wraps.
C. waxed cotton cord, nylon cord, or fiberglass cord.

4-59) AMP006

Splicing of individual aircraft electrical wires

A. must be staggered so that the bundle does not become excessively large.
B. is allowed but the splice must be located within 12″ of the wire end.
C. is not allowed.

4-60) AMP026

When using hand crimped wire terminals,

A. copper is preferred and should be used on aluminum or copper wires.
B. only aluminum terminals should be used on aluminum wire.
C. aluminum is preferred and should be used on aluminum or copper wires.

4-61) AMP006

Which of the following are true concerning emergency solder repairs of broken wires?
1. Solder repair of broken wires is only allowed on aluminum wires.
2. A permanent crimped splice connector is preferred to a solder repair.
3. A solder repair is preferred to a terminal splice.
4. Some manufacturers prohibit splicing.
5. Potting compound and a sleeve are used to complete a soldered wire repair.

A. 1, 3, and 5.
B. 2, 4, and 5.
C. 3, and 5 only.

4-62) AMP006

Terminal lugs

A. are too small to be torqued with a torque wrench and must be finger tight plus ¼ turn.
B. cannot be aluminum if used with on a copper terminal block.
C. should be installed so they are locked against movement in the direction of loosening.

4-57) C.
When wiring must be routed parallel to combustible fluid or oxygen lines for short distances, as much separation as possible should be maintained. The wires should be on a level with or above the plumbing lines. Clamps should be spaced so that, if a wire is broke at a clamp, it will not contact the fluid line.
[For more detailed information refer to Powerplant Handbook H-8083-32-ATB, Chapter 4 p.54]

4-58) C.
All wire groups or bundles should be tied where supports are more than 12 inches apart. Ties are made using waxed cotton cord, nylon cord, or fiberglass cord. Some manufacturers permit the use of pressure-sensitive vinyl electrical tape. When permitted, the tape should be wrapped around the bundle and the ends heat sealed to prevent unwinding of the tape. Whether lacing or tying, bundles should be secured tightly enough to prevent slipping but not so tightly that the cord cuts into or deforms the insulation.
[For more detailed information refer to Powerplant Handbook H-8083-32-ATB, Chapter 4 p.56]

4-59) A.
Splicing of aircraft cable should be kept to a minimum and avoided entirely in locations subject to extreme vibrations. Individual wires in a group or bundle can usually be spliced if the completed splice is where it can be inspected periodically. The splices should be staggered so that the bundle does not become excessively large.
[For more detailed information refer to Powerplant Handbook H-8083-32-ATB, Chapter 4 p.58]

4-60) B.
Aluminum wire is being used increasingly in aircraft systems because of its weight advantage over copper. However, bending aluminum causes work hardening of the metal making it brittle. Only aluminum terminals should be used on aluminum wire. To counter the formation of aluminum oxide, aluminum terminal lugs are filled with petrolatum-zinc dust compound. This removes the oxide film from the aluminum by a grinding process during the crimping operation.
[For more detailed information refer to Powerplant Handbook H-8083-32-ATB, Chapter 4 p.60]

4-61) B.
Broken wires can be repaired by means of crimped splices or by soldering together and potting broken strands. These repairs are applicable to copper wire. Aluminum wire must not be temporarily spliced. Some manufacturers prohibit splicing. The applicable manufacturer's instruction should always be consulted. A sleeve is installed on one piece of the broken wire so when soldering is complete, it can be pulled over the repair, filled with potting compound and tied securely.
[For more detailed information refer to Powerplant Handbook H-8083-32-ATB, Chapter 4 p.60-61]

4-62) C.
Terminal lugs should be installed on terminal blocks in such a manner that they are locked against movement in the direction of loosening. Aluminum and copper lugs can be used on the same block as long as washers of the specified material are installed between each. As a general rule, use a torque wrench to tighten nuts to ensure sufficient contact pressure. Manufacturer's instructions provide installation torques for all types of terminals.
[For more detailed information refer to Powerplant Handbook H-8083-32-ATB, Chapter 4 p.62]

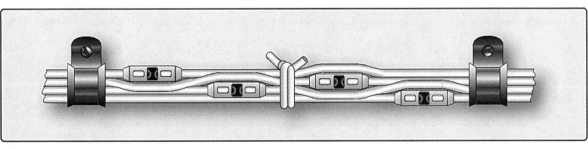

Figure 4-86. Staggered splices in wire bundle.

4-63) AMP026

Bonding jumpers should be designed and installed in such a manner that they

A. are not subject to flexing by relative motion of airframe or engine components.
B. provide a low electrical resistance in the ground circuit.
C. prevent build-up of a static electrical charge between the airframe and the surrounding atmosphere.

4-64) AMP006

In order to reduce the possibility of ground shorting the circuits when the connectors are separated for maintenance, the AN and MA electrical connectors should be installed with the

A. socket section on the ground side of the electrical circuit.
B. pin section on the ground side of the electrical circuit.
C. pin section on the positive side of the electrical circuit.

4-65) AMP044

When more than one generator is used in parallel, the total rated output

A. can be 100% of a single generator.
B. must be 80% of both generator outputs combined.
C. is the combined output of both generators.

4-66) AMP006

Automatic reset circuit breakers

A. reduce the load on the pilot.
B. reset themselves periodically and should not be used on aircraft.
C. reset after the initial surge of current has passed.

4-67) AMP006

Regarding the following statements about ON-OFF two-position engine electrical switches, which of the following statements is true?
1. The toggle should move in the same direction as the desired motion of the unit controlled.
2. Inadvertent operation of a switch can be prevented by a guarded switch.
3. The ON position is reached by a forward or upward motion.

A. 2 and 3 are correct.
B. 1 and 3 are correct.
C. 1, 2, and 3 are correct.

4-68) AMP006

When installing an electrical switch, under which of the following conditions should the switch be derated from its nominal current rating?

A. Direct current motor circuits.
B. Capacitive circuits.
C. Conductive circuits.

4-63) B.

Bonding is the electrical connecting of two or more conducting objects not otherwise connected adequately. Bonding jumpers should be made as short as practicable and installed so that the resistance of each connection does not exceed 0.003 ohm. The jumper should not interfere with the operation of moveable aircraft elements, such as surface controls; normal movement of these elements should not result in damage to the bonding jumper.

[For more detailed information refer to Powerplant Handbook H-8083-32-ATB, Chapter 4 p.62]

4-64) B.

Connectors (plugs and receptacles) facilitate maintenance when frequent disconnection is required. When replacing connector assemblies, the socket-type insert should be used on the half of the connector that is "live" or "hot" which means that the pin section of the connector should be on the ground side of the circuit. Thus, after the connector is disconnected, unintentional grounding will not occur if an exposed pin of the connector touches a conductive surface.

[For more detailed information refer to Powerplant Handbook H-8083-32-ATB, Chapter 4 p.65]

4-65) C.

When more than one generator is used in parallel, the total rated output is the combined output of the installed generators. The results in the requirement for quickly coping with sudden overloads which could be caused by a generator failure when the total connected system load exceeds the rated output of one generator. A quick load-reduction system can be employed or a specified procedure must be followed for reducing the total load to a quantity that is less than the rated output of the remaining functional generators.

[For more detailed information refer to Powerplant Handbook H-8083-32-ATB, Chapter 4 p.67]

4-66) B.

All resettable circuit breakers should open the circuit in which they are installed when an overload or circuit fault exists. This should occur regardless of the position of the operating control. This is known as a "trip-free" circuit breaker. This means one cannot hold the control switch in the ON position and obtain current flow if there is something wrong in the circuit. Automatic reset circuit breakers automatically reset themselves periodically. They should not be used as circuit protection devices in aircraft.

[For more detailed information refer to Powerplant Handbook H-8083-32-ATB, Chapter 4 p.67]

4-67) C.

Hazardous errors in switch operation can be avoided by logical and consistent installation. Two position ON-OFF switches should be mounted so that the ON position is reached by an upward or forward movement of the toggle. When the switch controls moveable aircraft elements, such as landing gear or flaps, the toggle should move in the same direction as the desired motion of the element. Also, inadvertent operation of a switch can be prevented by mounting a suitable guard over the switch.

[For more detailed information refer to Powerplant Handbook H-8083-32-ATB, Chapter 4 p.68]

4-68) A.

The nominal current rating of the conventional aircraft switch is usually stamped on the switch housing. This rating represents the continuous current rating with the contacts closed. Switches should be derated from their nominal current rating for high rush-in circuits such as incandescent lamp circuits. Inductive circuits, which release magnetic energy when the switch is opened, should employ derated switches as should DC motor circuits. Motors draw several times their rated current during starting. Magnetic energy stored in the armature and field coils is released when the control switch is opened.

[For more detailed information refer to Powerplant Handbook H-8083-32-ATB, Chapter 4 p.68]

Applicants for powerplant certification are required to answer oral examination questions before, after, or in conjunction with the practical examination portion of the airman certification process. The oral examination is used to establish knowledge. The practical examination is used to establish skill, which is the application of knowledge. Use the following questions to prepare for the oral examination. The questions are examples aligned with Practical Test Standards subject matter from which the examiner will choose topics for oral examination.

4-1(O). If the ignition switch is place in the OFF position but the aircraft engine continues to run, what is the probable cause of the problem?

4-2(O). During an engine run-up magneto check, what is the range of RPM drop considered to be normal when the mag switch is placed in the LEFT or RIGHT position?

4-3(O). A reciprocating engine either fails to start, fails to idle properly, or has low power and runs unevenly. All of these conditions could be caused by what common defective ignition system part(s)?

4-4(O). What can be done to verify if a turbine engine igniter is firing?

4-5(O). What precautions need to be taken when removing an igniter plug from an engine?

4-6(O). What is the purpose of checking the "P" lead for a proper ground?

4-7(O). What are two types of spark plug fouling and what causes each?

4-8(O). What are the components in the primary electrical circuit of a magneto?

4-9(O). What is "E" gap?

4-10(O). How is the p-lead circuit related to the production of a spark in a magneto?

4-11(O). What is the difference between a low-tension and a high-tension ignition system?

4-12(O). What is the procedure for locating the correct electrical cable/wire size needed to fabricate a replacement cable/wire?

4-13(O). What are some installation practices for wires running close to exhaust stacks or heating ducts?

4-14(O). What procedures must be adhered to when operating electrical system components.

4-1(O). The "P" lead is not grounded.
Reference: FAA-H-8083-32-ATB Chapter 4 p.28

4-2(O). 25-75 RPM.
Reference: FAA-H-8083-32-ATB Chapter 4 p.27

4-3(O). Defective or improperly gapped spark plugs.
Reference: FAA-H-8083-32-ATB Chapter 10 p.37

4-4(O). The igniter can be heard snapping while rotating the engine or the igniter can be removed from the engine and the spark can be observed while activating the start cycle.
Reference: FAA-H-8083-32-ATB Chapter 4 p.43

4-5(O). The low voltage lead to the exciter box should be disconnected and wait one minute (minimum) before removing the ignition lead from the plug.
Reference: FAA-H-8083-32-ATB Chapter 4 p.44

4-6(O). A grounded "P" lead disables the ignition and the magneto will not fire. An ungrounded "P" lead results in the ignition being "hot" and movement of the propeller could cause the engine to start.
Reference: FAA-H-8083-32-ATB Chapter 4 p.28

4-7(O). Carbon fouling – fuel/air mixtures too rich to burn or extremely lean.
Oil fouling – oil past the rings and valve guides into the cylinder.
Lead fouling – when using leaded fuel, lead oxide forms during combustion when cylinder temperature is low.
Graphite fouling – excessive application of anti-seize compound on spark plug threads.
Reference: FAA-H-8083-32-ATB Chapter 4 p.30 to 31

4-8(O). The breaker contact points, a condenser, and an insulated coil.
Reference: FAA-H-8083-32-ATB Chapter 4 p.4

4-9(O). The rotational position of a permanent magnet a few degrees past the neutral position where the breaker points are opened.
Reference: FAA-H-8083-32-ATB Chapter 4 p.4

4-10(O). Current is induced in the p-lead circuit by a rotating magnet. This creates a magnetic field. When the breaker points open the p-lead circuit, the field collapses across the secondary coil windings. This produces a high-voltage current that is directed to the spark plug to jump the electrode gap.
Reference: FAA-H-8083-32-ATB Chapter 4 p.4

4-11(O). The low-tension ignition system creates a low-voltage that is distributed to a transformer coil near each spark plug where it is changed to high voltage to fire the plug. A high-tension ignition system uses a secondary coil inside the magneto to create the high voltage which is distributed to every spark plug.
Reference: FAA-H-8083-32-ATB Chapter 4 p.2 to 12

4-12(O). Wire size considerations take into account allowable power loss, permissible voltage drop, and the current carrying capability of the conductor. Allowance must also be made for the influence of external heating on the wire. Replacement wire can be the same wire as the original wire. Wire can be measured with a wire gauge. It can also be found by consulting a table produced by the American Wire Gauge if the circuit load information is known. Additionally, wires often contain identification markings. Consulting the manufacturer's data can reveal exactly which wire is required by deciphering the markings which are typically coded.
Reference: FAA-H-8083-32-ATB Chapter 4 p.45 to 47

4-13(O). If possible, wires should be kept separate from high-temperature equipment. When wires must be run through hot areas, the wires must be insulated with high-temperature rated material such as asbestos, fiberglass or Teflon. Running coaxial cables through hot area should be avoided. To guard against abrasion, asbestos wires should be in a conduit lined with a high temperature rubber liner or they can be individually enclosed in high temperature plastic tubes before being installed in the conduit.
Reference: FAA-H-8083-32-ATB Chapter 4 p.53

4-14(O). The maximum load from the operation of electrical equipment should not exceed the rated limits of the wiring or protection devices. If loads can exceed the output limits of the alternator or generator, the load should be reduced so that an overload does not occur. If a battery is part of the electrical power system, it should be continuously charged in flight except for momentary intermittent heavy loads such as the operation of a landing gear motor or flaps, etc. Placards should be used to alert flight crews concerning operations that may cause an overload. The total continuous load should be held to 80% of the rated generator or alternator output when assurance is needed that the battery power source is being charged in flight. When two generators are in use, a specified procedure for quick load-reduction should be employed if, for whatever reason, only one generator is functioning and the load must be reduced to that which the single generator can handle without overload.
Reference: FAA-H-8083-32-ATB Chapter 4 p.67

4 - Engine Ignition and Electrical Systems
Practical

Applicants for powerplant certification are required to demonstrate the ability to apply knowledge by performing maintenance related tasks for the examiner. The Practical Test Standards (PTS) list the subject areas from which the skill elements to be performed by the applicant are chosen. The following examples resemble tasks an examiner may ask an applicant to perform. The Performance Level required to be demonstrated for each skill element is listed. Consult the PTS for Level descriptions.

4-1(P). Given an actual aircraft engine or mockup, appropriate publications, and tooling, flash a generator field. [Level 3]

4-2(P). Given an actual aircraft engine or mockup, appropriate publications, and tooling install an engine driven generator or alternator and record maintenance. [Level 3]

4-3(P). Given an engine electrical wiring schematic and an unknown discrepancy, explain the schematic's layout and symbols and demonstrate how it can be used to troubleshoot for the cause of the discrepancy. [Level 2]

4-4(P). Given an actual aircraft engine or mockup, appropriate publications, and tooling install a tachometer generator and record maintenance. [Level 3]

4-5(P). Given an actual aircraft engine or mockup, appropriate publications, materials, and tooling fabricate an electrical system cable. [Level 3]

4-6(P). Given an actual aircraft engine or mockup, appropriate publications, materials, and tooling repair damaged engine electrical system wire and record maintenance. [Level 3]

4-7(P). Given an actual aircraft engine or mockup, appropriate publications, materials, and tooling replace and check a current limiter and record maintenance. [Level 3]

4-8(P). Given an actual aircraft engine or mockup, appropriate publications, materials, and tooling complete a functional or operational check of one or more specified engine electrical system components and record maintenance. [Level 3]

4-9(P). Given an actual aircraft engine or mockup, appropriate publications, materials, and tooling service one or more specified engine electrical system components and record maintenance. [Level 3]

4-10(P). Given an actual aircraft engine or mockup, appropriate publications, materials, and tooling complete an adjustment on one or more specified engine electrical system components and record maintenance. [Level 3]

4-11(P). Given an actual aircraft engine or mockup, appropriate publications, required tooling, equipment, and an unknown discrepancy troubleshoot an engine electrical system component and record your findings. [Level 3]

4-12(P). Given an actual aircraft engine or mockup, appropriate publications, and tooling inspect a turbine engine ignition system for proper installation and record your findings. [Level 3]

4-13(P). Given an actual aircraft engine or mockup, appropriate publications, and tooling inspect a starter/generator for proper installation and record your findings. [Level 3]

4-14(P). Given an actual aircraft engine or mockup, appropriate publications, and tooling inspect magneto points and record your findings. [Level 3]

4-15(P). Given an actual aircraft engine or mockup, appropriate publications, and tooling perform a functional check of the engine timing and record maintenance. [Level 3]

4-16(P). Given an actual aircraft engine or mockup, appropriate publications, and tooling perform an operational check of a magneto switch and record maintenance. [Level 3]

4-17(P). Given an actual aircraft engine or mockup, appropriate publications, and tooling install a magneto, set the timing and record maintenance. [Level 3]

4-18(P). Given an actual aircraft engine or mockup, appropriate publications, materials, and tooling, repair an engine starter system and record maintenance.
[Level 3]

4-19(P). Given an actual aircraft engine or mockup, appropriate publications, materials, and tooling, repair an engine ignition system and record maintenance.
[Level 3]

4-20(P). Given an actual aircraft engine or mockup, appropriate publications, materials, and tooling, complete the following: remove and inspect turbine engine igniter plugs and record findings, install turbine engine igniter plugs, perform a functional check of the igniter system, and record maintenance.
[Level 3]

4-21(P). Given an actual aircraft engine or mockup, appropriate publications, materials, and tooling, inspect generator or starter-generator brushes and record findings. [Level 3]

4-22(P). Given an actual aircraft engine or mockup, appropriate publications, and tooling install brushes in a starter or starter-generator and record maintenance. [Level 3]

4-23(P). Given an actual aircraft engine or mockup, appropriate publications, and tooling install breaker points in a magneto, internally time the magneto, and record maintenance. [Level 3]

4-24(P). Given an actual aircraft engine or mockup, appropriate publications, materials, and tooling, repair an engine direct drive electric starter and record maintenance. [Level 3]

4-25(P). Given an ignition harness with a high-tension lead tester, appropriate publications, materials, equipment, and tooling, inspect and test the harness and record your findings. [Level 3]

4-26(P). Given an aircraft spark plug(s), appropriate publications, materials, equipment, and tooling, inspect them and record your findings. [Level 3]

4-27(P). Given an aircraft spark plug(s), appropriate publications, materials, equipment, and tooling, service and install them and record maintenance.
[Level 3]

4-28(P). Given an ignition system component, appropriate publications, materials, and tooling, bench test the component and record your findings.
[Level 2]

Engine Starting Systems

Reciprocating Engine Starting Systems, Gas Turbine Engine Starters, Electric Starting Systems, Air Turbine Starters

5-1) AMP063
In older reciprocating aircraft inertia starting systems, energy for cranking the engine is stored in the

- A. flywheel.
- B. battery.
- C. generator.

5-2) AMP025
What type of electric motor is used with a direct-cranking engine starter?

- A. Direct current shunt-wound motor.
- B. Direct current series-wound motor.
- C. Synchronous motor.

5-3) AMP063
The starter gear section on the typical direct cranking starter used for starting a large reciprocating aircraft engine

- A. converts the low starter motor speed into low torque to crank the engine.
- B. uses oil pressure to engage and disengage with the flywheel.
- C. uses a sun and planetary gear reduction system to transfer the energy of the starter motor to the engine flywheel.

5-4) AMP063
What assists the starter jaw in retracting after the starter motor is disengaged on a typical direct cranking reciprocating engine starter?

- A. Centrifugal force.
- B. Return spring.
- C. Oil pressure.

5-5) AMP063
Reciprocating engine starters

- A. are capable of continuous cranking for up to five minutes.
- B. have starting limits which restrict continuous cranking to one minute.
- C. use a two minute ON, two minute OFF cranking cycle.

5-6) AMP063
In automatic starting systems on small reciprocating engine aircraft,

- A. a starter solenoid is energized to allow current to flow to the starter motor.
- B. current flows through the ignition switch directly to the starter.
- C. starter current passes through the induction vibrator to ensure a hot spark is available before cranking.

5-1) A.

In the inertia starter, energy is stored slowly during an energizing process by a manual hand crank or electrically with a small motor. During the energizing of the starter, all movable parts within it, including the flywheel, are set in motion. When the starter is engaged, or meshed, flywheel energy is transferred to the engine through sets of reduction gears and a torque overload release clutch.
[For more detailed information refer to Powerplant Handbook H-8083-32-ATB, Chapter 5 p.2]

5-2) B.

The most widely used starting system on all types of reciprocating engines utilizes the direct cranking electric starter. The direct cranking electric starter consists of an electric motor, reduction gears, and an automatic engaging and disengaging mechanism. The typical starter motor is a 12- or 24-volt, series-wound motor that develops high starting torque.
[For more detailed information refer to Powerplant Handbook H-8083-32-ATB, Chapter 5 p.2-3]

5-3) C.

The starter gear section consists of an external housing with an integral mounting flange, planetary gear reduction, a sun and integral gear assembly, a torque-limiting clutch, and a jaw and cone assembly. The torque developed in the starter motor is transmitted to the starter jaw through the reduction gear train and clutch. The starter gear train converts the high speed low torque of the motor to the low speed high torque required to crank the engine. A sun gear drives three planetary gears which transmit torque to the starter jaw.
[For more detailed information refer to Powerplant Handbook H-8083-32-ATB, Chapter 5 p.3-4]

5-4) B.

When the engine starts, the rapidly moving engine jaw teeth (of the starter ring gear), striking the slower moving starter jaw teeth hold the starter jaw disengaged. As soon as the starter comes to rest, the engaging force is removed and the small return spring throws the starter jaw into its fully retracted position where it remains until the next start.
[For more detailed information refer to Powerplant Handbook H-8083-32-ATB, Chapter 5 p.5]

5-5) B.

All starting systems have operating time limits because of the high energy used during cranking or rotating the engine. These limits are referred to as starting limits and must be observed or overheating and damage to the starter occurs. After energizing the starter for 1 minute, it should be allowed to cool for at least one minute. After a second or subsequent cranking period of one minute, it should cool for five minutes.
[For more detailed information refer to Powerplant Handbook H-8083-32-ATB, Chapter 5 p.6]

5-6) A.

A small aircraft automatic starting systems, or remote solenoid engaged starting system, employs an electric starter mounted on an engine adapter. A starter solenoid is activated by either a push-button or by turning the ignition key on the instrument panel. When the solenoid is activated, its contacts close and electrical energy energizes the starter motor. Initial rotation of the starter motor engages the starter to the engine via the starter adapter and reduction gears.
[For more detailed information refer to Powerplant Handbook H-8083-32-ATB, Chapter 5 p.7]

5-7) AMP006

As a general rule, starter brushes should be replaced when they are approximately

    A.   one-half their original length.
    B.   one-third their original length.
    C.   two-thirds their original length.

5-8) AMP064

What is used to polish commutators or slip rings?

    A.   Very fine sandpaper.
    B.   Crocus cloth or fine oilstone.
    C.   Aluminum oxide or garnet paper.

5-9) AMP063

On a typical gas turbine engine, the starter

    A.   cuts off when ignition of the fuel takes place.
    B.   remains engaged until turned off in the cockpit.
    C.   continues to crank until after self-accelerating speed has been reached.

5-10) AMP068

The purpose of the undercurrent relay in a starter-generator system is to

    A.   provide back-up for the starter relay.
    B.   disconnect power from the starter-generator and ignition when sufficient engine speed is reached.
    C.   keep current flow to the starter–generator under the circuit capacity maximum.

5-11) AMP065

In a typical starter-generator system, under which of the following starting circumstances may it be necessary to use the stop-start switch?

    A.   Hung start.
    B.   Hot start.
    C.   Contacts stick open.

5-12) AMP063

The primary advantage of pneumatic (air turbine) starters over comparable electric starters for turbine engines is

    A.   a decreased fire hazard.
    B.   reduction gearing not required.
    C.   high power-to-weight ratio.

5 - Engine Starting Systems
Answers

5-7) A.
Most starting system maintenance practices include replacing the starter motor brushes and brush springs, cleaning dirty commutators, and turning down burned or out-of-round starter commutators. As a rule, starter brushes should be replaced when worn down to approximately one-half their original length.
[For more detailed information refer to Powerplant Handbook H-8083-32-ATB, Chapter 5 p.8]

5-8) A.
A glazed or dirty starter commutator can be cleaned by holding a strip of double 0 sandpaper or a brush seating stone against the commutators as it is turned. The sandpaper or stone should be moved back and forth across the commutators to avoid wearing a groove. Emery paper and carborundum should never be used for this purpose because of their possible shorting acting.
[For more detailed information refer to Powerplant Handbook H-8083-32-ATB, Chapter 5 p.8]

5-9) C.
As soon as the starter has accelerated the compressor sufficiently to establish airflow through the engine, the ignition is turned on followed by the fuel. At low engine cranking speeds, fuel flow rate is not sufficient to enable the engine to accelerate; for this reason, the starter continues to crank the engine until after the self-accelerating speed has been attained. The starter must continue to assist the engine considerably above the self accelerating speed to avoid a delay in the starting cycle, which would result in a hot or hung start, or a combination of both. At the proper points in the sequence, the starter and ignition are automatically cut off.
[For more detailed information refer to Powerplant Handbook H-8083-32-ATB, Chapter 5 p.9]

5-10) B.
In a starter generator system, as the starter motor builds up speed, the current draw of the starter decreases. As it decreases to less than 200 amps, the undercurrent relay opens. This action breaks the circuit from the positive bus to the coils of the motor, ignition and battery cutout relays. The de-energizing of these relay coils halts the start operation.
[For more detailed information refer to Powerplant Handbook H-8083-32-ATB, Chapter 5 p.12]

5-11) A.
On a normal start on an engine with a starter-generator system, once the starter speed reaches a speed due to the engine having started, the undercurrent relay opens and the starter (and ignition) is taken off line. The engine should be operating efficiently and ignition should be self sustaining. If the engine fails to reach sufficient speed to halt starter operation (hung start), the start-stop switch can be used to break the circuit from the positive battery bus to the main circuit of the undercurrent relay.
[For more detailed information refer to Powerplant Handbook H-8083-32-ATB, Chapter 5 p.12]

5-12) C.
Air turbine starters are designed to provide high starting torque from a small lightweight source. The typical air turbine starter weighs from ½ to ¼ as much as an electric starter capable of starting the same engine. It is capable of developing considerably more torque than the electric starter as well.
[For more detailed information refer to Powerplant Handbook H-8083-32-ATB, Chapter 5 p.13]

5-13) AMP063

Pneumatic starters are usually designed with what type of airflow impingement system?

A. Axial flow turbine.
B. Centrifugal flow compressor and axial flow compressor.
C. Double entry centrifugal outward flow compressor and axial flow turbine.

5-14) AMP064

Pneumatic starters contain a turbine which is driven by air and rotates the reduction gear train through a sprag clutch. The clutch is

A. manually engaged and automatically disengaged.
B. automatically engaged and manually disengaged.
C. automatically engaged and automatically disengaged.

5-15) AMP064

Inspection of pneumatic starters by maintenance technicians usually includes checking the

A. oil level and magnetic drain plug condition.
B. stator and rotor blades for FOD.
C. rotor alignment.

5-16) AMP063

On many turbine powered aircraft, the start valve works in conjunction with what other valve to supply the correct flow of air to the pneumatic starter?

A. Starter outflow valve.
B. Bleed air backflow regulator valve.
C. Pressure-regulating and shutoff valve.

5-13) A.

The typical air turbine starter consists of an axial flow turbine that turns a drive coupling through a reduction gear train and a starter clutch mechanism. The air to operate the starter is supplied from either a ground source or an onboard source (i.e. APU, bleed air from another engine). Only one source of 30-50 psi air is used at a time to start the engine. The starter is operated by introducing air into the starter inlet. The air passes into the starter turbine housing where it is directed against the axial flow turbine blades causing the starter to rotate.

[For more detailed information refer to Powerplant Handbook H-8083-32-ATB, Chapter 5 p.13]

5-14) C.

As the rotor of a pneumatic clutch turns, it drives the reduction gears and carrier, sprag clutch assembly, output shaft assembly, and drive coupling. The sprag clutch assembly engages automatically as soon as the rotor starts to turn but disengages as soon as the drive coupling turns more rapidly than the rotor side of the starter. When the starter reaches this overrun speed, the action of the sprag clutch allows the gear train to coast to a halt.

[For more detailed information refer to Powerplant Handbook H-8083-32-ATB, Chapter 5 p.13]

5-15) A.

Normal maintenance for air turbine starters includes checking the oil level, inspecting the magnetic chip detector, and checking for leaks. The starter housing incorporates a sight gauge that is used to check the oil quantity. A magnetic drain plug in the transmission drain opening attracts any ferrous particles that may be in the oil. The starter uses turbine oil, the same as the engine, but starter oil does not circulate through the engine.

[For more detailed information refer to Powerplant Handbook H-8083-32-ATB, Chapter 5 p.14]

5-16) C.

The starting air path is directed through a combination pressure-regulating and shutoff valve (PRSOV) that controls all duct pressure flowing to the starter inlet ducting. This valve regulates the pressure of the starter operating air and shuts off the supply of operating air when required. Downstream of the PRSOV, the start valve, usually mounted at the inlet to the starter, opens and closes to control the airflow into the starter.

[For more detailed information refer to Powerplant Handbook H-8083-32-ATB, Chapter 5 p.14-16]

Applicants for powerplant certification are required to answer oral examination questions before, after, or in conjunction with the practical examination portion of the airman certification process. The oral examination is used to establish knowledge. The practical examination is used to establish skill, which is the application of knowledge. Use the following questions to prepare for the oral examination. The questions are examples aligned with Practical Test Standards subject matter from which the examiner will choose topics for oral examination.

5-1(O). Name two possible causes of a starter motor that drags.

5-2(O). Name two starter maintenance procedures to keep a starter in proper operational condition.

5-3(O). What is the purpose for the undercurrent relay in a starter generator circuit?

5-4(O). What are the sources of air for a pneumatic starter as used on a gas turbine engine?

5-5(O). Why is an air turbine starter cut out after engine self-accelerating speed?

5-6(O). Explain the inspection and replacement criterion for brushes on a starter-generator.

5-7(O). Explain the operation of a turbine engine starter-generator.

5-1(O). Low battery, starter switch or relay controls burned or dirty, defective starter, and inadequate brush spring tension.
Reference: FAA-H-8083-32-ATB Chapter 5 p.9

5-2(O). Replacing brushes and brush springs, surfacing or turning down the commutator, checking the security of the mounting bolts, ensuring the drive gear and the flywheel ring gear are in good condition, and checking the electrical connection for security and corrosion.
Reference: FAA-H-8083-32-ATB Chapter 5 p.8

5-3(O). To open the circuit causing current flow to the motor for its use as a starter so that it can be used as a generator.
Reference: FAA-H-8083-32-ATB Chapter 5 p.12

5-4(O). A ground operated cart, an APU, or, cross-bleed from a running engine on the aircraft.
Reference: FAA-H-8083-32-ATB Chapter 5 p.13

5-5(O). To prevent overspeed since the engine turns at a higher RPM.
Reference: FAA-H-8083-32-ATB Chapter 5 p.10 to 14

5-6(O). Inspection of starter-generator bushes and brush springs is standard starting system maintenance. Typically, brushes are replaced when worn to approximately one-half the original length. Brush spring tension should be sufficient to give brushes a good, firm contact with the commutator. The brush leads should also be inspected to ensure that they are unbroken and that the lead terminal connection is tight.
Reference: FAA-H-8083-32-ATB Chapter 5 p.8

5-7(O). A starter-generator is a shunt generator with an additional heavyseries winding. This series winding is electrically connected to produce a strong field and results in high torque for starting. The starter generator is engaged with the engine at all times. The two-in-one configuration saves both space and weight. To engage the starter, the master switch must first be closed. Then, closing the battery and start switch energizes the starter portion of the unit through an undercurrent relay. As the motor builds up speed, the current draw or the motor begins to decrease. As it decreases to less than 200 amps, the undercurrent relay opens and thus the circuit from the positive bus to the series winding of the starter motor is interrupted. This halts the start operation and the shut generator comes on line.
Reference: FAA-H-8083-32-ATB Chapter 5 p.11 to 12

5 - Engine Starting Systems
Practical

Applicants for powerplant certification are required to demonstrate the ability to apply knowledge by performing maintenance related tasks for the examiner. The Practical Test Standards (PTS) list the subject areas from which the skill elements to be performed by the applicant are chosen. The following examples resemble tasks an examiner may ask an applicant to perform. The Performance Level required to be demonstrated for each skill element is listed. Consult the PTS for Level descriptions.

5-1(P). Given an actual aircraft engine or mockup, appropriate publications, and tooling inspect a starter for proper installation and record findings. [Level 3]

5-2(P). Given an actual aircraft engine or mockup, appropriate publications, materials, and tooling, repair an engine starter system and record maintenance. [Level 3]

5-3(P). Given an actual aircraft engine or mockup, appropriate publications, and tooling inspect a starter-generator and record findings. [Level 3]

5-4(P). Given an actual aircraft engine or mockup, appropriate publications, and tooling install brushes in a starter and record maintenance. [Level 3]

5-5(P). Given an actual aircraft engine or mockup, appropriate publications, and tooling install brushes in a starter-generator and record maintenance. [Level 3]

5-6(P). Given an actual aircraft engine or mockup, appropriate publications, materials, and tooling, repair an engine direct drive electric starter and record maintenance. [Level 3]

6-1) AMP029
In addition to lubricating (reducing friction between moving parts), engine oil performs what functions?
1. Cools.
2. Seals.
3. Cleans.
4. Prevents corrosion.
5. Cushions impact (shock) loads.

    A.   1, 2, 3, and 4.
    B.   1, 2, 3, 4, and 5.
    C.   1, 3, and 4.

6-2) AMP030
What is the source of most of the heat that is absorbed by the lubricating oil in a reciprocating engine?

    A.   Crankshaft and main bearings.
    B.   Exhaust valves.
    C.   Pistons and cylinder walls.

6-3) AMP029
The viscosity of a liquid is a measure of its

    A.   resistance to flow.
    B.   rate of change of internal friction with change in temperature.
    C.   weight, or density.

6-4) AMP029
Which of the following has the greatest effect on the viscosity of lubricating oil?

    A.   Temperature.
    B.   Engine RPM.
    C.   System Pressure.

6-5) AMP029
Which of the following factors helps determine the proper grade of oil to use in a particular engine?

    A.   Adequate lubrication in various attitudes of flight.
    B.   Positive introduction of oil to the bearings.
    C.   Operating speeds of bearings.

6-6) AMP029
Upon what quality or characteristic of a lubricating oil is its viscosity index based?

    A.   Its resistance to flow at a standard temperature as compared to high grade paraffin-base oil at the same temperature.
    B.   Its rate of change in viscosity with temperature change.
    C.   Its rate of flow through an orifice at a standard temperature.

6-7) AMP029
Specific gravity is a comparison of the weight of a substance to the weight of an equal volume of

    A.   oil at a specific temperature.
    B.   distilled water at a specific temperature.
    C.   mercury at a specific temperature.

6 - Lubrication and Cooling Systems
Answers

6-1) B.
In addition to reducing friction, the oil film acts as a cushion between metal parts. This is particularly important for such parts as crankshaft and connecting rods which are subject to shock loads. Oil cools by absorbing heat from the pistons and cylinder walls and also provides the sealing between the piston and the cylinder wall. Oil cleans the engine by reducing abrasive wear. It picks up foreign particles and carries them to a filter where they are removed. Oil also prevents corrosion on the interior of the engine by leaving a coating of oil on parts when the engine is shut down.
[For more detailed information refer to Powerplant Handbook H-8083-32-ATB, Chapter 6 p.2]

6-2) C.
As oil circulates through the engine, it absorbs heat from the pistons and cylinder walls. In reciprocating engines, these components are especially dependent on the oil for cooling. Crankshafts and main bearings are not exposed to the high temperature of the combustion chamber. Exhaust valves have no significant contact with the oil in a reciprocating engine.
[For more detailed information refer to Powerplant Handbook H-8083-32-ATB, Chapter 6 p.2]

6-3) A.
While there are several important properties that satisfactory reciprocating engine oil must possess, its viscosity is most important in engine operation. The resistance of an oil to flow is known as viscosity. Oil that flows slowly is viscous or has high viscosity; if it flows freely, the oil has low viscosity.
[For more detailed information refer to Powerplant Handbook H-8083-32-ATB, Chapter 6 p.2]

6-4) A.
The viscosity of oil is affected by temperature. Early grades of oil became practically solid in cold weather, increasing drag and making circulation almost impossible. Other oils may become so thin at high temperatures that the oil film is broken, causing a low load carrying ability resulting in rapid wear of the moving parts.
[For more detailed information refer to Powerplant Handbook H-8083-32-ATB, Chapter 6 p.2]

6-5) C.
Several factors must be considered in determining the proper grade of oil to use in a particular engine, the most important of which are the operating load, rotational speeds, and operating temperatures. The grade of the lubricating oil to be used is determined by the operating conditions to be met in the various types of engines.
[For more detailed information refer to Powerplant Handbook H-8083-32-ATB, Chapter 6 p.3]

6-6) B.
The viscosity index is a number that indicates the effect of temperature changes on the viscosity of the oil. When oil has a low viscosity index, it signifies a relatively large change of viscosity across temperature variations. The oil becomes thin at high temperatures and thick at low temperatures. Oils with a high viscosity index have small changes in viscosity over a wide temperature index. The best oil for most purposes is one that maintains a constant viscosity throughout temperature changes (high viscosity index).
[For more detailed information refer to Powerplant Handbook H-8083-32-ATB, Chapter 6 p.3]

6-7) B.
Specific gravity is a comparison of the weight of a substance to the weight of an equal volume of distilled water at a specified temperature. As an example, water weighs approximately 8 pounds to the gallon. Oil with a specific gravity of .9 would weigh 7.2 pounds to the gallon (8 X .9 = 7.2).
[For more detailed information refer to Powerplant Handbook H-8083-32-ATB, Chapter 6 p.4]

6-8) AMP029

What type of oil do most engine manufacturers recommend for new reciprocating engine break-in?

  A. Ashless-dispersant oil.
  B. Straight mineral oil.
  C. Semi-synthetic oil.

6-9) AMP029

What type of oil do most engine manufacturers recommend after new reciprocating engine break-in?

  A. Metallic ash detergent oil.
  B. Ashless-dispersant oil.
  C. Straight mineral oil.

6-10) AMP030

Engine oil lubricating systems on aircraft reciprocating engines are

  A. splash type or spray type.
  B. pressure type or a combination of pressure and splash type.
  C. pressure type only.

6-11) AMP030

An oil tank having a capacity of 5 gallons, must have an expansion space of

  A. 2 quarts.
  B. 4 quarts.
  C. 5 quarts.

6-12) AMP056

Oil tank fillers on reciprocating engines are marked with the word

  A. 'oil,' type, and grade, in accordance with 14 CFR part 33.
  B. 'oil,' and tank capacity, in accordance with 14 CFR part 45.
  C. 'oil,' in accordance with 14 CFR part 23.

6-13) AMP030

Why is an aircraft reciprocating engine oil tank on a dry sump lubricating system equipped with a vent line?

  A. To prevent pressure buildup in the reciprocating engine crankcase.
  B. To eliminate foaming in the oil tank.
  C. To prevent pressure buildup in the oil tank.

6-14) AMP030

What is the primary purpose of the hopper located in the oil supply tank of some dry sump engine installations?

  A. To reduce the time required to warm the oil to operating temperature.
  B. To reduce surface aeration of the hot oil and thus reduce oxidation and the formation of sludge and varnish.
  C. To impart a centrifugal motion to the oil entering the tank so that the foreign particles in the oil will separate more readily.

6 - Lubrication and Cooling Systems
Answers

6-8) B.

Oil grades 65, 80, and 120 are straight mineral oils blended from select high viscosity index base oil. These oils do not contain any additives except for very small amounts of pour point depressant, which helps improve fluidity at very low temperatures and an antioxidant. This type of oil is used during the break-in period of a new aviation piston engine or those recently overhauled. The additives in some of the ashless dispersant oils may retard the break in of the piston rings and cylinder walls causing high oil consumption. This condition can be avoided by the use of mineral oil until normal oil consumption is obtained, then change to ashless dispersant oil.
[For more detailed information refer to Powerplant Handbook H-8083-32-ATB, Chapter 6 p.4]

6-9) B.

The ashless-dispersant grades of oil are recommended for aircraft engines subject to wide variations of ambient temperature, particularly the turbocharged series engines that require oil to activate the various turbo controllers. The ashless dispersant grades contain additives which extend operating temperature range and improve cold weather starting. They permit flight through wider ranges of climactic changes without the necessity of changing oil.
[For more detailed information refer to Powerplant Handbook H-8083-32-ATB, Chapter 6 p.4]

6-10) B.

The lubricating oil is distributed to the various moving parts of a typical internal combustion engine by one of the following methods: pressure, splash, or a combination of pressure and splash. The pressure lubricating system is the principle method. Usually, the pressure type lubricating system combined with splash lubrication is used.
[For more detailed information refer to Powerplant Handbook H-8083-32-ATB, Chapter 6 p.5]

6-11) A.

Each oil tank used with a reciprocating engine must have expansion space of not less than the greater of 10 percent of the tank capacity or .5 gallons. A 5 gallon tank has a 20 quart capacity. 10 percent of 20 quarts is 2 quarts (.1 X 20 = 2) Since this is the same as .5 gallons, neither is larger, so the required expansion space is 2 quarts.
[For more detailed information refer to Powerplant Handbook H-8083-32-ATB, Chapter 6 p.5]

6-12) C.

Each filler cap of an oil tank that is used with an aircraft reciprocating engine must provide an oil-tight seal. The filler cap or cover is marked with the word "OIL".
[For more detailed information refer to Powerplant Handbook H-8083-32-ATB, Chapter 6 p.5]

6-13) C.

Oil tank vent lines are provided to ensure proper tank ventilation in all altitude of flight. These lines are usually connected to the engine crankcase to prevent the loss of oil through the vents. This indirectly vents the tanks to the atmosphere through the crankcase breather.
[For more detailed information refer to Powerplant Handbook H-8083-32-ATB, Chapter 6 p.5]

6-14) A.

To help with engine warm up, some oil tanks have a built-in hopper or temperature accelerating unit. This well extends from the oil return fitting on top of the oil tank to the outlet fitting in the sump in the bottom of the tank. By separating the circulating oil from the surrounding oil in the tank, less oil is circulated. This hastens the warming of the oil when the engine is started. Very few of these tanks are still in use and most are associated with radial engines installations.
[For more detailed information refer to Powerplant Handbook H-8083-32-ATB, Chapter 6 p.5-6]

6-15) AMP030

The main oil filters strain the oil at which point in the system?

- A. Immediately after it leaves the scavenge pump.
- B. Immediately before it enters the pressure pump.
- C. Just as it leaves the pressure pump.

6-16) AMP030

If a full-flow oil filter is used on an aircraft engine, and the filter becomes completely clogged, the

- A. oil supply to the engine will be blocked.
- B. oil will be bypassed back to the oil tank hopper where larger sediments and foreign matter will settle out prior to passage through the engine.
- C. bypass valve will open and the oil pump will supply unfiltered oil to the engine.

6-17) AMP030

In order to relieve excess pump pressure in an engine's internal oil system, most engines are equipped with a

- A. vent.
- B. bypass valve.
- C. relief valve.

6-18) AMP056

Where is the oil temperature bulb located on a dry sump reciprocating engine?

- A. Oil inlet line.
- B. Oil cooler.
- C. Oil cooler outlet line.

6-19) AMP056

The purpose of the flow control valve in a reciprocating aircraft engine oil system is to

- A. direct oil through or around the oil cooler.
- B. deliver cold oil to the hopper tank.
- C. compensate for the volumetric increases due to the foaming of the oil.

6 - Lubrication and Cooling Systems

Answers

6-15) C.
Full flow oil filters are the most widely used oil filters on aircraft reciprocating engines. The filter is positioned between the oil pump and the engine bearings which filters the oil of any contaminants before they pass through the engine bearing surfaces.
[For more detailed information refer to Powerplant Handbook H-8083-32-ATB, Chapter 6 p.8]

6-16) C.
Full flow spin-on filters contain an anti-drain back valve and a pressure relief valve all in a disposable housing. The relief valve is used in case the filter becomes clogged. It opens to allow the oil to bypass, preventing the engine components from oil starvation.
[For more detailed information refer to Powerplant Handbook H-8083-32-ATB, Chapter 6 p.7-8]

6-17) C.
An oil pressure regulating valve limits oil pressure to a predetermined value, depending on the installation. This valve is sometimes called a relief valve but its real function is to regulate the oil pressure at a preset pressure level.
[For more detailed information refer to Powerplant Handbook H-8083-32-ATB, Chapter 6 p.8]

6-18) A.
In dry sump lubricating systems, the oil temperature bulb may be anywhere in the oil inlet line between the supply tank and the engine. The bulb is located so that it measures the temperature of the oil before it enters the hot sections of the engine.
[For more detailed information refer to Powerplant Handbook H-8083-32-ATB, Chapter 6 p.10]

6-19) A.
The oil cooler flow control valve determines which of two possible paths the oil takes through the oil cooler. When the oil is cold, a bellows within the flow control valve contracts and lifts a valve from its seat. The oil flows around the oil cooler jacket to the tank. As the oil heats up, the bellows of the thermostat expands and closes the outlet from the bypass jacket. The oil control valve must now flow oil through the core of the oil cooler.
[For more detailed information refer to Powerplant Handbook H-8083-32-ATB, Chapter 6 p.10]

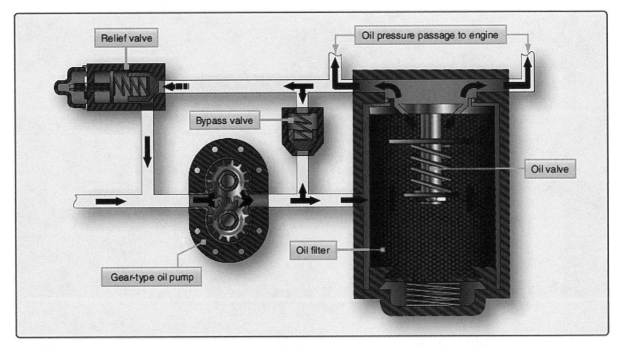

Figure 6-6. Engine oil pump and associated units.

6-20) AMP030

If the oil in the oil cooler core and annular jacket becomes congealed, what unit prevents damage to the cooler?

A. Oil pressure relief valve.
B. Airflow control valve.
C. Surge protection valve.

6-21) AMP030

The floating control thermostat used on some reciprocating aircraft engine installations helps regulate oil temperature by

A. controlling oil flow through the oil cooler.
B. recirculating hot oil back through the sump.
C. controlling airflow through the oil cooler.

6-22) AMP030

Cylinder walls are usually lubricated by

A. splashed or sprayed oil.
B. a direct pressure system fed through the crankshaft, connecting rods, and piston pins to the oil control ring groove in the piston.
C. oil that is picked up by the oil control ring when the piston is at bottom center.

6-23) AMP056

The oil temperature regulator is usually located between which of the following on a dry sump reciprocating engine?

A. The engine oil supply pump and the internal lubrication system.
B. The scavenge pump outlet and the oil storage tank.
C. The oil storage tank and the engine oil supply pump.

6-24) AMP030

The pumping capacity of the scavenger pump in a dry sump aircraft engine's lubrication system

A. is greater than the capacity of the oil supply pump.
B. is less than the capacity of the oil supply pump.
C. is usually equal to the capacity of the oil supply pump in order to maintain constant oiling conditions.

6-25) AMP031

What is the primary purpose of changing aircraft engine lubricating oils at predetermined periods?

A. The oil becomes diluted with gasoline washing past the pistons into the crankcase.
B. The oil becomes contaminated with moistures, acids, and finely divided suspended solid particles.
C. Exposure to heat and oxygen causes a decreased ability to maintain a film under load.

6-26) AMP031

Low oil pressure can be detrimental to the internal engine components. However, high oil pressure

A. should be limited to the manufacturer's recommendations.
B. has a negligible effect.
C. will not occur because of pressure losses around the bearings.

6-27) AMP029

Compared to reciprocating engine oils, the types of oils used in turbine engines

A. are required to carry and disperse a higher level of combustion by-products.
B. may permit a somewhat higher level of carbon formation in the engine.
C. have less tendency to produce lacquer or coke.

6 - Lubrication and Cooling Systems

Answers

6-20) C.

When oil in the system is congealed, the scavenger pump may build up a very high pressure in the oil return line. To prevent this high pressure from bursting the oil cooler or blowing off the hose connections, some aircraft have surge protection valves in the engine lubricating systems. One type of surge valve is incorporated in the oil cooler flow control valve; another type is a separate unit in the oil return line.

[For more detailed information refer to Powerplant Handbook H-8083-32-ATB, Chapter 6 p.10-11]

6-21) C.

One of the most widely used automatic oil temperature control devices is a floating control thermostat that provides manual and automatic control of the engine oil inlet temperatures. With this type of control, the oil cooler air exit door is opened and closed. This regulates the amount of air flowing through the cooler and thus the temperature of the oil that passes through the cooler on its way to the engine.

[For more detailed information refer to Powerplant Handbook H-8083-32-ATB, Chapter 6 p.11]

6-22) A.

The engine cylinder surfaces receives oil sprayed from the crankshaft and also from the crankpin bearings. Since oil seeps slowly through the small crankpin clearances before it is sprayed on the cylinder walls, considerable time is required for enough oil to reach the cylinder walls, especially on a cold day when oil flow is more sluggish.

[For more detailed information refer to Powerplant Handbook H-8083-32-ATB, Chapter 6 p.13]

6-23) B.

Oil collected in the sump is picked up by the scavenge pump as quickly as it accumulates On dry sump engines, this oil leaves the engine, passes through the oil cooler and returns to the supply tank.

[For more detailed information refer to Powerplant Handbook H-8083-32-ATB, Chapter 6 p.13]

6-24) A.

Oil collected in the sump is picked up by the scavenge pump as quickly as it accumulates. These pumps have a greater capacity than the pressure pump. This is needed because the volume of the oil has generally increased due to foaming (mixing with air).

[For more detailed information refer to Powerplant Handbook H-8083-32-ATB, Chapter 6 p.13]

6-25) B.

Oil in service is constantly exposed to many harmful substances that reduce its ability to protect moving parts. The main contaminants are: gasoline, moisture, acids, dirt, carbon, and metallic particles. Because of the accumulation of these harmful substances, common practice is to drain the entire lubrication system at regular intervals and refill with new oil.

[For more detailed information refer to Powerplant Handbook H-8083-32-ATB, Chapter 6 p.17-18]

6-26) A.

The oil pressure must be high enough to ensure adequate lubrication of the engine and accessories at high speeds and power settings. On the other hand, the pressure must not be too high, since leakage and damage to the oil system may result. The oil pressure reading should be between the limits prescribed by the manufacturer at all throttle settings.

[For more detailed information refer to Powerplant Handbook H-8083-32-ATB, Chapter 6 p.17]

6-27) C.

The many requirements for lubricating oils are met in the synthetic oils developed specifically for turbine engines. Synthetic oil has principle advantages over petroleum oil. It has a lower tendency to deposit lacquer and coke (solids left after solvents from the oil have been evaporated) because it does not evaporate the solvents from the oil at high temperature.

[For more detailed information refer to Powerplant Handbook H-8083-32-ATB, Chapter 6 p.19]

6-28) AMP029

In regards to using a turbine engine oil analysis program, which of the following is NOT true?

A. Generally, an accurate trend forecast may be made after an engine's first oil sample analysis.

B. It is best to start an oil analysis program on an engine when it is new.

C. A successful oil analysis program should be run over an engine's total operating life so that normal trends can be identified.

6-29) AMP030

What type of oil system is found on turbine engines?

A. Wet sump.

B. Dry sump.

C. Wet or dry pump depending on design.

6-30) AMP068

Oil picks up the most heat from which of the following turbine engine components?

A. Rotor coupling.

B. Turbine bearing.

C. Compressor bearing.

6-31) AMP027

Which of the following is a function of the fuel oil heat exchanger on a turbojet engine?

A. Aerates the fuel.

B. Emulsifies the oil.

C. Increases fuel temperature.

6-32) AMP068

The purpose of a relief valve installed in the tank venting system of a turbine engine oil tank is to

A. prevent oil pump cavitation by maintaining a constant pressure on the oil pump inlet.

B. maintain internal tank air pressure at the ambient atmospheric level regardless of altitude or rate of change in altitude.

C. maintain a positive internal pressure in the oil tank after shutdown to prevent oil pump cavitation on engine start.

6-33) AMP068

The type of oil pump most commonly used on turbine powered engines are classified as

A. positive displacement.

B. variable displacement.

C. constant speed.

6-34) AMP068

What is the purpose of a last chance oil filter?

A. To prevent damage to the oil pump gears.

B. To prevent clogging of the oil spray nozzles that spray the main bearings.

C. To assure a clean supply of oil to the lubrication system.

6-35) AMP030

What is the primary purpose of the oil breather pressurization system that is used on turbine engines?

A. Prevents foaming of the oil.

B. Allows aeration of the oil for better lubrication because of the air/oil mist.

C. Provides a proper oil spray pattern from the main bearing oil jets.

6-28) C.
Oil analysis programs allow an oil sample to be analyzed and searched for the presence of minute metallic elements. The analyzed elements can be grouped into categories such as wear metals and additives. Expert analysis can use this information to determine engine condition. If the amount of wear metals increase beyond a normal rate, a repair or maintenance can be ordered before engine failure occurs. Thus, it is best to start an oil analysis program on an engine when it is new and continue it throughout its total operating life to be able to distinguish normal and abnormal trends and conditions.
[For more detailed information refer to Powerplant Handbook H-8083-32-ATB, Chapter 6 p.21]

6-29) C.
Both wet- and dry-sump lubrication systems are used in gas turbine engines. Wet-sump engines store the lubricating oil in the engine proper, while dry-sump engines utilize an external tank mounted on the engine or somewhere in the aircraft structure near the engine.
[For more detailed information refer to Powerplant Handbook H-8083-32-ATB, Chapter 6 p.12-14]

6-30) B.
The exhaust turbine bearing is the most critical lubricating point in a gas turbine engine because of the high temperature normally present. In some engines, air cooling is used in addition to oil cooling of the turbine bearings.
[For more detailed information refer to Powerplant Handbook H-8083-32-ATB, Chapter 6 p.21]

6-31) C.
When an oil cooler is required on a gas turbine engine, a greater quantity of oil is required to provide for circulation between the cooler and the engine. To ensure proper temperature, oil is routed through either an air-cooled or fuel-cooled oil cooler. The fuel-cooled system is also used to heat (regulate) the fuel to prevent ice in the fuel.
[For more detailed information refer to Powerplant Handbook H-8083-32-ATB, Chapter 6 p.22]

6-32) A.
In most oil tanks, a pressure buildup is desired within the tank to ensure a positive flow of oil to the oil pump inlet. The pressure buildup is made possible by running the vent line through an adjustable check relief valve. The check relief valve is usually set to relieve at about 4 psi, keeping positive pressure on the oil pump inlet.
[For more detailed information refer to Powerplant Handbook H-8083-32-ATB, Chapter 6 p.23]

6-33) A.
Turbine engine oil pumps may be one of several types, each having certain advantages and limitations. The two most common oil pumps are the gear and gerotor, with the gear-type being the most commonly used. Both gear and gerotor pumps are constant displacement pumps since they deliver a fixed volume of oil with each rotation of the gears.
[For more detailed information refer to Powerplant Handbook H-8083-32-ATB, Chapter 6 p.23]

6-34) B.
Main oil filters strain the oil as it leaves the pump before being piped to the various points of lubrication in the engine. In addition to main oil filters, there are also secondary filters. Fine-mesh screens called last chance filters are used to strain the oil just before it passes from spray nozzles onto the main bearing surfaces. These filters are located at each bearing and help screen out contaminants that could plug the oil spray nozzles.
[For more detailed information refer to Powerplant Handbook H-8083-32-ATB, Chapter 6 p.24-25]

6-35) C.
Breather subsystems are used to remove excess air from the bearing cavities and return the air to the oil tank where it is separated from any oil mixed in the vapor of air and oil by the deaerator. Then, the air is vented overboard. This allows air free oil to be pumped to engine lubrication points to provide the required lubrication.
[For more detailed information refer to Powerplant Handbook H-8083-32-ATB, Chapter 6 p.26]

6-36) AMP030

Which type of valve prevents oil from entering the main accessory case when the engine is not running?

    A. Bypass.
    B. Relief.
    C. Check.

6-37) AMP069

What is used on most turbine engines to monitor engine wear possibly providing notification in advance of an internal engine problem?

    A. Sight gauges at the bearings and accessory housing.
    B. Magnetic chip detectors at key oil scavenge locations.
    C. Oil conductivity transmitters in the sump or oil reservoirs.

6-38) AMP031

Turbine engine lubrication system maintenance intervals are

    A. set by the operator.
    B. set by the manufacturer.
    C. every 100 hours.

6-39) AMP027

The greatest portion of heat generated by combustion in a typical aircraft reciprocating engine is

    A. converted into useful power.
    B. carried out with the exhaust gases.
    C. dissipated through the cylinder walls and heads.

6-40) AMP027

What is the function of a blast tube as used on aircraft reciprocating engines?

    A. A means of cooling the engine by utilizing the propeller backwash.
    B. A tube used to load a cartridge starter.
    C. A device to cool an engine accessory.

6-41) AMP056

The primary purpose of baffles and deflectors installed around cylinders of air-cooled aircraft engines is to

    A. create a low pressure area aft of the cylinders.
    B. force cooling air into close contact with all parts of the cylinders.
    C. increase the volume of air used to cool the engine.

6-36) C.
Check valves are sometimes used in the oil supply lines of dry-sump oil systems to prevent reservoir oil from seeping (by gravity) through the oil pump elements and high pressure lines into the engine after shutdown. Check valves, by stopping flow in an opposite direction, prevent accumulations of undue amounts of oil in the accessory gearbox, compressor rear housing, and the combustion chamber.
[For more detailed information refer to Powerplant Handbook H-8083-32-ATB, Chapter 6 p.27]

6-37) B.
Magnetic chip detectors are used in the oil system to detect and catch ferrous (magnetic) particles present in the oil. Chip detectors are placed in several locations but generally are in the scavenge lines for each scavenge pump, oil tank, and in the oil sumps. If metal is found on a chip detector, an investigation should be made to find the source of the metal on the detector.
[For more detailed information refer to Powerplant Handbook H-8083-32-ATB, Chapter 6 p.28]

6-38) B.
Maintenance of gas turbine lubrication systems consists mainly of adjusting, removing, cleaning and replacing various components. Oil filter maintenance and oil change intervals for turbine engines vary widely from model to model, depending on the severity of the oil temperature conditions imposed by the specific airframe installation and engine configuration. The applicable manufacturer's instructions should be followed.
[For more detailed information refer to Powerplant Handbook H-8083-32-ATB, Chapter 6 p.32]

6-39) B.
About one-fourth of the heat released by combustion in a reciprocating aircraft engine is converted into useful power. The remainder of the heat must be dissipated so that it is not destructive to the engine. In a typical powerplant, half of the heat goes out with the exhaust and the remainder is absorbed by the engine to be redistributed by the oil or the cooling air.
[For more detailed information refer to Powerplant Handbook H-8083-32-ATB, Chapter 6 p.33]

6-40) C.
Blast tubes are built into the engine compartment baffles to direct jets of cooling air onto engine accessories to prevent overheating. Most often the tubes route air to areas with heat sensitive components that may not receive adequate cooling air. Rear spark plug elbows are often the focus of blast tube air as are alternators.
[For more detailed information refer to Powerplant Handbook H-8083-32-ATB, Chapter 6 p.2]

6-41) B.
Cowling and baffles are designed to force air over the cylinder cooling fins. The baffles direct the air close around cylinders and prevent air from forming hot pools of stagnant air while the main streams rush by unused. The air baffle blocks the flow of air and forces it to circulate between the cylinder and the deflector.
[For more detailed information refer to Powerplant Handbook H-8083-32-ATB, Chapter 6 p.33 & 38]

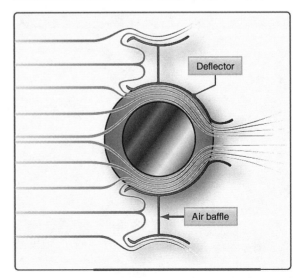

Figure 6-50. Cylinder baffle and deflector system.

6-42) AMP056
During ground operation of an engine, the cowl flaps should be in what position?

    A. Fully closed.
    B. Fully open.
    C. Opened according to ambient conditions.

6-43) AMP027
1. Some exhaust systems include an augmenter system to draw additional air over the engine for cooling.
2. Augmenter systems are used to create a low pressure area at the lower rear of the aircraft engine cowling.
Regarding the above statements,

    A. only No. 1 is true.
    B. both No. 1 and No. 2 are true.
    C. only No. 2 is true.

6-44) AMP027
Where are cooling fins located on the outside of air-cooled engines?

    A. Crankcase and oil sump.
    B. Cylinder heads and cylinder barrels.
    C. Cylinder barrels and engine cowl baffles.

6-45) AMP056
Which of the following defects would likely cause a hot spot on a reciprocating engine cylinder?

    A. Too much cooling fin area broken off.
    B. A cracked cylinder baffle.
    C. Cowling air seal leak.

6-46) AMP009
Cylinder head temperatures are measured by means of an indicator and a

    A. resistance bulb sensing device.
    B. Wheatstone bridge sensing device.
    C. thermocouple sensing device.

6-47) AMP027
How are combustion liner walls cooled in a gas turbine engine?

    A. By secondary air flowing through the combustion chamber.
    B. By the pattern of holes and louvers cut in the diffuser section.
    C. By bleed air vented from the engine air inlet.

6-48) AMP027
What air is used to cool the exterior and nacelle of a turbofan engine?

    A. Compressor bleed air.
    B. Conditioned air from the air cycle machine.
    C. Fan air.

6 - Lubrication and Cooling Systems
Answers

6-42) B.
When extended for increased cooling, the cowl flaps produce drag. During ground operation however, drag does not matter and cooling needs to be set at maximum. Therefore during ground operation, the cowl flaps should be opened wide (fully open).
[For more detailed information refer to Powerplant Handbook H-8083-32-ATB, Chapter 6 p.34]

6-43) B.
Some aircraft use augmenters to provide additional cooling airflow. The exhaust gas mixes with air that has passed over the engine and heats it to form a high temperature, low pressure, jet like exhaust. The low pressure area in the augmenters draws additional cooling air over the engine.
[For more detailed information refer to Powerplant Handbook H-8083-32-ATB, Chapter 6 p.34]

6-44) B.
The cylinder fins radiate heat from the cylinder walls and heads. As the air passes over the fins, it absorbs this heat, carries it away from the cylinder, and is exhausted overboard through the bottom rear of the cowl.
[For more detailed information refer to Powerplant Handbook H-8083-32-ATB, Chapter 6 p.35]

6-45) A.
If total fins broken on any cylinder head exceed a certain number of square inches of area, the cylinder is removed and replaced. The reason for removal is that missing fin area of a large size would cause a hot spot on the cylinder since very little heat transfer would occur. Applicable manufacturer's instructions should be consulted when determining allowable fin area missing or damaged.
[For more detailed information refer to Powerplant Handbook H-8083-32-ATB, Chapter 6 p.38]

6-46) C.
Cylinder temperature indicating systems usually consist of an indicator, electrical wiring , and a thermocouple. The thermocouple connects to the cylinder head and is either the bayonet-type or the gasket type. They are inserted or installed on the hottest cylinder of the engine as determined in the block test.
[For more detailed information refer to Powerplant Handbook H-8083-32-ATB, Chapter 6 p.38]

6-47) A.
The secondary air passing through the engine cools the combustion chamber liners. The liners are constructed to induce a thin, fast-moving film of air over both the inner and outer surfaces of the liner.
[For more detailed information refer to Powerplant Handbook H-8083-32-ATB, Chapter 6 p.39]

6-48) C.
Internal bleed air from the engine compressor section is vented to the bearings and other parts of the engine for cooling. The engine exterior and the engine nacelle are cooled by passing fan air around the engine and the nacelle.
[For more detailed information refer to Powerplant Handbook H-8083-32-ATB, Chapter 6 p.39-40]

Applicants for powerplant certification are required to answer oral examination questions before, after, or in conjunction with the practical examination portion of the airman certification process. The oral examination is used to establish knowledge. The practical examination is used to establish skill, which is the application of knowledge. Use the following questions to prepare for the oral examination. The questions are examples aligned with Practical Test Standards subject matter from which the examiner will choose topics for oral examination.

6-1(O). Name two items to be inspected to ensure adequate cooling of a reciprocating aircraft engine.

6-2(O). In what position should cowl flaps be placed for ground operation and why?

6-3(O). How is the combustion section of a turbine engine cooled?

6-4(O). What cools the bearings on a turbine engine?

6-5(O). What would be the effect of removing the engine baffles and seals from around a reciprocating air-cooled aircraft engine and why?

6-6(O). What are the two common types of heat exchangers used to cool engine oil on turbine engine aircraft?

6-7(O). What is the function and operation of an augmenter cooling system?

6-8(O). What is the difference between straight mineral oil, ashless-dispersant oil, and synthetic oil?

6-9(O). What types of oils are used for different climates?

6-10(O). What are the functions of engine oil?

6-11(O). How can the technician identify and select the proper lubricants?

6-12(O). Name two maintenance actions that are part of servicing an aircraft engine lubrication system.

6-13(O). What is the reason for changing engine oil at specified intervals?

6-14(O). What are two reasons for excessive oil consumption on a reciprocating engine that shows no signs of oil leakage?

6-1(O). Cowling, cowling seals, cowl flaps, cylinder fins, cylinder baffles, and deflector system.
Reference: FAA-H-8083-32-ATB Chapter 6 p.36 to 38

6-2(O). Fully OPEN because in this position they provide for the greatest amount of airflow over the engine and thus the greatest amount of cooling.
Reference: FAA-H-8083-32-ATB Chapter 6 p.34 to 35

6-3(O). Using air that has been drawn through the compressor which is routed through combustion chamber liners that provide a thin, fast-moving film of air that carries the heat away. Air is also routed to join with the burned gases aft of the burners to cool the hot gases before they enter the turbines.
Reference: FAA-H-8083-32-ATB Chapter 6 p.39

6-4(O). Air that is bled from the compressor section of the engine and sometimes air that is drawn from outside the engine for cooling purposes is routed to the bearings. Heat is also transferred to the oil that lubricates the bearings.
Reference: FAA-H-8083-32-ATB Chapter 6 p.27 to 39

6-5(O). The engine would overheat because the baffles and seals are designed to route cooling air close by and past the engine cylinders and thus draw away heat from the engine.
Reference: FAA-H-8083-32-ATB Chapter 6 p.33 to 38

6-6(O). Fuel – oil heat exchangers and air – oil heat exchangers.
Reference: FAA-H-8083-32-ATB Chapter 6 p.28 to 29

6-7(O). The function is to draw ambient air through the engine compartment for better cooling. It is accomplished with augmenter tubes or ejector tubes into which the exhaust gas is directed. This causes a low pressure and increases the flow of ambient air through augmenter and, thus, through the nacelle.
Reference: FAA-H-8083-32-ATB Chapter 6 p.34 to 35

6-8(O). Straight mineral oil is blended from specifically selected petroleum based stocks. It has no additives except small amounts of pour point depressant and an antioxidant. It is used during the break-in period of a new or recently overhauled engine. Ashless dispersant oil is straight mineral oil with non-metallic, non-ash forming polymeric additives such as viscosity stabilizers. It extends operating temperature range and improves cold engine starting and lubrication during warm-up. It permits flight through a wide range of climactic changes without having to change oils. Synthetic oil is specially formulated and is used in turbine engines. It is more viscous than ashless or straight mineral oil and has a lower tendency to deposit lacquer and coke. It also resists oxidation and has superior load carrying ability. It provides long service life and prevents seal wear.
Reference: FAA-H-8083-32-ATB Chapter 6 p.4 to 19

6-9(O). Ashless dispersant grades of oil are recommended for aircraft engines subject to wide variations of ambient temperatures. However, below 20 °F, preheating the engine and oil supply tank is normally required regardless of the type of oil used. In all cases, refer to the manufacturer's specifications.
Reference: FAA-H-8083-32-ATB Chapter 6 p.4

6-10(O). Engine oil acts as a cushion between metal parts and reduces friction. It cools the engine, seals, cleans, and reduces abrasive wear. Oil also prevents corrosion on the inside of the engine.
Reference: FAA-H-8083-32-ATB Chapter 6 p.1 to 2

6-11(O). Aircraft oils are classified by a numbering system that is an approximation of their viscosity. There are different systems in use such as SAE and MIL-spec. Letters, such as a W, are also used to describe the oil or its characteristics. Many factors are considered when determining the proper oil for a particular engine including operating load, rotational speeds, and operating temperatures. In all cases, refer to the engine manufacturer's information when oil type or time in service is being considered.
Reference: FAA-H-8083-32-ATB Chapter 6 p.2 to 4

6-12(O). Periodic oil changes, oil filter change, inspection of oil filter contents, inspection and cleaning of oil screen(s), checking and adjustment of oil pressure relief valve, cleaning oil cooler of obstructions.
Reference: FAA-H-8083-32-ATB Chapter 6 p.14 to 19

6-13(O). Oil in service accumulates contaminants such as gas, moisture, acids, dirt, carbon, and metallic particles which reduce the ability of the oil to protect moving parts. Replacing the oil periodically ensure the oil can do what it is designed to do.
Reference: FAA-H-8083-32-ATB Chapter 6 p.17 to 18

6-14(O). Low grade oil or improper oil such as ashless dispersant oil used in a new or overhauled engine, failing or failed crankshaft bearing(s).
Reference: FAA-H-8083-32-ATB Chapter 6 p.4, 6-20

6 - Lubrication and Cooling Systems
Practical

Applicants for powerplant certification are required to demonstrate the ability to apply knowledge by performing maintenance related tasks for the examiner. The Practical Test Standards (PTS) list the subject areas from which the skill elements to be performed by the applicant are chosen. The following examples resemble tasks an examiner may ask an applicant to perform. The Performance Level required to be demonstrated for each skill element is listed. Consult the PTS for Level descriptions.

6-1(P). Given an actual aircraft engine or mockup, appropriate publications, and tooling inspect an engine lubrication system to ensure continued operation and record your findings. [Level 3]

6-2(P). Given an actual aircraft engine or mockup, appropriate publications, and tooling inspect oil lines and filter/screen for leaks and record your findings. [Level 3]

6-3(P). Given an actual aircraft engine or mockup, appropriate publications, and tooling replace a defective oil cooler and record maintenance. [Level 3]

6-4(P). Given an actual aircraft engine or mockup, appropriate publications, and tooling replace a defective oil cooler component and record maintenance.
[Level 3]

6-5(P). Given an actual aircraft engine or mockup, appropriate publications, and tooling replace a gasket in the oil system, accomplish a leak check, and record maintenance. [Level 3]

6-6(P). Given an actual aircraft engine or mockup, appropriate publications, and tooling replace a seal in the oil system, accomplish a leak check, and record maintenance. [Level 3]

6-7(P). Given an actual aircraft engine or mockup, appropriate publications, and tooling adjust the oil pressure and record maintenance. [Level 3]

6-8(P). Given an actual aircraft engine or mockup, appropriate publications, equipment, tooling and supplies complete the following: change engine oil, inspect screen(s) and/or filter, leak check the engine, and record maintenance. [Level 3]

6-9(P). Given an actual aircraft engine or mockup, and appropriate publications, pre-oil an engine. [Level 2]

6-10(P). Given an actual aircraft engine or mockup, appropriate publications, and tooling inspect an engine cooling system and record your findings. [Level 3]

6-11(P). Given an actual aircraft engine or mockup, appropriate publications, and tooling check cowl flap operation, inspect rigging and record maintenance. [Level 3]

6-12(P). Given an actual aircraft engine or mockup, appropriate publications, materials, and tooling, repair one or more cylinder cooling fins and record maintenance. [Level 3]

6-13(P). Given an actual aircraft engine or mockup, appropriate publications, materials, and tooling, repair an engine pressure baffle plate and record maintenance. [Level 3]

6-14(P). Given an actual aircraft engine or mockup, appropriate publications, and tooling inspect a heat exchanger and record your findings. [Level 3]

6-15(P). Given an actual aircraft engine or mockup, appropriate publications, tooling, equipment and an unknown discrepancy troubleshoot an engine cooling system and record your findings. [Level 3]

6-16(P). Given an actual rotorcraft engine or mockup, locate and identify specified rotorcraft cooling system components. [Level 3]

Propellers

Propeller Aerodynamics, Propeller Placement, Types of Propellers, Propeller Governors, Vibration and Balancing, Servicing and Overhaul

7-1) AMP053
Which of the following is identified as the cambered or curved side of a propeller blade corresponding to the upper surface of a wing airfoil section.

A. Blade back.
B. Blade chord.
C. Blade face.

7-2) AMP053
The primary purpose of the propeller is to

A. create lift on the fixed airfoils of an aircraft.
B. change engine horsepower into thrust.
C. provide static and dynamic stability of an aircraft in flight.

7-3) AMP053
Geometric pitch of a propeller is defined as

A. effective pitch minus slippage.
B. effective pitch plus slippage.
C. angle between the blade chord and the plane of rotation.

7-4) AMP053
The actual distance a propeller moves forward through the air during one revolution is known as the

A. effective pitch.
B. geometric pitch
C. relative pitch.

7 - Propellers
Answers

7-1) A.
The basic nomenclature for a propeller is illustrated in Figure 7-1 of FAA-H-8083-32. The curved surface of a propeller, the side that most resembles the curved upper surface of a wing airfoil, is known as the blade back. The blade face resembles the bottom surface of a wing airfoil in that it is relatively flat.
[For more detailed information refer to Powerplant Handbook H-8083-32-ATB, Chapter 7 p.2]

7-2) B.
The propeller is mounted on a shaft which may be an extension of the crankshaft on low-horsepower engines. On high horsepower engines, it is mounted on a propeller shaft which is geared to the engine crankshaft. In either case, the engine rotates the airfoils of the blades through the air at high speeds and the propeller transforms the rotary power of the engine into thrust.
[For more detailed information refer to Powerplant Handbook H-8083-32-ATB, Chapter 7 p.2-3]

7-3) B.
Pitch is not the same as blade angle but pitch is largely determined by blade angle. Geometric pitch is the distance the propeller should advance in one revolution with no slippage. Effective pitch is the distance the propeller actually advances. Thus, geometric pitch is theoretical. It is the effective pitch plus the slippage. Geometric pitch is usually expressed in inches.
[For more detailed information refer to Powerplant Handbook H-8083-32-ATB, Chapter 7 p.3]

7-4) A.
Propeller slip is the difference between geometric pitch of the propeller and its effective pitch. Geometric pitch is the distance the propeller should advance in one revolution with no slippage; effective pitch is the distance it actually advances. Thus, geometric pitch is based on no slippage. Effective (or actual) pitch recognizes propeller slippage in the air.
[For more detailed information refer to Powerplant Handbook H-8083-32-ATB, Chapter 7 p.3]

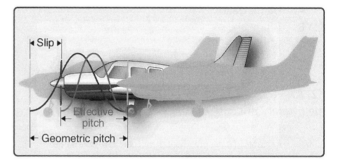

Figure 7-4. Effective pitch and geometric pitch.

7-5) AMP053

Blade angle is an angle formed by a line perpendicular to the crankshaft and a line formed by the

    A.   relative wind.

    B.   chord of the blade.

    C.   blade face.

7-6) AMP053

Propeller blade station numbers increase from

    A.   hub to tip.

    B.   tip to hub.

    C.   leading edge to trailing edge.

7 - Propellers
Answers

7-5) B.

Although blade angle and propeller pitch are closely related, blade angle is the angle between the chord of a blade section and the plane in which the propeller rotates. Therefore, blade angle, usually measured in degrees, is the angle between the chord line of the blade and the plane of rotation. Note that the plane of rotation is perpendicular to the crankshaft.

[For more detailed information refer to Powerplant Handbook H-8083-32-ATB, Chapter 7 p.3]

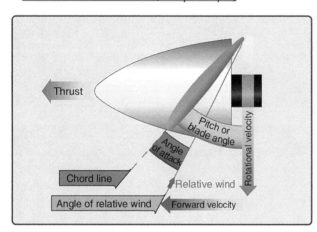

Figure 7-5. Propeller aerodynamic factors.

7-6) A.

For purposes of analysis and maintenance, a propeller blade can be divided into segments that are located by station numbers in inches from the center of the blade hub. Thus, the station numbers increase from hub to tip.

[For more detailed information refer to Powerplant Handbook H-8083-32-ATB, Chapter 7 p.3]

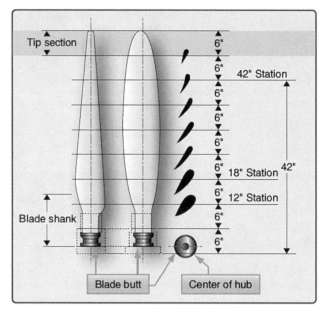

Figure 7-6. Typical propeller blade elements.

7-7) AMP053
What operational force causes the greatest stress on a propeller?

   A. Aerodynamic twisting force.
   B. Centrifugal force.
   C. Thrust bending force.

7-8) AMP053
What operational force causes propeller blade tips to lag in the opposite direction of rotation?

   A. Thrust bending.
   B. Aerodynamic twisting.
   C. Torque bending.

7-9) AMP053
What operational force tends to bend the propeller blades forward at the tips?

   A. Torque bending force.
   B. Centrifugal-twisting force.
   C. Thrust bending force.

7-10) AMP053
How does the aerodynamic twisting force affect operating propeller blades?

   A. It tends to turn the blades to a high blade angle.
   B. It tends to bend the blades forward.
   C. It tends to turn the blades to a low blade angle.

7-11) AMP053
The centrifugal twisting moment of an operating propeller tends to

   A. increase the pitch angle.
   B. reduce the pitch angle.
   C. bend the blades in the direction of rotation.

7-12) AMP053
The angle of attack of a rotating propeller blade is measured between the blade chord or face and which of the following?

   A. Plane of blade rotation.
   B. Full low-pitch blade angle.
   C. Relative airstream.

7-13) AMP053
The thrust produced by rotating a propeller is a result of

   A. an area of low pressure behind the propeller blades.
   B. an area of decreased pressure immediately in front of the propeller blades.
   C. the angle of the relative wind and rotational velocity of the propeller.

7-7) B.
Centrifugal force is a physical force that tends to throw the rotating propeller blades away from the hub. This is the most dominant force on the propeller.
[For more detailed information refer to Powerplant Handbook H-8083-32-ATB, Chapter 7 p.4]

7-8) C.
Torque bending force, in the form of air resistance, tends to bend the propeller blade in the direction opposite that of rotation.
[For more detailed information refer to Powerplant Handbook H-8083-32-ATB, Chapter 7 p.4]

7-9) C.
Thrust bending force is the thrust load that tends to bend propeller blades forward as the aircraft is pulled through the air.
[For more detailed information refer to Powerplant Handbook H-8083-32-ATB, Chapter 7 p.4]

7-10) A.
Aerodynamic twisting force tends to turn the blades to a high blade angle.
[For more detailed information refer to Powerplant Handbook H-8083-32-ATB, Chapter 7 p.4]

7-11) B.
Centrifugal twisting force, being greater than the aerodynamic twisting force, tends to force the blades towards a low blade angle.
[For more detailed information refer to Powerplant Handbook H-8083-32-ATB, Chapter 7 p.4]

7-12) C.
The angle at which the air, the relative wind, strikes the propeller blade is called the angle of attack (AOA).
[For more detailed information refer to Powerplant Handbook H-8083-32-ATB, Chapter 7 p.5]

7-13) B.
The shape of the propeller blade creates thrust because it is shaped like a wing. As the air flows past the propeller, the pressure on one side is less than that on the other. As in a wing, this difference in pressure produces a reaction force in the direction of the lesser pressure. The area above a wing has less pressure and the force, lift, is upward. The area of decreased pressure is in front of a propeller which is mounted in a vertical instead of horizontal position. Thus, the force, thrust, is in a forward direction.
[For more detailed information refer to Powerplant Handbook H-8083-32-ATB, Chapter 7 p.5]

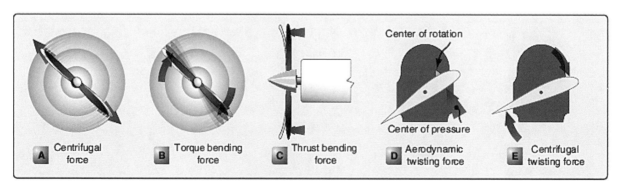

Figure 7-8. Forces acting on a rotating propeller.

7-14) AMP053

Which of the following best describes the blade movement of a feathering propeller that is in the HIGH RPM position when reversing?

    A.   Low pitch directly to reversing.
    B.   Low pitch through high pitch to reverse pitch.
    C.   Low pitch through feathering position to reverse pitch.

7-15) AMP053

What are the rotational speed and blade pitch angle requirements of a constant-speed propeller during takeoff?

    A.   Low speed and high pitch angle.
    B.   High speed and low pitch angle.
    C.   High speed and high pitch angle.

7-16) AMP053

A constant-speed propeller provides maximum efficiency by

    A.   increasing blade pitch as the aircraft speed decreases.
    B.   adjusting blade angle for most conditions encountered in flight.
    C.   increasing the lift coefficient of the blade.

7-17) AMP053

Counterweights on constant-speed propellers are generally used to aid in

    A.   increasing blade angle.
    B.   decreasing blade angle.
    C.   un-feathering the propellers.

7 - Propellers
Answers

7-14) A.
Regardless of which aircraft it is mounted on, a a propeller that can change blade position (blade angle) to match the flight conditions is known as a constant speed propeller. The available blade angles range from feathered, when the angle is between 85° and 90° to the plane of rotation, to reverse pitch when the blade angle is -2° to -8° to the plane of propeller rotation. A HIGH RPM position is one in which the blade angle is low. To reverse the propeller, the blade angle moves directly from a low blade angle, through zero degrees blade angle to a negative blade angle.
[For more detailed information refer to Powerplant Handbook H-8083-32-ATB, Chapter 7 p.2-6]

7-15) B.
During takeoff, when maximum power and thrust are required, the constant-speed propeller is at low propeller blade angle or pitch. The low blade angle keeps the AOA small and efficient with respect to the relative wind. This light load allows the engine to turn at high speed. and convert the maximum amount of fuel into heat energy. The high RPM also creates maximum thrust. The mass of air handled per revolution of the propeller is small due to the low blade angle, however, with high RPM, the slipstream velocity is high and, combined with the low speed of the aircraft, thrust is at maximum.
[For more detailed information refer to Powerplant Handbook H-8083-32-ATB, Chapter 7 p.5]

7-16) B.
To provide an efficient propeller, the speed is kept as constant as possible.
If the throttle setting is changed, instead of changing the speed of the aircraft by climbing or diving, the blade angle increases or decreases as required to maintain a constant engine RPM. The power output, not the RPM, changes in accordance with changes in throttle setting. The constant-speed propeller changes the blade angle automatically keeping engine RPM constant.
[For more detailed information refer to Powerplant Handbook H-8083-32-ATB, Chapter 7 p.8]

7-17) A.
Each constant-speed propeller has an opposing force that operates against oil pressure from the governor. Flyweights (counterweights) mounted to the blades move the blades in the high pitch direction as the propeller turns. Other forces used to move the blades toward the high pitch direction include air pressure (contained in the front dome), springs, and aerodynamic twisting moment.
[For more detailed information refer to Powerplant Handbook H-8083-32-ATB, Chapter 7 p.8]

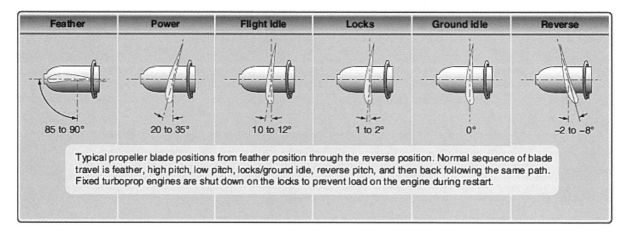

Feather	Power	Flight idle	Locks	Ground idle	Reverse
85 to 90°	20 to 35°	10 to 12°	1 to 2°	0°	−2 to −8°

Typical propeller blade positions from feather position through the reverse position. Normal sequence of blade travel is feather, high pitch, low pitch, locks/ground idle, reverse pitch, and then back following the same path. Fixed turboprop engines are shut down on the locks to prevent load on the engine during restart.

Figure 7-3. Propeller range positions.

7-18) AMP053

The primary purpose of a feathering propeller is to

A. prevent further engine damage when an engine fails in flight.
B. prevent propeller damage when an engine fails in flight.
C. eliminate the drag created by a windmilling propeller when an engine fails in flight.

7-19) AMP053

How do small feathering propellers prevent feathering when the engine is shut down?

A. Latches lock the propeller in low pitch to prevent excess load on the engine at start-up.
B. Oil pressure is held against the pitch change mechanism.
C. Aerodynamic twisting moment prevents feathering.

7-20) AMP053

Reverse pitch propellers

A. turn in the opposite direct than that of the crankshaft.
B. produce a negative blade angle to slow the aircraft after touchdown.
C. go beyond feathering position to provide thrust for stopping.

7-21) AMP053

The propeller governor controls the

A. oil to and from the pitch changing mechanism.
B. spring tension on the boost pump speeder spring.
C. linkage and counterweights from moving in and out.

7-22) AMP053

During the on-speed condition of a propeller, the

A. centrifugal force acting on the governor flyweights is greater than the tension of the speeder spring.
B. tension on the speeder spring is less than the centrifugal force acting on the flyweights.
C. centrifugal force of the governor flyweights is equal to the speeder spring tension.

7-23) AMP023

When the centrifugal force acting on the propeller governor flyweights overcomes the tension on the speeder spring, a propeller is in what speed condition?

A. On speed.
B. Under-speed.
C. Over-speed.

7-24) AMP053

What is the primary purpose of the metal tipping which covers the blade tips and extends along the leading edge of each wood propeller blade?

A. To increase the lateral strength of the blade.
B. To prevent impact damage to the tip and leading edge of the blade.
C. To increase longitudinal strength of the blade.

7 - Propellers
Answers

7-18) C.
A feathering propeller is a constant-speed propeller used on multi-engine aircraft that has a mechanism to change pitch to an angle of approximately 90°. By rotating the propeller blade angle parallel to the line of flight, the drag on the aircraft is greatly reduced.
[For more detailed information refer to Powerplant Handbook H-8083-32-ATB, Chapter 7 p.8]

7-19) A.
Almost all small feathering propellers use oil pressure to take the propeller to low pitch and blade flyweights, springs and compressed air to take the blades to high pitch. Since the blades would go to feather position during shutdown, latches lock the propeller in the low pitch position as the propeller slows down at shutdown. The latches are needed to prevent excess load on the engine at start up.
[For more detailed information refer to Powerplant Handbook H-8083-32-ATB, Chapter 7 p.8]

7-20) B.
The purpose of the reversible pitch feature is to produce a negative blade angle that produces thrust opposite to the normal forward direction. Normally, when the landing gear is in contact with the runway after landing, the propeller blades can be moved to negative pitch (reversed), which creates thrust opposite of the aircraft direction and slows the aircraft. Engine power can be applied to increase the negative thrust.
[For more detailed information refer to Powerplant Handbook H-8083-32-ATB, Chapter 7 p.9]

7-21) A.
A governor is an engine rpm-sensing device and high-pressure oil pump. In a constant-speed propeller system, the governor responds to a change in engine RPM by directing oil under pressure to the propeller hydraulic cylinder. The change in oil volume in the hydraulic cylinder changes the blade angle and maintains the propeller system RPM. The governor is set for a specific RPM via the cockpit propeller control, which compresses or releases the governor speeder spring.
[For more detailed information refer to Powerplant Handbook H-8083-32-ATB, Chapter 7 p.8]

7-22) C.
In an on speed condition, the centrifugal force acting on the flyweights is balanced by the speeder spring and the pilot valve is neither directing oil to or from the propeller hydraulic cylinder.
[For more detailed information refer to Powerplant Handbook H-8083-32-ATB, Chapter 7 p.10]

7-23) C.
In an over-speed condition, the centrifugal force acting on the flyweights is greater than the speeder spring force. Therefore, the flyweights tilt outward. This raises the pilot valve and allows oil to flow to the piston so as to increase blade pitch and reduce RPM.
[For more detailed information refer to Powerplant Handbook H-8083-32-ATB, Chapter 7 p.10]

7-24) B.
A metal tipping is fastened to most of the leading edge and tip of each blade on a wood propeller to protect the propeller from damage caused by flying particles in the air during landing, taxiing, or takeoff.
[For more detailed information refer to Powerplant Handbook H-8083-32-ATB, Chapter 7 p.13]

7-25) AMP053

What is the basic purpose of the three small holes (No. 60 drill) in the tipping of wood propeller blades?

A. To provide a means for inserting balancing shot when necessary.
B. To provide a means for periodically impregnating the blade with preservation materials.
C. To allow the moisture which may collect between the tipping and the wood to escape (vent the tipping).

7-26) AMP053

Constant speed non-feathering McCauley, Hartzell, and other propellers of similar design without counterweights increase pitch angle using

A. oil pressure.
B. spring pressure.
C. centrifugal twisting moment.

7-27) AMP053

What normally prevents a Hartzell Compact propeller from going to feather when the engine is shut down on the ground?

A. Propeller cylinder pressure.
B. A latch mechanism composed of springs and lock pins.
C. Accumulator provided oil pressure.

7-28) AMP016

Ice formation on propellers, when an aircraft is in flight, will

A. decrease thrust and cause excessive vibration.
B. increase aircraft stall speed and increase noise.
C. decrease available engine power.

7-29) AMP016

How is anti-ice fluid ejected from the slinger ring on a propeller?

A. By pump pressure.
B. By centripetal force.
C. By centrifugal force.

7-30) AMP016

Propeller fluid anti-icing systems generally use which of the following?

A. Ethylene glycol.
B. Isopropyl alcohol.
C. Ethyl alcohol.

7-31) AMP053

How is aircraft electrical power for propeller deicer systems transferred from the engine to the propeller hub assembly?

A. By slip rings and segment plates.
B. By slip rings and brushes.
C. By flexible electrical connectors.

7-32) AMP053

Propeller deicer boots are

A. "ON" continuously in icing conditions.
B. used to prevent ice before it builds on the propeller surfaces.
C. energized for short periods by a cycling timer.

7 - Propellers
Answers

7-25) C.
Since moisture condenses on tipping between the metal and the wood, the tipping is provided with small holes near the blade tip to allow this moisture to drain away or be thrown out by centrifugal force. It is important that these drain holes be kept open at all times.
[For more detailed information refer to Powerplant Handbook H-8083-32-ATB, Chapter 7 p.13]

7-26) A.
In the absence of governor oil pressure, centrifugal twisting moment tends to move propeller blades into low pitch. Most Hartzell and other constant speed propellers with aluminum and steel hubs use centrifugal force acting on blade counterweights to increase blade pitch and governor oil pressure to move the blades towards low pitch. However, the constant speed, non-feathering models without counterweights use oil pressure to move the blades toward high pitch.
[For more detailed information refer to Powerplant Handbook H-8083-32-ATB, Chapter 7 p.15]

7-27) B.
In order to prevent feathering spring and counterweights from feathering the propeller when the engine is shut down and the engine stopped, automatically removable high-pitch stops were incorporated in the design. These consist of spring-loaded latches fastened to the stationary hub that engage high-pitch stop plates bolted to the movable blade clamps.
[For more detailed information refer to Powerplant Handbook H-8083-32-ATB, Chapter 7 p.17]

7-28) A.
Ice formation on a propeller blade, in effect, produces a distorted blade airfoil section that causes a loss in propeller efficiency and a decrease in thrust. Generally, as ice collects asymmetrically on a propeller blade it unbalances the propeller causing destructive vibration while it increases the weight of the blades.
[For more detailed information refer to Powerplant Handbook H-8083-32-ATB, Chapter 7 p.17]

7-29) C.
Fluid is transferred from a stationary nozzle on the engine nose case into a circular U-shaped channel (slinger ring) mounted on the rear of the propeller assembly. The fluid under pressure of centrifugal force is transferred through nozzles to each blade shank.
[For more detailed information refer to Powerplant Handbook H-8083-32-ATB, Chapter 7 p.17]

7-30) B.
Isopropyl alcohol is used in some anti-icing systems because of its availability and low cost. Phosphate compounds are comparable to isopropyl alcohol in performance and have reduced flammability, however, they are more expensive.
[For more detailed information refer to Powerplant Handbook H-8083-32-ATB, Chapter 7 p.18]

7-31) B.
A slip ring rotates with the propeller and provides a current path to the blades deice boots. A brush block, mounted on the engine just behind the propeller is used to transfer electricity to the slip ring.
[For more detailed information refer to Powerplant Handbook H-8083-32-ATB, Chapter 7 p.19]

7-32) C.
Electric deicing systems are usually designed for intermittent application of power to the heating elements to remove ice after formation but before excessive accumulation. Cycling timers are used to energize the heating element circuits for periods of 15 to 20 seconds, with a complete cycle time of 2 minutes. A cycling timer is an electric motor driven contactor that controls power contactors in separate sections of the circuit.
[For more detailed information refer to Powerplant Handbook H-8083-32-ATB, Chapter 7 p.19-20]

7-33) AMP053

What is the function of the automatic propeller synchronizing system on multiengine aircraft?

  A. To control the tip speed of all propellers.
  B. To control engine RPM and reduce vibration.
  C. To control the power output of all engines.

7-34) AMP052

How can a steel propeller hub be tested for cracks?

  A. By anodizing.
  B. By magnetic particle inspection.
  C. By etching.

7-35) AMP052

Which of the following generally renders an aluminum alloy propeller un-repairable?

  A. Any repair that would require shortening and re-contouring the blades.
  B. Any slag inclusions or cold shuts.
  C. Transverse cracks of any size.

7-36) AMP052

Inspection of propeller blades by dye-penetrant inspection is accomplished to detect

  A. cracks or other defects.
  B. corrosion at the blade tip.
  C. torsional stress.

7-37) AMP052

Propeller blade tracking is the process of determining

  A. the plane of rotation of the propeller with respect to the aircraft longitudinal axis.
  B. that the blade angles are within the specified tolerance of each other.
  C. the positions of the tips of the propeller blades relative to each other.

7-38) AMP052

Which of the following functions requires the use of propeller blade station?

  A. Measuring blade angle.
  B. Indexing blades.
  C. Propeller balancing.

7-39) AMP052

Propeller aerodynamic (thrust) imbalance can be largely eliminated by

  A. correct blade contouring and angle setting.
  B. static balancing.
  C. keeping the propeller blades within the same plane of rotation.

7-40) AMP052

Propellers exposed to salt spray should be flushed with

  A. stoddard solvent.
  B. fresh water.
  C. soapy water.

7 - Propellers
Answers

7-33) B.
Most multi-engine aircraft are equipped with propeller synchronization systems. Synchronization systems provide a means of controlling and synchronizing engine RPM. Synchronization reduces vibration and eliminates the unpleasant beat produced by unsynchronized propeller operation.
[For more detailed information refer to Powerplant Handbook H-8083-32-ATB, Chapter 7 p.20]

7-34) B.
The inspection of steel blades may be accomplished by either visual, fluorescent penetrant, or magnetic particle inspection. The full length of the leading edge (especially near the tip), the full length of the trailing edge, the grooves and shoulders on the shank, and all dents and scars should be examined with a magnifying glass to decide whether defects are scratches or cracks.
[For more detailed information refer to Powerplant Handbook H-8083-32-ATB, Chapter 7 p. 21]

7-35) C.
Carefully inspect aluminum propellers and blades for cracks and other flaws. A transverse crack or flaw of any size is cause for rejection. Multiple deep nicks and gouges on the leading edge and face of the blade are cause for rejection. Use dye penetrant or fluorescent dye penetrant to confirm suspected cracks found in the propeller.
[For more detailed information refer to Powerplant Handbook H-8083-32-ATB, Chapter 7 p.21]

7-36) A.
Use of dye penetrant or fluorescent dye penetrant is used to confirm suspected cracks found in a propeller.
[For more detailed information refer to Powerplant Handbook H-8083-32-ATB, Chapter 7 p.21]

7-37) C.
Blade tracking is the process of determining the positions of the tips of the propeller blades relative to each other (blades rotating in the same plane of rotation). An out of track propeller may be due to one or more of the blades being bent, a bent propeller flange, or propeller mounting bolts that or improperly torqued.
[For more detailed information refer to Powerplant Handbook H-8083-32-ATB, Chapter 7 p.22]

7-38) A.
Due to the twist of most propellers, blade angle must be measured at the same blade station on each blade to ensure comparable readings. The manufacturer's instructions are used to obtain the blade angle setting and the station at which the blade angle is checked.
[For more detailed information refer to Powerplant Handbook H-8083-32-ATB, Chapter 7 p.22]

7-39) A.
Dynamic imbalance of a propeller resulting from improper mass distribution is negligible provided the track tolerance requirements are met. Aerodynamic unbalance, however, results when the thrust (or pull) of the blades is unequal. This type of unbalance can be largely eliminated by checking blade contour and blade angle setting.
[For more detailed information refer to Powerplant Handbook H-8083-32-ATB, Chapter 7 p.24]

7-40) B.
If a propeller has been subjected to salt water, flush it with fresh water until all traces of salt have been removed. This should be accomplished as soon as possible after the salt water has splashed on the propeller regardless of whether the propeller parts are aluminum alloy, steel or wood.
[For more detailed information refer to Powerplant Handbook H-8083-32-ATB, Chapter 7 p.27]

7-41) AMP052

When lubricating a Hartzell propeller blade with grease, to prevent damage to the blade seals, the service manual may recommend on some models to

A. pump grease into both zerk fittings for the blade simultaneously.
B. remove the seals prior to greasing and reinstall them afterwards.
C. remove one of the two zerk fittings for the blade and grease the blade through the remaining fitting.

7-42) AMP052

Which of the following determines oil and grease specifications for lubrication of propellers?

A. Airframe manufacturers.
B. Engine manufacturers.
C. Propeller manufacturers.

7-43) AMP052

Cold straightening of a bent aluminum propeller blade

A. may be accomplished by any certified powerplant mechanic.
B. requires specialized tooling and precision measuring equipment.
C. renders it unairworthy.

7-44) AMP053

How is a propeller controlled in a large aircraft with a turboprop installation?

A. Independently of the engine.
B. By varying the engine RPM except for feathering and reversing.
C. By the engine power lever.

7-45) AMP053

On a typical Pratt and Whitney PT-6 turboprop engine, oil for the propeller governor is supplied by

A. a separate reservoir from the main engine oil supply.
B. the aircraft hydraulic system.
C. the engine oil supply.

7-46) AMP053

A Hydromatic propeller differs from most constant-speed propellers in that

A. engine oil pressure balances governor oil pressure.
B. the blade counterweights are larger for rapid feathering.
C. it has a single acting governor completely enclosed in the spinner housing.

7 - Propellers
Answers

7-41) C.
Redistribution of grease may result in voids in the blade bearing area where moisture can collect. Remove one of the lubrication fittings for each blade hub. Pump grease into the fitting located nearest the leading edge of the blade on a tractor propeller installation, or nearest the trailing edge on a pusher installation, until grease emerges from the hole where the fitting was removed. Always follow specific manufacturer's instructions for the specified model propeller undergoing maintenance.
[For more detailed information refer to Powerplant Handbook H-8083-32-ATB, Chapter 7 p.28]

7-42) C.
Proper propeller lubrication procedures, with oil and grease specifications, are usually published in the propeller manufacturer's instructions. The greasing schedule must be followed to ensure proper lubrication of moving parts and protection from corrosion.
[For more detailed information refer to Powerplant Handbook H-8083-32-ATB, Chapter 7 p.28]

7-43) B.
Occasionally, blade straightening is required during propeller overhaul. The manufacturer's specifications dictate certain allowable limits within which damaged blades can be straightened and returned to airworthy condition. Specialized tooling and precision measuring equipment permit pitch changes or corrections of less than one-tenth of one degree.
[For more detailed information refer to Powerplant Handbook H-8083-32-ATB, Chapter 7 p.29]

7-44) C.
The turboprop engine produces thrust indirectly because the compressor and turbine assembly furnish torque to a propeller producing the major portion of the propulsive force that drives the aircraft. The turboprop fuel control and the propeller governor are connected and operate in coordination with each other. The power lever directs a signal from the cockpit to the fuel control for a specific amount of power from the engine. The fuel control and the propeller governor together establish the correct combination of rpm, fuel flow, and propeller blade angle to create sufficient propeller thrust to provide the desired power.
[For more detailed information refer to Powerplant Handbook H-8083-32-ATB, Chapter 7 p.30-31]

7-45) C.
Engine oil is supplied to the propeller governor from the engine oil supply. A gear pump mounted at the base of the governor increases flow and pressure as demanded.
[For more detailed information refer to Powerplant Handbook H-8083-32-ATB, Chapter 7 p.32]

7-46) A.
A Hydromatic propeller has a double acting governor that uses oil pressure on both sides of the propeller piston. In the pitch changing mechanism, no counterweights are used. Engine oil pressure on one side of the piston is used against propeller governor oil on the other side of the piston to change blade angle or pitch. Hydromatic propellers can be found on some older radial engines but also on large new turboprop systems.
[For more detailed information refer to Powerplant Handbook H-8083-32-ATB, Chapter 7 p.35]

Applicants for powerplant certification are required to answer oral examination questions before, after, or in conjunction with the practical examination portion of the airman certification process. The oral examination is used to establish knowledge. The practical examination is used to establish skill, which is the application of knowledge. Use the following questions to prepare for the oral examination. The questions are examples aligned with Practical Test Standards subject matter from which the examiner will choose topics for oral examination.

7-1(O). How does a propeller function?

7-2(O). Why are constant speed propellers used?

7-3(O). What are the components of a propeller governor and how does it operate?

7-4(O). What is a test club propeller? When and why is it used?

7-5(O). What is the maximum interval between lubrication of a propeller and where does the technician find the proper procedures for lubrication of a particular propeller?

7-6(O). How is the angle of a propeller blade measured while the propeller is mounted on the engine?

7-7(O). In general, what is the procedure for removing a propeller?

7-8(O). What is the function of a typical propeller synchronization system and how does it operate?

7-9(O). Explain why is ice a problem for propeller operation. Then, name a means for anti-icing and a means of deicing aircraft propellers.

7-10(O). A propeller is essentially a rotating wing. As the engine turns it, the air moving past the curved forward surface of the propeller causes a low pressure when compared to the area on the aft side of the propeller, which is relatively flat. As in a wing, the difference in pressure causes a reactive force in the direction of the lesser pressure. On a wing, this force is upward and is called lift. On a propeller, this force is forward and is called thrust. It is this force that moves the aircraft.
Reference: FAA-H-8083-32-ATB Chapter 7 p.5

7-11(O). To obtain maximum efficiency from the propeller by rotating it at a constant speed and to keep the engine RPM constant while adjusting the power output with the throttle lever.
Reference: FAA-H-8083-32-ATB Chapter 7 p.8

7-12(O). A typical propeller governor consists of a drive gear to engage the engine, an oil pump, a pilot valve controlled by flyweights, a relief valve system, a piston connected mechanically to the blades, a speeder spring, and an adjusting rack for control from the flight deck. The governor senses the RPM of the engine/propeller assembly via the flyweights. The force of the flyweights is counterbalanced against the force of the speeder spring that is set via the adjusting rack. If the speed of the engine and propeller increase, the flyweight force increases and they move outward. This opens the pilot valve and oil is pumped against the piston. The piston motion transmits the force to the blades which increase pitch angle. At a higher pitch angle, the force of the air striking the blades increases. This increases the load on the engine and serves to suppress engine RPM and keep it constant.
Reference: FAA-H-8083-32-ATB Chapter 7 p.10

7-13(O). A test club propeller is a four-bladed, fixed pitch propeller used during ground testing or break-in of a reciprocating engine. The blades are short and designed to put the correct amount of load on the engine during the test break-in period. The multi-blade design also provides additional cooling airflow.
Reference: FAA-H-8083-32-ATB Chapter 7 p.7

7-14(O). Propellers must be lubricated every 100 hours or at 12 calendar months, whichever occurs first. If annual operation is significantly less than 100 hours, calendar lubrication intervals should be reduced 6 months. Also, if the propeller is exposed to adverse atmospheric conditions, such as high humidity and, salt air, the calendar interval should be shortened to 6 months. The manufacturer's instructions should be consulted for the proper propeller lubrication procedures as well as oil and grease specifications.
Reference: FAA-H-8083-32-ATB Chapter 7 p.28

7-15(O). Propeller blade angle is measure at a blade station(s) specified by the manufacturer. Blade stations are measured in inches from the base of the blade toward the tip. Using a propeller or universal protract placed at the correct blade station, follow the manufacturer's instruction. The angle between the plane of rotation and the propeller blade face at the specified station is what is being measured.
Reference: FAA-H-8083-32-ATB Chapter 7 p.23 to 24

7-16(O). Always follow manufacturer's instruction. In general, remove the spinner dome. Then cut and remove the safety wire on the propeller mounting studs. Support the propeller assembly with a sling. Make an alignment mark on the hub and engine flange to maintain dynamic balance during reinstallation. Unscrew the four mounting bolts from the engine bushings. Unscrew the two mounting nuts and the attached studs from the engine bushings. If the propeller is removed between overhauls, mounting studs, nuts, and washers may be reused if not damaged or corroded. Using care and supporting the weight of the propeller assembly with the sling, remove the propeller from the mounting flange.
Reference: FAA-H-8083-32-ATB Chapter 7 p.27

7-17(O). Propeller synchronization is used to eliminate the unpleasant beat produced by unsynchronized propeller operation. A typical synchrophasing system is an electronic system. It functions to match the RPM of both engines and establish a blade phase relationship between the left and right propellers to reduce cabin noise. A switch on the flight deck controls the system. When in the "ON" position, pick-ups on each propeller send a signal to a control box. The control box sends a command signal to an RPM trimming coil on the propeller governor of the slow engine to adjust the RPM to equal that of the other propeller.
Reference: FAA-H-8083-32-ATB Chapter 7 p.20

7-18(O). Ice formation on a propeller blade in effect produces a distorted blade airfoil section and makes the propeller inefficient. Ice collects asymmetrically and produces propeller unbalance resulting in destructive vibration and increased blade weight. A typical propeller anti-icing system includes an on-board reservoir of anti-icing fluid that is pumped to a slinger ring mounted on the rear of the assembly and distributed to the blades by centrifugal force. A typical propeller de-icing system includes electric heating elements adhered to the leading edge of each blade. Power is transferred to the propeller elements through brushes and a slip ring. A timer cycles the elements on and off in sequence or this can be controlled by the pilot.
Reference: FAA-H-8083-32-ATB Chapter 7 p.17 to 19

Applicants for powerplant certification are required to demonstrate the ability to apply knowledge by performing maintenance related tasks for the examiner. The Practical Test Standards (PTS) list the subject areas from which the skill elements to be performed by the applicant are chosen. The following examples resemble tasks an examiner may ask an applicant to perform. The Performance Level required to be demonstrated for each skill element is listed. Consult the PTS for Level descriptions.

7-1(P). Given an actual aircraft propeller or mockup, appropriate publications, and tooling inspect a propeller installation and make a minor repair on an aluminum propeller and record maintenance. [Level 3]

7-2(P). Given an appropriate type certificate data sheet determine what minor propeller alterations are acceptable. [Level 2]

7-3(P). Given an actual aircraft propeller or mockup, appropriate publications, and tooling service a constant speed propeller with lubricant and record maintenance. [Level 2]

7-4(P). Given an actual aircraft propeller or mockup, appropriate publications, a propeller protractor determine correct blade angle and record findings. [Level 3]

7-5(P). Given an actual aircraft propeller or mockup, appropriate publications, and tooling leak check a constant speed propeller installation and record findings. [Level 3]

7-6(P). Given an actual aircraft propeller or mockup, appropriate publications, and tooling install a fixed pitch propeller and check the tip tracking and record maintenance.
[Level 3]

7-7(P). Given an actual aircraft propeller or mockup, appropriate publications, and tooling inspect a spinner/bulkhead for defects and proper alignment and installation and recording findings. [Level 3]

7-8(P). Given an actual aircraft propeller or mockup, appropriate publications, and dye-penetrant complete an inspection the propeller to determine the amount of any damage and record findings. [Level 2]

7-9(P). Given an actual aircraft propeller or mockup, appropriate publications, and tooling inspect a propeller governor and record findings. [Level 3]

7-10(P). Given an actual aircraft propeller or mockup, appropriate publications, and tooling adjust a propeller governor and record maintenance. [Level 3]

7-11(P). Given an actual aircraft propeller or mockup, appropriate publications, and tooling inspect a wood propeller and record findings. [Level 3]

7-12(P). Given an actual aircraft propeller or mockup, appropriate publications, and tooling troubleshoot a propeller system and record findings. [Level 3]

Engine Removal and Replacement

General Procedures, Inspection and Replacement of External Systems, Mounting Engines for Replacement, Rigging and Adjustments

8-1) AMP068

Who establishes the recommended operating time between overhauls (TBO) of a turbine engine used in general aviation?

- A. The engine manufacturer.
- B. The operator (utilizing manufacturer data and trend analysis) working in conjunction with the FAA.
- C. The FAA.

8-2) AMP057

Engine crankshaft run-out is usually checked
1. during engine overhaul.
2. during annual inspection.
3. after a prop strike or sudden engine stoppage.
4. during the 100 hour inspection.

- A. 1, 3, and 4.
- B. 1 and 3.
- C. 1, 2, and 3.

8-3) AMP048

A ground incident that results in propeller sudden stoppage may require a crankshaft run-out inspection. What publication would be used to obtain crankshaft run-out tolerance?

- A. Current manufacturer's maintenance instructions.
- B. Type certificate data sheet.
- C. AC43.13-1A Acceptable Methods, Techniques, and Practices Aircraft Inspection and Repair.

8-4) AMP007

If metallic particles are found in the oil filter during an inspection,

- A. it is an indication of normal engine wear unless the particles are nonferrous.
- B. the cause should be identified and corrected before the aircraft is released for flight.
- C. it is an indication of normal engine wear unless the deposit exceeds a specific amount.

8-5) AMP057

A QECA (quick-engine-change-assembly) is

- A. used mostly for unscheduled, unexpected engine changes.
- B. used whenever the most efficient and expeditious replacement of an aircraft engine is relied upon.
- C. must be pre-approved by the administrator or an airframe and powerplant mechanic with inspection authorization.

8-6) AMP050

In addition to its primary purpose of confining a potential fire to engine compartment, the engine firewall also

- A. provides mounting surfaces for the engine and accessories.
- B. acts as a heat sink for the engine nacelle.
- C. is used as a ground plain for radio antenna reception.

8-1) A.
Engine life is dependent upon such factors as operational use, the quality of manufacture or overhaul, the type of aircraft in which the engine is installed, the kind of operation being carried out, and the degree to which maintenance is accomplished. Thus, the engine manufacturer sets engine removal times. Based on service experience, it is possible to establish a maximum expected time before overhaul (TBO) or span of time within which an engine needs to be overhauled. Regardless of condition, an engine should be removed when it has accumulated the recommended maximum allowable time since the last overhaul or since new.
[For more detailed information refer to Powerplant Handbook H-8083-32-ATB, Chapter 8 p.2]

8-2) B.
When sudden reduction in RPM occurs such as in a prop strike or sudden engine stoppage, the propeller should be removed and the crankshaft (or propeller drive shaft on a reduction gear engine) should be checked for misalignment. This run-out should be within manufacturer's limits for the engine to continue in service. Crankshaft run-out is also used during engine overhaul when the engine is disassembled as one of the criterion to ensure the crankshaft is serviceable. It is not required during annual or 100 hour inspection as per CFR Title 14, PART 43, Appendix D.
[For more detailed information refer to Powerplant Handbook H-8083-32-ATB, Chapter 8 p.2]

8-3) A.
When sudden stoppage occurs, the engine usually requires replacement or disassembly and inspection as per manufacturer's instructions. When a crankshaft or propeller drive shaft run-out is performed, consult the applicable manufacturer's instructions for permissible limits.
[For more detailed information refer to Powerplant Handbook H-8083-32-ATB, Chapter 8 p.2]

8-4) B.
Metal particles in the engine oil screens is generally an indication of partial internal failure of the engine. Before removing an engine for suspected internal failure, determine the probable extent of any internal damage. For example, if only small particles are found that are similar to filings, drain the oil system and refill it. Ground-run the engine and re-inspect the oil screens and magnetic chip detectors. If no further evidence of foreign material is found, continue the engine in service or per manufacturer's instructions. Engine performance should be closely observed for any indication of difficulty or internal failure.
[For more detailed information refer to Powerplant Handbook H-8083-32-ATB, Chapter 8 p.3]

8-5) B.
After the decision has been made to remove an engine, the preparation of the replacement engine must be considered. Commercial operators, whose maintenance requires the most efficient and expeditious replacement of aircraft engines, usually rely on a system that utilizes the quick-engine-change-assembly, also sometimes referred to as the engine power package. The QECA is essentially a powerplant and the necessary accessories installed with the engine.
[For more detailed information refer to Powerplant Handbook H-8083-32-ATB, Chapter 8 p.3]

8-6) A.
The engine firewall also provides a mounting surface for units within the engine nacelle and a point of disconnect for lines, linkages, and electrical wiring that are routed between the engine and aircraft.
[For more detailed information refer to Powerplant Handbook H-8083-32-ATB, Chapter 8 p.4]

8-7) AMP057

When preparing an engine for service that has been preserved, care should be taken to

    A.   not tilt the engine while placing it in the engine stand.
    B.   ensure all corrosion-preventative compound is drained from the engine cylinders.
    C.   prefilled oil filters with ashless dispersant oil.

8-8) AMP057

When installing a new engine after internal failure of the previous engine, many engine accessories may need to be removed and cleaned. Other components may require replacement, such as

    A.   the oiler cooler and propeller governor.
    B.   the alternator and the starter.
    C.   the carburetor and the tachometer.

8-9) AMP042

When preparing to remove an engine, fuel valves must be

    A.   removed first.
    B.   fully opened.
    C.   fully closed even if they are solenoid operated.

8-10) AMP057

When mounting a replacement engine, always

    A.   install AN bolts of the correct diameter and length while the weight of the engine is still on the engine hoist.
    B.   secure the engine first with starter bolts, remove the engine hoist and replace the starter bolts with the manufacturer's specified bolts.
    C.   install the manufacturer specified bolts and torque to the manufacturer recommended value.

8-11) AMP057

When tightening the exhaust system clamps,

    A.   torque the clamp nuts, run the engine, and then torque the nuts again.
    B.   tapping the clamps with a rawhide mallet prevents binding.
    C.   tighten the nuts, back them off and tighten them again.

8-12) AMP031

Which of the following engine servicing operations generally requires engine pre-oiling prior to starting the engine?

    A.   Engine oil and filter change.
    B.   Engine installation.
    C.   Replacement of oil lines.

8-7) B.

On radial engines, the inside of the lower cylinders and intake pipes should be carefully checked for the presence of excessive corrosion-preventative compound that has drained throughout the interior of the engine and settled at these low points. This excessive compound, if not removed, could cause the engine to become damaged from hydraulic lock (also referred to as liquid lock) when a starting attempt is made.

[For more detailed information refer to Powerplant Handbook H-8083-32-ATB, Chapter 8 p.5]

8-8) A.

If an engine has been removed for internal failure, usually some units in the oil system must be replaced and others thoroughly cleaned and inspected. The oil cooler and temperature regulator must be removed and sent to a repair facility for overhaul. The propeller governor and feathering pump mechanism must also be replaced if these units are operated by oil pressure. There is a high probability that contaminants from the internal engine failure may have lodged in these parts.

[For more detailed information refer to Powerplant Handbook H-8083-32-ATB, Chapter 8 p.6]

8-9) C.

When preparing to remove an engine, check to see that all fuel selectors or solenoid operated fuel shutoff valves are closed. The fuel selector valves are either manually or solenoid operated. If solenoid operated fuel shutoff valves are installed, it may be necessary to turn the battery switch ON to close the valves. These valves close the fuel line at the firewall between the engine and the aircraft. After ensuring all fuel to the engine is shut off, disconnect the battery to eliminate the possibility of a hot wire starting a fire.

[For more detailed information refer to Powerplant Handbook H-8083-32-ATB, Chapter 8 p.7]

8-10) C.

When the engine has been aligned correctly in the nacelle, insert the mounting bolts into their holes and start all of the nuts on them. Always use the type of bolt and nut recommended by the manufacturer. Never use an unauthorized substitution of a different type or specification of nut and bolt than that prescribed. The nuts on the engine mount bolts must be tightened to the torque recommended by the aircraft manufacturer. While the nuts are being tightened, the hoist should support the engine weight sufficiently to allow alignment of the mounting bolts.

[For more detailed information refer to Powerplant Handbook H-8083-32-ATB, Chapter 8 p.10]

8-11) B.

During assembly of the exhaust system, the nuts should be gradually and progressively tightened to the correct torque. The clamps should be tapped with a rawhide mallet as they are being tightened to prevent binding at any point.

[For more detailed information refer to Powerplant Handbook H-8083-32-ATB, Chapter 8 p.11]

8-12) B.

To prevent failure of the engine bearings during the initial start, the engine should be pre-oiled. When an engine has been idle for an extended period of time, its internal bearing surfaces are likely to become dry at points where the corrosion-preventative mixture has dried out or drained away from the bearings. Hence, it is necessary to force oil throughout the entire engine oil system. If the bearings are dry when the engine is started, the friction at high RPM destroys the bearings before lubricating oil from the engine driven oil pump can reach them.

[For more detailed information refer to Powerplant Handbook H-8083-32-ATB, Chapter 8 p.13]

8-13) AMP057

How may it be determined that a reciprocating engine with a dry sump is pre-oiled sufficiently?

    A. The engine oil pressure gauge will indicate normal oil pressure.

    B. Oil will flow from the engine return line or indicator port.

    C. When the quantity of oil specified by the manufacturer has been pumped into the engine.

8-14) AMP052

Once an engine has been installed satisfactorily, the propeller can be installed. It should be

    A. tested before, during, and after the engine has been ground operated.

    B. mounted with the blades in the feathered position.

    C. a low pitch test propeller during ground test operation of the engine.

8-15) AMP057

Typical engine mounts on a reciprocating engine

    A. bolt firmly to the frame so vibration is kept to a minimum.

    B. are studs mounted in the rear of the engine and bolts used in the front of the engine.

    C. utilize a rubber shock mount to reduce vibration.

8-16) AMP018

Many APU engine hoists

    A. are the same as used on the main engine of the aircraft.

    B. attach to fittings in the APU compartment.

    C. are electric over hydraulic in operation.

8-17) AMP069

After a turbofan engine has been replaced, it must be trimmed. What other actions or conditions mandate that a turbofan engine be re-trimmed?

    A. Annual inspection or replacement of the fuel control.

    B. Replacement of the fuel control or after an in-flight shutdown.

    C. Replacement of fuel control, engine not developing maximum thrust, or excessive throttle stagger.

8-18) AMP069

Under which of the following conditions will the trimming of a turbine engine be most accurate?

    D. High wind and high moisture.

    E. High moisture and low wind.

    F. No wind and low moisture.

8-19) AMP069

For what primary purpose is a turbine engine fuel control unit trimmed?

    A. To obtain maximum thrust output when desired.

    B. To properly position the thrust levers.

    C. To adjust idle RPM.

8 - Engine Removal and Replacement
Answers

8-13) B.
In using some types of pre-oilers, the oil line from the inlet side of the engine oil pump must be disconnected to permit the pre-oiler tank to be connected at this point. Then, a line must be disconnected, or an opening made in the oil system at the nose of the engine to allow oil to flow out of the engine. Oil flowing out of the engine indicates the completion of the pre-oiling operation since the oil has now passed through the entire system.
[For more detailed information refer to Powerplant Handbook H-8083-32-ATB, Chapter 8 p.13]

8-14) A.
The propeller must be checked before, during, and after the engine has been ground operated. The propeller should be checked for proper torque on the mounting bolts, leaks, vibration, and for correct safety. A propeller whose pitch-changing mechanism is electrically actuated may be checked before the engine is operated. Propellers whose pitch-changing mechanisms are oil actuated must be checked during engine operation after the normal operating temperature of the oil has been reached. In addition to checking the increase or decrease in RPM, the feathering cycle of the propeller should also be checked.
[For more detailed information refer to Powerplant Handbook H-8083-32-ATB, Chapter 8 p.14]

8-15) C.
Most reciprocating engines are bolted to the engine mount with the use of rubber engine mount pads. This helps dissipate the vibration developed by the engine.
[For more detailed information refer to Powerplant Handbook H-8083-32-ATB, Chapter 8 p.15]

8-16) B.
Many modern APU's are positioned for mounting from below in the very aft portion of the fuselage. Manufacturers equip the APU nacelle with mounting holes where a specifically designed APU hoist can be mounted. This hand-operated hoist cradles the APU from front to rear and allows slow, controlled raising and lowering of the APU as necessary during the removal and installation procedures.
[For more detailed information refer to Powerplant Handbook H-8083-32-ATB, Chapter 8 p.16-17]

8-17) C.
The fuel control of the engine is adjusted to trim the engine to obtain maximum thrust output of the engine when desired. The engine must be re-trimmed after a fuel control unit is replaced, the engine does not develop maximum thrust, engine change, or excessive throttle stagger.
[For more detailed information refer to Powerplant Handbook H-8083-32-ATB, Chapter 8 p.21]

8-18) C.
If wind velocity is a factor, the aircraft should be headed into the wind while trimming or checking the trim on a turbine engine. Since trimming accuracy decreases as wind speed and moisture content increase, the most accurate trimming is obtained under conditions of no wind and clear, moisture-free air.
[For more detailed information refer to Powerplant Handbook H-8083-32-ATB, Chapter 8 p.21]

8-19) A.
All of the above are accomplished when trimming an engine. However, the primary purpose the fuel control unit of the engine is adjusted to trim the engine is to obtain maximum thrust output of the engine when desired.
[For more detailed information refer to Powerplant Handbook H-8083-32-ATB, Chapter 8 p.21]

8-20) AMP069

On a typical engine trim check chart included in the manufacturer's maintenance data, what are the two main variables for which trim valves are adjusted?

A. Ambient temperature and wind speed.
B. Ambient temperature and barometric pressure.
C. Ambient temperature and humidity.

8-21) AMP008

A characteristic of Dyna-focal engine mounts as applied to aircraft reciprocating engines is that the

A. shock mounts eliminate the torsional flexing of the powerplant.
B. engine attached to the shock mounts at the engine's center of gravity.
C. shock mounts point towards the engines center of gravity.

8-22) AMP068

The engine mounts on a turbofan engine

A. are solid steel due to the weight of the engine.
B. isolate the aircraft structure from adverse engine vibration.
C. block the centrifugal force of the rotating fan mass.

8-23) AMP056

Engines that are not flown regularly may not achieve normal service life due to corrosion

A. of the interior parts of the carburetor.
B. of the crankshaft and bearing journals.
C. in and around the cylinders.

8-24) AMP056

An aircraft engine having at least one continuous hour of operation with an oil temperature of at least 165°F within 30 days is said to be in

A. temporary storage.
B. active storage.
C. indefinite storage.

8-25) AMP056

Light corrosion preventative compounds

A. are intended to preserve an engine for less than 30 days and to spray cylinders.
B. can be used to dip metal parts in for long-term storage.
C. do not mix with the oil but cover surfaces where oil has been removed.

8-26) AMP008

To prevent moisture from aiding in corroding engine cylinders when stored or shipped, spark plugs are remove and dehydrator plugs installed. When the dehydrator plugs are blue, it is an indication

A. of high humidity with corrosion likely.
B. of low humidity with corrosion unlikely.
C. the limited life of the desiccant has been reached.

8-20) B.

An actual trim check is done based on barometric pressure and temperature. For given temperatures and pressures, target parameter values vary slightly. A chart is developed by the manufacturer for use during the trim check and the values are checked against the tolerances given on the chart.

[For more detailed information refer to Powerplant Handbook H-8083-32-ATB, Chapter 8 p.22]

8-21) C.

Dyna-focal engine mounts, or vibration isolators, are units that give directional support to the engines. Dyna-focal engine mounts have the mounting pad angled to point to the CG (center of gravity) of the engine mass.

[For more detailed information refer to Powerplant Handbook H-8083-32-ATB, Chapter 8 p.24]

8-22) B.

Vibration isolator engine mounts are used on turbofan engines. They isolate the airplane structure from adverse engine vibrations. Vibration isolators consist of a resilient material permanently enclosed in a metal case. As an engine vibrates, the resilient material deforms slightly, thereby dampening the vibrations before they reach the airplane structure. If complete failure or loss of the resilient material occurs, the isolators will continue to support the engine.

[For more detailed information refer to Powerplant Handbook H-8083-32-ATB, Chapter 8 p.24]

8-23) C.

An engine must receive daily care and attention to detect and correct early stages of corrosion. Engines that are not flown regularly may not achieve normal service life because of corrosion in and around the cylinders. The normal combustion process creates moisture and corrosive byproducts that attack the unprotected surfaces of the cylinder walls, valves, and any other exposed areas that are unprotected.

[For more detailed information refer to Powerplant Handbook H-8083-32-ATB, Chapter 8 p.24]

8-24) B.

There are three types of engine storage: active, temporary and indefinite. Active storage is defined as having at least one continuous hour of operation with an oil temperature of at least 165°F to 200°F and storage time not to exceed 30 days. Temporary storage describes an aircraft and engine that is not flown for 30 to 90 days. Indefinite storage is for an aircraft not to be flown for over 90 days or is removed from the aircraft for extended time.

[For more detailed information refer to Powerplant Handbook H-8083-32-ATB, Chapter 8 p.25]

8-25) A.

Corrosion preventative compounds are petroleum-based products that form a wax-like film over metal to which they are applied. Several types are manufactured according to different specifications to fit various aviation needs. The type mixed with engine oil is a relatively light compound that readily blends with the oil when the mixture is heated. The light mixture is intended for use when a preserved engine is to remain inactive for less than 30 days. It is also used to spray cylinders and other designated areas.

[For more detailed information refer to Powerplant Handbook H-8083-32-ATB, Chapter 8 p.25]

8-26) B.

Cobalt chloride is added to the silica gel used in dehydrator plugs. This makes it possible for the plugs to indicate moisture content in the cylinders. The cobalt chloride treated silica gel remains a bright blue color with low relative humidity. As humidity increases, the shade of blue becomes progressively lighter, becoming lavender at 30 percent humidity and fading through various shades of pink until at 60 percent humidity, the dehydrator plug is natural or white in color. When humidity is less than 30 percent, corrosion does not normally take place.

[For more detailed information refer to Powerplant Handbook H-8083-32-ATB, Chapter 8 p.25]

8-27) AMP008

When preparing to place an engine in temporary or indefinite storage

    A.   the engine should be operated to normal operating temperature with corrosion-preventative mixture oil for at least one hour.

    B.   the engine should be operated to normal operating temperature then corrosion-preventative oil should be added.

    C.   regular engine oil should be drained and replaced with corrosion-preventative oil without operating the engine.

8-28) AMP008

Regardless of the type of shipping container used for an engine,

    A.   it should be vacuum sealed.

    B.   it should be pressurized.

    C.   it should contain a visible humidity indicator.

8-27) A.

Before an engine is placed in temporary or indefinite storage, it should be operated and filled with a corrosion-preventative oil mixture added in the oil system to retard corrosion by coating the engine's internal parts. Drain the normal lubricating oil from the sump or system, and replace with a preservative oil mixture according to the manufacturer's instructions. Operate the engine until normal operating temperatures are obtained for at least one hour.

[For more detailed information refer to Powerplant Handbook H-8083-32-ATB, Chapter 8 p.26]

8-28) C.

When lowering a wooden shipping case cover into position, be sure the humidity indicator card is placed so it can be seen through the inspection window. Engines in wooden shipping containers typically have an envelope that is vacuumed to remove excess air. Metal shipping containers are sealed and pressurized to about 5 psi with dehydrated air. However, a humidity indicator should be fastened inside the container at the inspection window provided.

[For more detailed information refer to Powerplant Handbook H-8083-32-ATB, Chapter 8 p.28]

8-1(O). What procedures are required *after* the installation of a turbine engine?

8-2(O). What are the reasons a turbine engine would require a trim check?

8-3(O). What is the procedure required to adjust (trim) a fuel control unit (FCU)?

8-4(O). Name three reasons for removal of an engine and what are the required inspections after a potentially damaging event occurs.

8-1(O). After installation, an engine run-up should be performed. On newer engines with electronic engine controls, verification of correct engine instrument indications is required. On engines with hydromechanical fuel controls, the engine must be manually trimmed. This is the process of adjusting the idle and maximum RPM and EPR settings in accordance with temperature and pressure adjusted values provided by the manufacturer.
Reference: FAA-H-8083-32-ATB Chapter 8 p.20 to 23

8-2(O). It has a hydromechanical fuel control and the engine or fuel control has just been changed. Also, if the engine is not developing maximum thrust or if there is excessive throttle stagger the engine should be trimmed.
Reference: FAA-H-8083-32-ATB Chapter 8 p.21

8-3(O). Ideally, trimming an engine should be done under conditions of no wind and clear, moisture-free air. Never trim when icing conditions exist because of the adverse effect on trimming accuracy. If there is wind, face the engine intake into the wind to avoid re-ingestion of the exhaust gases. Accurate ambient temperature and pressure readings need to be taken. These are used to compute the desired EPR indication(s) from charts in the maintenance manual. Idle RPM and maximum speed adjustments are made as well as acceleration and deceleration checks according to the specific instructions provided by the manufacturer.
Reference: FAA-H-8083-32-ATB Chapter 8 p.21

8-4(O). Reasons for removal of an engine include: Engine or components lifespan exceeded; sudden stoppage; sudden reduction in speed; metal particles in oil; negative spectrometric oil analysis; operational problems such as excessive vibration; low power output caused by low compression or internal engine deterioration or damage; turbine engine parameters exceeded; and, turbine engine condition monitoring program trends. A sudden reduction does not automatically result in an engine change. Additional test such as a complete visual inspection should be performed - especially of the engine mounts and the nose section of the engine, crankshaft run-out, and oil filter, sump, and screen checks for metal in the oil. If these all prove negative, the engine may be able to stay in service. Also, just the presence of metal in the oil does not mean the engine has to be removed. The quantity and type of metal particles must be further analyzed. Any ferrous metal in an oil screen is cause for concern. Small non-ferrous particles could be normal. A complete oil and filter/screen change should be performed and the engine should be ground-run and filters and screens rechecked.
Reference: FAA-H-8083-32-ATB Chapter 8 p.2 to 3

Applicants for powerplant certification are required to demonstrate the ability to apply knowledge by performing maintenance related tasks for the examiner. The Practical Test Standards (PTS) list the subject areas from which the skill elements to be performed by the applicant are chosen. The following examples resemble tasks an examiner may ask an applicant to perform. The Performance Level required to be demonstrated for each skill element is listed. Consult the PTS for Level descriptions.

8-1. Given an actual aircraft engine or mockup, appropriate publications, and tooling, perform a crankshaft runout on a reciprocating engine installation and record findings. [Level 3]

8-2. Given an actual aircraft engine or mockup, appropriate publications, and tooling, inspect a reciprocating aircraft engine as though it had experienced a sudden reduction in speed during operation and record findings. [Level 3]

8-3. Given an actual aircraft engine or mockup, appropriate publications, and tooling, inspect a reciprocating engine for suspected internal engine damage and record findings. [Level 3]

8-4. Given an actual aircraft engine or mockup, appropriate publications, and tooling, inspect an engine mounting frame assembly and mounting bolts for serviceability and record findings. [Level 3]

8-5. Given an actual aircraft engine or mockup, appropriate publications, and required tooling, prepare an engine for removal. [Level 3]

8-6. Given an actual aircraft engine or mockup, appropriate publications, and tooling, inspect the intake ducting and exhaust system of an aircraft engine and record findings. [Level 3]

8-7. Given an actual aircraft engine or mockup, appropriate publications, and tooling, disconnect and inspect the engine controls including control rods, cables, pulleys, bell cranks, and linkages. Record findings. [Level 3]

8-8. Given an actual aircraft engine or mockup, appropriate publications, and tooling, properly remove an aircraft engine from the aircraft or test stand. [Level 3]

8-9. Given an actual aircraft engine or mockup, appropriate publications, and tooling, properly mount an aircraft engine to the aircraft or a test stand. [Level 3]

8-10. Given an actual aircraft engine or mockup, appropriate publications, and tooling, properly connect the engine controls to a newly mounted engine and record the maintenance activity. [Level 3]

8-11. Given an actual aircraft engine or mockup, appropriate publications, and tooling, inspect and connect electrical wiring to engine mounted components on a newly mounted engine and record maintenance activity. [Level 3]

8-12. Given an actual aircraft engine or mockup, appropriate publications, and tooling, properly connect all fluid lines to a newly mounted engine and record the maintenance activity. [Level 3]

8-13. Given an actual aircraft engine or mockup, appropriate publications, and tooling, properly connect all intake ducting and the exhaust system to a newly mounted engine and record the maintenance activity. [Level 3]

8-14. Given an actual aircraft engine or mockup, appropriate publications, and tooling, perform the final inspection and preparation of a newly installed engine for run-up and record the maintenance activity. [Level 3]

8-15. Given an actual aircraft engine or mockup, appropriate publications, and tooling, run-up a newly installed engine. Check and record all performance parameters per manufacturer's data . [Level 3]

8-16. Given an actual aircraft engine or mockup, appropriate publications, and tooling, perform a post run-p inspection of a newly installed engine and record findings. [Level 3]

8-17. Given an actual aircraft engine or mockup, appropriate publications, and tooling, perform fuel control rigging, adjustments, and trimming of a turbine engine. Record the maintenance activity. [Level 3]

Engine Fire Protection Systems

Engine Fire Detection, Extinguishers, Troubleshooting, Fire Detection System Maintenance

9-1) AMP034
Which of the following fire detectors are commonly used in the power section of engine nacelles?

   A. CO detectors.
   B. Smoke detectors.
   C. Rate-of-temperature-rise detectors.

9-2) AMP034
Which of the following are features of an ideal fire detection system?
1. Illuminates a light on the flight deck which indicates the location of the fire.
2. Sets off an audible alarm.
3. Low number or no false alarms.
4. Resettable when the fire is out.
5. Minimum electrical current requirements.

   A. 1, 3, 5.
   B. 2, 3, 4, and 5.
   C. 1, 2, 3, 4, and 5.

9-3) AMP034
What is the operating principle of the spot detector sensor in a fire detection system?

   A. Resistant core material that prevents current flow at normal temperatures.
   B. A conventional thermocouple that produces a current flow.
   C. A bimetallic thermal switch that closes when heated to a high temperature.

9-4) AMP034
Which of the following fire detection systems measure temperature rise compared to a reference temperature?

   A. Thermocouple.
   B. Thermal switch.
   C. Lindberg continuous element.

9-5) AMP034
Optical fire detection systems

   A. can be infrared or ultraviolet.
   B. must be used out of the way of direct sunlight.
   C. give a false alarm if not disarmed before an incandescent light strikes the sensor.

9 - Engine Fire Protection Systems
Answers

9-1) C.

Fires are detected in aircraft by using one or more of the following: overheat detectors, rate-of-temperature-rise detectors, and flame detectors. In addition to these methods, other types of detectors are used in aircraft fire protection systems but are NOT used to detect engine fires. For example, smoke detectors are better suited to monitor areas such as baggage compartments or lavatories where materials burn slowly or smolder. Other types of detectors in this category include carbon monoxide (CO) detectors.

[For more detailed information refer to Powerplant Handbook H-8083-32-ATB, Chapter 9 p.2]

9-2) C.

There are many desirable features of a fire detection system. A system that does not cause false warnings under any flight or ground condition is important as is rapid indication that there is a fire and where it located. Good fire detection systems set off audible and visual alarms to notify flight crew of the fire. Accurate indication that the fire is out and the ability to indicate that a fire has reignited are also desired features. Low electrical requirements for the detection system are also desirable so when aircraft power is compromised, reliable fire indication is still available.

[For more detailed information refer to Powerplant Handbook H-8083-32-ATB, Chapter 9 p.2]

9-3) C.

Thermal switches are heat sensitive units that complete electrical circuits at a certain temperature. They are connected in parallel with each other, but in series with the indicator lights. If the temperature rises above a set value in any area where a thermal switch is located, the switch closes completing the light circuit to indicate a fire or overheat condition.

[For more detailed information refer to Powerplant Handbook H-8083-32-ATB, Chapter 9 p.3]

9-4) A.

A thermocouple depends on the rate of temperature rise and does not give a warning when an engine slowly overheats or a short circuit develops. The thermocouple is constructed of a junction of two dissimilar metals that produce current flow when heated. In addition to the thermocouple sensors, there is a reference junction of dissimilar metals enclosed in a dead air space between two insulation blocks. This reference junction box is in the engine nacelle. Current flow of the thermocouple sensor(s) is compared to the current flow at the reference junction. Only the sensor temperature increasing a faster rate than the reference junction temperature produces enough resultant current flow to close the fire warning indicator circuit.

[For more detailed information refer to Powerplant Handbook H-8083-32-ATB, Chapter 9 p.3]

9-5) A.

Optical sensors are often referred to as flame detectors. They are designed to alarm when they detect the presence of prominent, specific radiation emissions from hydrocarbon flames. The two types of optical sensors available are infrared (IR) and ultraviolet, based on the specific emission wavelengths they are designed to detect. A window in the unit allows light to strike a detector. The processing electronics are tailored exactly to the time signature of all known hydrocarbon flame sources and ignores false alarms sources such as incandescent lights and sunlight.

[For more detailed information refer to Powerplant Handbook H-8083-32-ATB, Chapter 9 p.4]

9-6) AMP034

A fire detection system operates on the principle of a buildup of gas pressure within a tube proportional to temperature. Which of the following systems does this statement define?

    A. Kidde continuous-loop system.
    B. Lindberg continuous-element system.
    C. Thermal switch system.

9-7) AMP034

What is the principle of operation of the continuous loop fire detection system sensor?

    A. Fuse material which melts at high temperatures.
    B. Core resistance material which prevents current flow at normal temperatures.
    C. A bimetallic thermoswitch which closes when heated to a high temperature.

9-8) AMP036

Which of the following is the safest fire-extinguishing agent to use from a standpoint of toxicity and corrosion hazards?

    A. Dibromodiflouromethane (Halon 1202).
    B. Bromochlorodiflouromethane (Halon 1211).
    C. Bromotriflouromethane (Halon 1301).

9-9) AMP036

How is the fire extinguishing agent distributed in the engine section?

    A. Spray nozzles and fluid pump.
    B. Nitrogen pressure and slinger rings.
    C. Spray nozzles and perforated tubing.

9-10) AMP036

In a fixed fire-extinguishing system, there are two small lines running from the system and exiting overboard. The line exit ports are covered with a blowout type indicator disc. Which of the following statements is true?

    A. When the red indicator is missing, it indicates the fire-extinguishing system has been normally discharged.
    B. When the yellow indicator disc is missing, it indicates the fire-extinguishing system has been normally discharged.
    C. When the green indicator disc is missing, it indicates the fire-extinguishing system has had a thermal discharge.

9-11) AMP035

A common visual check of fire detection elements includes

    A. the contact points in the control box.
    B. cracked or broken sections.
    C. the color of missing blowout disks.

9-6) B.
Pneumatic detectors are based on the principle of gas laws. The sensing element consists of a closed helium-filled tube connected at one end to a responder assembly. As the element is heated, the gas pressure inside the tube increases until the alarm threshold is reached. An internal switch in the responder closes and an alarm is reported on the flight deck. Thermal switches are spot detectors and the Kidde continuous-loop system consists of two wires imbedded in an inconel tube with a thermistor core material. Therefore, the gas-filled continuous element, sometimes called Lindberg from the name of its long-time manufacturer, is the answer.
[For more detailed information refer to Powerplant Handbook H-8083-32-ATB, Chapter 9 p.5]

9-7) B.
In the Kidde continuous-loop system, two wire conductors are imbedded in an inconel tube filled with a thermistor core material. One conductor has a ground connection to the tube, the other conductor connects to the fire detection control unit. As the temperature of the core increases, electrical resistance of the thermistor core decreases. Current can flow to ground completing the overheat or fire warning circuit which warns the crew on the flight deck.
[For more detailed information refer to Powerplant Handbook H-8083-32-ATB, Chapter 9 p.5]

9-8) C.
The most common extinguishing agent still used today is Halon 1301 because of its effective firefighting capability and relatively low toxicity. Noncorrosive Halon 1301 does not effect the material it contacts and requires no clean-up when discharged.
[For more detailed information refer to Powerplant Handbook H-8083-32-ATB, Chapter 9 p.8]

9-9) C.
Many systems use perforated tubing or discharge nozzles to distribute the extinguishing agent. High rate of discharge (HRD) systems use open-end tubes to deliver a large quantity of extinguishing agent in 1 to 2 seconds.
[For more detailed information refer to Powerplant Handbook H-8083-32-ATB, Chapter 9 p.8]

9-10) B.
If the flight crew activates the fire extinguishing system, a yellow disk is ejected from the skin of the aircraft fuselage (blowout type indicator at the line exit port). This is an indication for the maintenance crew that the fire extinguishing system was activated by the flight crew, and that the fire extinguishing container needs to be replaced before the next flight.
[For more detailed information refer to Powerplant Handbook H-8083-32-ATB, Chapter 9 p.10]

9-11) B.
An inspection and maintenance program for all types of continuous-loop systems should include the following visual checks and others. 1) Inspect for cracked or broken sections caused by crushing or squeezing between inspection plates, cowl panels, or engine components, 2) Inspect for abrasion caused by rubbing of the element on the cowling, accessories, or structural members, 3) Check the condition of rubber grommets in mounting clamps which may be softened from exposure to oils or hardened from excessive heat, 4) Look for dents and kinks in sensing element sections.
[For more detailed information refer to Powerplant Handbook H-8083-32-ATB, Chapter 9 p.11]

9-12) AMP035

If a continuous-loop fire detection system is giving a false alarm, how can it be determined if the problem is in the control unit or in the sensing loop?

   A. By disconnecting the loop from the control box and observing if the false alarm stops.
   B. By connecting a voltmeter across the connected loop terminals.
   C. By resetting the warning lights and timing the interval until the next false alarm.

9-13) AMP036

The explosive cartridge in the discharge valve of a fire extinguisher container is

   A. a life dated unit.
   B. not a life dated unit.
   C. mechanically fired.

9-14) AMP036

Using the chart in FAA-H-8083-32, Figure 9-18, what are the fire-extinguisher container pressure limits when the temperature is 40 F?

   A. 448psi minimum and 598psi maximum.
   B. 405psi minimum and 560psi maximum.
   C. 477psi minimum and 650psi maximum.

9-15) AMP034

Engine fire detection on a Boeing 777 aircraft is accomplished with two loops which are monitored by the fire detection card file. When is a BITE test performed?

   A. When one of the loops fails to have continuity and the other one has continuity.
   B. Before starting the engine and before it is shut down.
   C. When power is applied, after a power interrupt, and every 5 minutes of operation.

9-16) AMP036

What is a squib as it relates to a fire extinguishing system?

   A. The signal sent through the discharge circuit during a BITE test.
   B. An electrically operated explosive device.
   C. An electronic circuit that verifies the authenticity of the fire warning signal.

9-17) AMP036

How is the engine fire extinguishing agent discharged on the Boeing 777 and most other transport category aircraft?

   A. By pulling the fire handle.
   B. By pulling the fire handle and rotating it to the mechanic stop.
   C. By pressing the extinguisher discharge button on the fire control panel.

9-12) A.

Fire alarms and warning lights can occur when no engine fire or overheat condition exists. Such false alarms can most easily be located by disconnecting the engine sensing loop from the control unit. If the false alarm ceases when the engine sensing loop is disconnected, the fault is in the disconnected sensing loop.

[For more detailed information refer to Powerplant Handbook H-8083-32-ATB, Chapter 9 p.12]

9-13) A.

The service life of fire extinguisher discharge cartridges is calculated from the manufacturer's date stamp, which is typically placed on the face of the cartridge. The cartridge service life recommended by the manufacturer is usually in terms of years. Cartridges are available with a service life of 5 years or more.

[For more detailed information refer to Powerplant Handbook H-8083-32-ATB, Chapter 9 p.13]

9-14) A.

To find the answer on the chart, locate the temperature on the bottom (horizontal) scale: 40°F. Go straight up the 40°F line until you intersect with the green arc. Follow this intersection point across to the vertical scale to obtain the minimum pressure reading (448psi). Now continue up the 40°F line until it intersects with the blue arc. This is the maximum pressure allowed in the extinguisher bottle at 40°F. From this intersection point, move horizontally to the vertical scale to obtain the maximum psi allowed in the bottle (598psi). So on a day where the temperature is 40°F, the pressure in the fire extinguisher bottle should between 448psi and 598psi. If it is not, the bottle should be replaced.

[For more detailed information refer to Powerplant Handbook H-8083-32-ATB, Chapter 9 p.13]

9-15) C.

The 777 has continuous fault monitoring of the fire detection loops. Built-in-test-equipment (BITE) performs a test of the engine fire detection system for these conditions: 1) when the system first gets power, 2) after a power interrupt, and 3) every 5 minutes of operation.

[For more detailed information refer to Powerplant Handbook H-8083-32-ATB, Chapter 9 p.14]

9-16) B.

The squib is installed in the discharge assembly at the bottom of the fire [extinguisher] container. A fire container has two squibs, one for each engine. The squib is an electrically operated explosive device. When the squib is activated, it fires a slug through the breakable disk and nitrogen pressure inside the bottle pushes the Halon through the discharge port. The squib fires when the fire switch is pulled and turned to the DISCH 1 or DISCH 2 position.

[For more detailed information refer to Powerplant Handbook H-8083-32-ATB, Chapter 9 p.16]

9-17) B.

When the fire switch is pulled, the push-pull switch contacts operate electrical circuits that stop the engine and isolate it from the airplane systems. With the switch pulled, it can be rotated to left or right to a mechanical stop at the discharge position. The rotary switch contacts close and operate the fire extinguishing system (discharges the agent).

[For more detailed information refer to Powerplant Handbook H-8083-32-ATB, Chapter 9 p.17]

Applicants for powerplant certification are required to answer oral examination questions before, after, or in conjunction with the practical examination portion of the airman certification process. The oral examination is used to establish knowledge. The practical examination is used to establish skill, which is the application of knowledge. Use the following questions to prepare for the oral examination. The questions are examples aligned with Practical Test Standards subject matter from which the examiner will choose topics for oral examination.

9-1(O). How would a technician verify proper operation of a fire extinguishing system?

9-2(O). How would a technician troubleshoot an engine fire detection system?

9-3(O). What are the basic inspection requirements for an engine fire extinguisher squib and the safety practices and precautions to be followed?

9-4(O). What are the components of a typical fire detection system?

9-5(O). Maintenance procedures for fire detection systems include extensive visual inspection of the components. Name three common items to look for on a visual inspection of a fire detection system.

9-1(O). By inspection and good maintenance practices. The fire extinguishing system contains agent containers that must be verified as fully charged by checking the pressure gauge mounted in each bottle against a chart containing temperature-adjusted values. The extinguisher bottle squib, which fires to discharge the agent, has a limited service life and must be changed if the date on the squib has been exceeded. The pressure switch mounted on the bottle sends a signal for an indication on the flight deck when low pressure exists in the bottle due to leakage or discharge. This indication should not be illuminated. An electrical wiring continuity check can also be performed to ensure that power will arrive at the squib when the switch on the flight deck is closed.
Reference: FAA-H-8083-32-ATB Chapter 9 p.13 to 14

9-2(O). A push-to-test button is provided on most fire detection systems. It should light all warning lights and sound the aural alarms. Failure to do so requires further investigation. A faulty test switch or control unit is possible. Also, lack of electric power, an inoperative indicator light, or opening in the sensor element or connecting wiring are possible. Continuity of the sensing element can be checked by measuring the resistance. Intermittent alarms can be traced by visual inspection and moving wires and the sensors in suspected areas to recreate the fault. Also, by disconnecting the sensing elements from the control unit, the fault can be isolated to the sensing elements if the false alarm stops.
Reference: FAA-H-8083-32-ATB Chapter 9 p.12 to 13

9-3(O). The squib must be inspected to insure it is within its serviceable life. It must be replaced if it is not. The date is stamped on the outside of the squib. Power to the discharge valve assembly should be disconnected when disassembled to access the squib. A discharge cartridge (squib) removed from an assembly should not be used in another discharge valve assembly. The distance that the contact points protrude may vary. The wrong length of protrusion could result in a loss of electrical continuity required to fire the squib and discharge the agent.
Reference: FAA-H-8083-32-ATB Chapter 9 p.13 to 14

9-4(O). There are different types of fire detection systems. All types have some sort of detection device and indication devices on the flight deck. Thermal switch systems are simple and typically will also contain a test switch, test relay, and a dimming relay for the indicator light(s). Thermocouple detection systems contain a control box with relays and a thermal test unit. Optical fire detection systems contain an amplifier and comparative circuits to decipher sensing data. Continuous loop systems also contain control boxes which decipher the analog signal from the sensor loops and signal warnings or supply the Aircraft In-flight Monitoring System. The most sophisticated systems contain a control module that uses control cards with various interpretive circuitry to decipher signals from each area where sensors are located. Some systems will initiate extinguishing automatically from the control module.
Reference: FAA-H-8083-32-ATB Chapter 9 p.2 to 7

9-5(O). Cracked or broken loop sections, abrasion of elements by rubbing, loose metal that might short a spot detector, condition of rubber grommets and mounting clamps, dents and kinks in loop elements, secure connections at the end of the sensing elements, integrity of shielded leads, and, proper routing and support of elements.
Reference: FAA-H-8083-32-ATB Chapter 9 p.11 to 12

9 - Engine Fire Protection Systems
Practical

Applicants for powerplant certification are required to demonstrate the ability to apply knowledge by performing maintenance related tasks for the examiner. The Practical Test Standards (PTS) list the subject areas from which the skill elements to be performed by the applicant are chosen. The following examples resemble tasks an examiner may ask an applicant to perform. The Performance Level required to be demonstrated for each skill element is listed. Consult the PTS for Level descriptions

9-1(P). Given an actual aircraft engine or mockup, appropriate publications, and tooling check an engine fire detection system for proper operation and record findings. [Level 2]

9-2(P). Given an actual aircraft engine or mockup, appropriate publications, and tooling check an engine fire extinguishing system for proper operation and record findings. [Level 2]

9-3(P). Given an actual aircraft engine or mockup, appropriate publications, and tooling accomplish a weight and pressure inspection of an engine fire bottle, verify hydrostatic inspection date and record findings. [Level 2]

9-4(P). Given an actual aircraft engine or mockup, appropriate publications, and tooling repair an engine fire detector heat sensing loop malfunction and record maintenance. [Level 3]

9-5(P). Given an actual aircraft engine or mockup, appropriate publications, and tooling check operation of firewall shut-off valve after a fire handle is pulled and record findings. [Level 2]

9-6(P). Given an actual aircraft engine or mockup, appropriate publications, and tooling troubleshoot an engine fire detection and record findings. [Level 2]

9-7(P). Given an actual aircraft engine or mockup, appropriate publications, and tooling troubleshoot an engine fire extinguishing system and record findings. [Level 2]

9-8(P). Given an actual aircraft engine or mockup, appropriate publications, and tooling inspect an engine fire detection and record findings. [Level 3]

9-9(P). Given an actual aircraft engine or mockup, appropriate publications, and tooling inspect an engine fire extinguishing system and record findings. [Level 3]

Engine Maintenance and Operation

Inspection Process, Disassembly, Cleaning, Reassembly,
Installation and Testing, Troubleshooting, Maintenance

10-1) AMP007
The major purpose of an engine overhaul is to

  A. extend the life of the cylinders and
     pistons.
  B. inspect, repair, and replace worn engine
     parts.
  C. evaluate the airworthiness of the
     crankshaft and bearings.

10-2) AMP007
The receiving inspection for an engine needing to
be overhauled

  A. includes checking the airworthiness
     directives, service bulletins and type
     certificate compliance.
  B. includes an ultra-sound or eddy current
     inspection of the unassembled engine.
  C. is performed in conjunction with tear-
     down of the engine.

10-3) AMP000
Indentations on bearing races caused by high static
loads are known as

  A. fretting.
  B. brinelling.
  C. galling.

10-4) AMP007
A severe condition of chafing or fretting in which a
transfer of metal from one part to another occurs
is called

  A. scoring.
  B. burning.
  C. galling.

10-5) AMP007
The breaking loose of small pieces of metal from
coated surfaces, usually caused by defective plating
or excessive loads is called

  A. flaking.
  B. chafing.
  C. brinelling.

10-6) AMP007
During visual inspection while overhauling an
engine, the pistons heads were depressed. This is
a sign that

  A. the engine was running normally.
  B. pre-ignition had occurred.
  C. detonation had occurred.

Powerplant Test Guide H-8083-32-ATB   Aircraft Technical Book Company 10-1

10 - Engine Maintenance and Operation
Answers

10-1) B.
Part of an engine overhaul will include evaluating the crankshaft, cylinders, and pistons for condition but the major purpose of overhauling an engine is to inspect, repair and replace worn engine parts.
[For more detailed information refer to Powerplant Handbook H-8083-32-ATB, Chapter 10 p.1]

10-2) A.
The receiving inspection is the first step in the complete engine overhaul process. It consists of determining the general condition of the engine as received, along with an inventory of the engine's components. The accessory information should be recorded, such as model and serial number, and the accessories should be sent to overhaul as needed. The overhaul records should be organized and the appropriate manuals obtained and reviewed along with a review of the engine's history (logbooks). The engine's service bulletins, airworthiness directives and type certificate compliance should be checked.
[For more detailed information refer to Powerplant Handbook H-8083-32-ATB, Chapter 10 p.2]

10-3) B.
Several terms are used to describe defects detected in engine parts during inspection. One common term is brinelling. Brinelling is one or more indentations on bearing races, usually caused by high static loads or application of force during installation or removal. Indentations are rounded or spherical due to the impression left by the contacting balls or rollers of the bearings.
[For more detailed information refer to Powerplant Handbook H-8083-32-ATB, Chapter 10 p.3]

10-4) C.
Several terms are used to describe defects detected in engine parts during inspection. One common term is galling. Galling is a severe condition of chafing or fretting in which a transfer of metal from one part to another occurs. It is usually caused by slight movement of the mated parts having limited relative motion and under high loads.
[For more detailed information refer to Powerplant Handbook H-8083-32-ATB, Chapter 10 p.4]

10-5) A.
Several terms are used to describe defects detected in engine parts during inspection. One common term is flaking. Flaking is the breaking loose of small pieces of metal or coated surface that is usually caused by defective plating or excessive loading.
[For more detailed information refer to Powerplant Handbook H-8083-32-ATB, Chapter 10 p.4]

10-6) C.
When applicable, check for flatness of the piston head using a straight edge and thickness gauge. If a depression is found, check for cracks on the inside of the piston. A depression in the top of the piston usually means that detonation has occurred within the cylinder.
[For more detailed information refer to Powerplant Handbook H-8083-32-ATB, Chapter 10 p.5]

10-7) AMP007

When cleaning aluminum and magnesium engine parts, it is inadvisable to soak them in solutions containing soap because

A. some of the soap will become impregnated in the surface of the material and subsequently cause engine oil contamination and foaming.
B. the soap can chemically alter the metals causing them to become more susceptible to corrosion.
C. the parts can be destroyed by dissimilar metal electrolytic action if they are placed together in the solution for more than a few minutes.

10-8) AMP030

Where are sludge chambers when used in aircraft engine lubrication systems usually located?

A. In the crankshaft throws.
B. Adjacent to the scavenger pumps.
C. In the oil storage tank.

10-9) AMP007

Which of the following are true concerning structural inspection of engine parts during an engine overhaul?
1. Dye penetrant can be used on aluminum, stainless, and titanium.
2. Eddy current inspection requires bare metal surfaces to be effective.
3. Resonance ultra-sound inspection is primarily used for thickness measurement.
4. Magnetic particle inspection requires fluorescent developer to see the results.
5. X-rays can be used to check the structural integrity of an engine component.

A. 1, 2, and 4.
B. 1, 3, and 4.
C. 1, 3, and 5.

10-10) AMP007

On which part of the cylinder walls of a normally operating engine will the greatest amount of wear occur?

A. Near the center of the cylinder where the piston velocity is greatest.
B. Near the top of the cylinder.
C. Wear is normally evenly distributed.

10-11) AMP007

During overhaul, reciprocating engine exhaust valves are checked for stretch

A. with a suitable inside spring caliper.
B. using a manufacturer's contour or radius gauge or by the stem diameter just behind the head.
C. by placing the valve on a surface plate and measuring its length with a vertical height gauge.

10-12) AMP007

Straightening nitride crankshafts is

A. recommended.
B. not recommended.
C. approved by the manufacturer.

10-7) A.
Degreasing can be done by spraying or immersing the part in a suitable commercial solvent. Extreme care must be used if any water-mixed degreasing solutions containing caustic compounds or soap are used. Such compounds, in addition to being potentially corrosive to aluminum and magnesium, may become impregnated in the pores of the metal and cause oil foaming when the engine is returned to service.
[For more detailed information refer to Powerplant Handbook H-8083-32-ATB, Chapter 10 p.6]

10-8) A.
Some older engines used sludge chambers in the crankshafts which were manufactured with hollow crankpins that serve as sludge removers. Sludge chambers are formed by means of spool-shaped tubes pressed into the hollow crankpins or by plugs pressed into each end of the crankpin.
[For more detailed information refer to Powerplant Handbook H-8083-32-ATB, Chapter 10 p.7]

10-9) C.
All of the answers contain a type of inspection that is used on aircraft engines. Eddy current inspection, however, can frequently be performed without removing the surface coatings, such as primer, paint, and anodized film. In magnetic particle inspection, tiny ferrous particles align with discontinuities in a material. Fluorescent developer is not used.
[For more detailed information refer to Powerplant Handbook H-8083-32-ATB, Chapter 10 p.7-8]

10-10) B.
The cylinder is usually worn larger at the top than at the bottom. At the top of the piston stroke (top of the cylinder), the piston is subjected to greater heat and pressure and more erosive environment than at the bottom of the stroke. Also there is a greater freedom of movement at the top of the stroke. Under these conditions, the piston wears the cylinder more at the top of the cylinder.
[For more detailed information refer to Powerplant Handbook H-8083-32-ATB, Chapter 10 p.9]

10-11) B.
Inspect a valve for stretch using a micrometer or a valve radius gauge. If a micrometer is used, stretch is found as a smaller diameter of the valve stem near the neck of the valve.
[For more detailed information refer to Powerplant Handbook H-8083-32-ATB, Chapter 10 p.10]

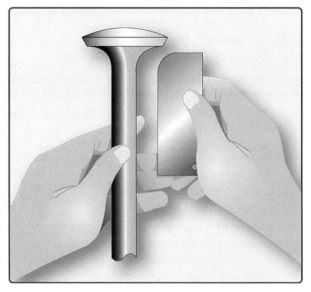

Figure 10-8. Checking valve stretch with a manufacturer's gauge.

10-12) B.
A bent crankshaft should not be straightened. Any attempt to do so results in rupture of the nitride surface of the bearing journals, a condition that causes eventual failure.
[For more detailed information refer to Powerplant Handbook H-8083-32-ATB, Chapter 10 p.11]

10-13) AMP057

In general, welding of engine parts is

    A.   not acceptable.
    B.   only allowed when approved by the manufacturer.
    C.   can be accomplished if listed in 14 CFR, Part 43.

10-14) AMP057

When overhauling a certified reciprocating aircraft engine

    A.   Only steel valve seats can be used.
    B.   new valve seats are required to be installed.
    C.   steel valve seats can be wet or dry grinded.

10-15) AMP057

Checking the valve seat to valve face fit can be done with

    A.   Prussian blue or by gently lapping the valve to the seat and examining the valve seat afterwards.
    B.   gasoline by checking for leaks around the interface while the two surfaces are mated.
    C.   a strong light held behind the valve head while examining the seat to valve interface from the other side.

10-16) AMP057

When grinding a valve to an interference fit, a

    A.   greater area of contact between the valve seat and valve face is created.
    B.   stronger set of valve springs is required.
    C.   narrow contact surface is created.

10-17) AMP057

Grinding the valves of a reciprocating engine to a feathered edge is likely to result in

    A.   normal operation and long life.
    B.   excessive valve clearance.
    C.   preignition and burned valves.

10-18) AMP056

Standard aircraft cylinder oversizes usually range from 0.010 inch to 0.030 inch. Oversize on automobile engine cylinders may range up to 0.100 inch. This is because aircraft engine cylinders

    A.   have more limited cooling capacity.
    B.   have relatively thin walls and may be nitrided.
    C.   operate at high temperatures.

10-13) B.

In general, welding of highly-stressed parts can be accomplished only when approved by the manufacturer. However, welding may be accomplished using methods that are approved by the engine manufacturer, and if it can be reasonably expected that the weld repair will not adversely affect the airworthiness of the engine.

[For more detailed information refer to Powerplant Handbook H-8083-32-ATB, Chapter 10 p.12]

10-14) C.

The valve seat inserts of an aircraft engine are usually in need of refacing at engine overhaul. They are refaced to provide a true, clean, and correct size seat for the valve. Steel valve seats are refaced by grinding equipment. It can be either wet or dry valve seat grinding equipment. The wet grinder uses a mixture of soluble oil and water to wash away the chips and to keep the stone and seat cool. This produces as smoother, more accurate job than the dry grinder. The grinding stones may be either silicon carbide or aluminum oxide.

[For more detailed information refer to Powerplant Handbook H-8083-32-ATB, Chapter 10 p.13]

10-15) A.

Prussian blue is used to check for contact transfer from one surface to another. To check the fit of the seat, spread a thin coat of Prussian blue evenly on the seat. Press the valve onto the seat. The blue transferred to valve indicates the contact surface. The contact surface should be one-third to two-thirds the width of the valve face and in the middle of the face. The same check may be made by lapping the valve lightly to the seat. Lapping is accomplished by using a small amount of lapping compound placed between the valve face and seat. The valve is then moved in a rotary motion back and forth until the lapping compound grinds slightly into the surface. After cleaning the lapping compound off, a contact area can be seen. It should be within the above parameters.

[For more detailed information refer to Powerplant Handbook H-8083-32-ATB, Chapter 10 p.14]

10-16) C.

The interference fit is used to obtain a more positive seal by means of a narrow contact surface between the valve face and the valve seat. Theoretically, there is a line contact between the valve and the seat. With this line contact, the load that the valve exerts against the seat is concentrated in a very small area, thereby increasing the unit load at any one spot. The interference fit is especially beneficial during the first few hours of operation after an overhaul because the positive seal prevents a burned valve or seat that a leaking valve might produce.

[For more detailed information refer to Powerplant Handbook H-8083-32-ATB, Chapter 10 p.16]

10-17) C.

After grinding, check the valve margin to be sure that the valve edge has not been ground too thin. A thin edge is called a feathered edge and can lead to preignition. The valve edge would burn away in a short period of time and the cylinder would have to be overhauled again.

[For more detailed information refer to Powerplant Handbook H-8083-32-ATB, Chapter 10 p.17]

10-18) B.

Aircraft cylinders have relatively thin walls and may have a nitrided surface that must not be ground away. Nitriding is a surface hardening process that hardens the steel surface to a depth of several thousandths of an inch. Any one manufacturer usually does not allow all of the above oversizes. Some manufacturers do not allow regrinding to an oversize at all. The manufacturer's overhaul manual or parts catalog usually lists the oversizes allowed for a particular make and model engine.

[For more detailed information refer to Powerplant Handbook H-8083-32-ATB, Chapter 10 p.18]

10-19) AMP057

Once an aircraft cylinder is ground to an oversize during overhaul,

- A. it must be resurfaced or honed to the desired finish.
- B. it is measured and installed on the engine.
- C. a chemical finish is imparted to the cylinder walls.

10-20) AMP057

A reassembled, overhauled engine must undergo testing before it can be released for service. The purposes of the test run include

- A. valve seating and crankshaft run-in.
- B. burnishing the crankshaft bearings and run-in of the piston rings.
- C. fuel consumption and oil pressure checks and adjustments.

10-21) AMP057

When an overhauled engine is test run before being put into service, a club propeller is used

- A. for proper cooling and the correct load on the engine.
- B. because the propeller to be installed is rarely available.
- C. to ensure maximum RPM can be achieved and the carburetor properly adjusted.

10-22) AMP009

Which instrument gives information concerning the extent to which an engine's fuel primer system should be used for starting?

- A. Fuel flow meter.
- B. Manifold pressure gauge.
- C. Carburetor air temperature.

10-23) AMP009

Engine oil temperature gauges indicate the temperature of the oil

- A. entering the oil cooler.
- B. entering the engine.
- C. in the oil storage.

10-24) AMP041

Fuel flow on many light aircraft with reciprocating engines is measured

- A. with a turbine sensor-based indicating system.
- B. using direct flow meters.
- C. with a pressure-based flow meter.

10-25) AMP009

A manifold pressure gauge is designated to

- A. maintain constant pressure in the intake manifold.
- B. indicate differential pressure between the intake manifold and atmospheric pressure.
- C. indicate absolute pressure in the intake manifold.

10-19) A.
The type of finish desired in the cylinder is an important consideration when ordering a regrind. Some engine manufacturers specify a fairly rough finish on the cylinder walls that allows the rings to seat even if they are not lapped to the cylinder. Other manufacturers desire a smooth finish to which a lapped ring seats without much change in ring or cylinder dimensions. Hones and deglazing hone are used to prepare the surface of the cylinder wall. Hones that remove material and change the dimension of the cylinder must be chosen before the cylinder is ground so that after it is honed the final dimension is correct.
[For more detailed information refer to Powerplant Handbook H-8083-32-ATB, Chapter 10 p.19]

10-20) B.
Engine run-in is as vital as any other phase of engine overhaul for it is the means by which the quality of a new or newly overhauled engine is checked and it is the final step in the preparation of an engine for service. Thus, the reliability and potential service life of an engine is in question until it has satisfactorily passed the test cell. The test serves a dual purpose. First, it accomplishes piston ring run-in and bearing burnishing. Second, it provides valuable information that is used to evaluate engine performance and determine engine condition.
[For more detailed information refer to Powerplant Handbook H-8083-32-ATB, Chapter 10 p.20]

10-21) A.
A test club (propeller) should be used when running in an engine after overhaul instead of a flight propeller. The club propeller provides more cooling airflow and the correct amount of load.
[For more detailed information refer to Powerplant Handbook H-8083-32-ATB, Chapter 10 p.21]

10-22) C.
The carburetor air temperature gauge should be noted before starting and just after shutdown. The temperature before starting is the best indication of the temperature of the fuel in the carburetor body and tells whether vaporizing is sufficient for the initial firing or whether the mixture must be augmented by priming. If the engine has been shut down for only a short time, the residual heat in the carburetor may make it possible to rely on the vaporizing heat in the fuel and powerplant. Priming would then be unnecessary.
[For more detailed information refer to Powerplant Handbook H-8083-32-ATB, Chapter 10 p.22]

10-23) B.
The oil temperature gauge line in the aircraft is connected at the oil inlet to the engine. However, during initial testing of an overhauled engine, engine oil temperature readings are taken at the oil inlet and the oil outlet. From these readings, it can be determined if the engine heat transferred to the oil is low, normal, or excessive.
[For more detailed information refer to Powerplant Handbook H-8083-32-ATB, Chapter 10 p.23]

10-24) C.
Reciprocating engines on light aircraft use a fuel pressure gauge that is also used for the fuel flow meter. This is because the fuel flow is proportional to the fuel pressure in these systems. Fuel flow is normally measured in gallons per hour. By calibrating the fuel pressure indicator in gallons per hour an acceptable, reliable measurement of fuel flow is obtained.
[For more detailed information refer to Powerplant Handbook H-8083-32-ATB, Chapter 10 p.23]

10-25) C.
The preferred type of instrument for measuring the manifold pressure on reciprocating engine is a gauge that records the pressure as an absolute pressure reading. Absolute pressure takes into account the atmospheric pressure plus the pressure in the intake manifold.
[For more detailed information refer to Powerplant Handbook H-8083-32-ATB, Chapter 10 p.24]

10-26) AMP066

Thermocouples are usually inserted or installed on the

- A. front cylinder of the engine.
- B. rear cylinder of the engine.
- C. hottest cylinder of the engine.

10-27) AMP031

When a reciprocating aircraft engine is started, what is the maximum time period to wait for an indication of oil pressure?

- A. 15 seconds.
- B. 30 seconds.
- C. 1 minute.

10-28) AMP057

What is the purpose of a power check on a reciprocating aircraft engine?

- A. To check magneto drop.
- B. To determine satisfactory performance.
- C. To determine if the fuel air mixture is adequate.

10-29) AMP023

An indication that the optimum idle mixture has been obtained occurs when the mixture control is moved to IDLE CUTOFF and manifold pressure

- A. decreases momentarily and RPM drops slightly before the engine ceases to fire.
- B. increases momentarily and RPM drops slightly before engine ceases to fire.
- C. decreases and RPM increases momentarily before the engine ceases to fire.

10-30) AMP056

1. Preignition is caused by improper ignition timing.
2. Detonation occurs when an area of the combustion chamber becomes incandescent and ignites the fuel air mixture in advance of normal timed ignition.

- A. only No. 1 is true.
- B. both No. 1 and No. 2 are true.
- C. both No. 1 and No. 2 are false.

10-31) AMP056

Which of the following would most likely cause a reciprocating engine to backfire through the induction system at low RPM?

- A. Idle mixture too rich.
- B. Clogged derichment valve.
- C. Lean mixture.

10-26) C.
Cylinder head temperatures are indicated by a gauge connected to a thermocouple attached to the cylinder that tests show to be the hottest on an engine in a particular installation. This is often a rear cylinder in an opposed engine configuration but it does not have to be. While normally it can be assumed that the remaining cylinder temperatures are lower, conditions such as detonation are not indicated unless they occur in the cylinder that has the thermocouple installed.
[For more detailed information refer to Powerplant Handbook H-8083-32-ATB, Chapter 10 p.24]

10-27) B.
During warm-up, watch the instruments associated with engine operation. This aids in making sure that all phases of engine operation are normal. Engine oil pressure should be indicated within 30 seconds after the start. Furthermore, if the oil pressure is not up to or above normal within one minute after the engine starts, the engine should be shut down.
[For more detailed information refer to Powerplant Handbook H-8083-32-ATB, Chapter 10 p.26]

10-28) B.
Specific RPM and manifold pressure relationship should be checked during each ground check. This can be done at the time the engine is run-up to make the magneto check. The purpose of the power check is to measure the performance of the engine against an established standard.
[For more detailed information refer to Powerplant Handbook H-8083-32-ATB, Chapter 10 p.28]

10-29) C.
When performing an idle speed and mixture check, as the mixture control lever is moved into IDLE CUTOFF, and before normal drop off, the engine speed may increase. An increase in RPM, but less than that recommended by the manufacturer (usually 20 RPM), indicates proper mixture strength. A greater increase indicates that the mixture is too rich. If the engine speed does not increase or drops immediately when the mixture control lever in moved into IDLE CUTOFF, the mixture is too lean.
[For more detailed information refer to Powerplant Handbook H-8083-32-ATB, Chapter 10 p.29]

10-30) C.
Preignition means that combustion takes place within the cylinder before the timed spark jumps across the spark plug terminals. Do not confuse preignition with the spark that occurs too early in the cycle. Preignition is caused by a hot spot in the combustion chamber and not by incorrect ignition timing. Detonation is the spontaneous combustion of the unburned charge ahead of the flame fronts after ignition of the charge.
[For more detailed information refer to Powerplant Handbook H-8083-32-ATB, Chapter 10 p.30-31]

10-31) C.
When a fuel air mixture does not contain enough fuel to consume all of the oxygen, it is called a lean mixture. An extremely lean mixture either does not burn at all or burns so slowly that combustion is not complete at the end of the exhaust stroke. The flame lingers in the cylinder and then ignites the contents in the intake manifold or the induction system when the intake valve opens. This causes an explosion known as backfiring which can damage the carburetor and other parts of the induction system.
[For more detailed information refer to Powerplant Handbook H-8083-32-ATB, Chapter 10 p.31]

10-32) AMP056

One cause of after firing in an aircraft engine is

    A.   an excessively rich mixture.
    B.   an excessively lean mixture.
    C.   sticking intake valve.

10-33) AMP056

Which statement relating to fuel/air ratios is true?

    A.   The mixture ratio which gives the best power is richer than the mixture ratio which gives maximum economy.
    B.   A rich mixture is faster burning than a normal mixture.
    C.   The mixture ratio which gives maximum economy may also be designated the best power mixture.

10-34) AMP056

An induction system leak near the cylinder will

    A.   cause back firing.
    B.   cause a lean mixture.
    C.   causes a rich mixture.

10-35) AMP008

Excessive valve clearance will cause the duration of valve opening to

    A.   increase for both intake and exhaust valves.
    B.   decrease for both intake and exhaust valves.
    C.   decrease for intake valves and increase for exhaust valves.

10-36) AMP057

At any given RPM, a change in power output can be noted by which engine monitoring instrument?

    A.   Manifold pressure gauge.
    B.   Fuel pressure gauge.
    C.   Cylinder head temperature.

10-37) AMP057

A hissing sound coming from the carburetor when the propeller is pulled through manually indicates

    A.   worn piston rings.
    B.   an induction leak.
    C.   intake valve blow-by.

10-38) AMP057

As the pressure is applied during a reciprocating engine compression check using a differential pressure tester, what would a movement of the propeller in the direction of engine rotation indicate?

    A.   The piston was on the compression stroke.
    B.   The piston was on the exhaust stroke.
    C.   The piston was positioned past top dead center.

10-32) A.

Overly rich mixtures are also slow burning, therefore charges of unburned fuel are present in the exhaust gases. Air from outside the exhaust stacks mixes with this unburned fuel that ignites. This causes an explosion in the exhaust system. After firing is perhaps more common where long exhaust ducting retains greater amounts of unburned charges. As in the case of back firing, the correction for after firing is the proper adjustment of the fuel/air mixture.

[For more detailed information refer to Powerplant Handbook H-8083-32-ATB, Chapter 10 p.31-32]

10-33) A.

For a given RPM, the power output of an engine is less with the best-economy setting (auto lean) than with the best-power mixture.

[For more detailed information refer to Powerplant Handbook H-8083-32-ATB, Chapter 10 p.33]

10-34) B.

Any leak in the induction system has an effect on the mixture reaching the cylinders. This is particularly true of a leak at the cylinder end of an intake pipe. At manifold pressures below atmospheric pressure, such a leak leans out the mixture. This occurs because additional air is drawn in from the atmosphere at the leaky point. The affected cylinder may overheat, fire intermittently, or even cut out altogether.

[For more detailed information refer to Powerplant Handbook H-8083-32-ATB, Chapter 10 p.34]

10-35) B.

Valve operation is only correct if valve clearances are set and remain at the value recommended by the engine manufacturer. If valve clearances are set wrong, the valve overlap period is longer or shorter than the manufacturer intended. Where there is too much valve clearance, the valves do not open as wide or remain open as long as they should. This reduces the valve overlap period.

[For more detailed information refer to Powerplant Handbook H-8083-32-ATB, Chapter 10 p.35]

10-36) A.

The cylinders of an engine, along with any type of supercharging, form an air pump. The power developed in the cylinders varies directly with the rate that air can be consumed by the engine. Therefore, a measure of air consumption into the engine is a measure of power input. Together, the manifold pressure gauge and the tachometer provide a measure of engine air consumption. For any given RPM, any change in power input is reflected by a corresponding change in manifold pressure.

[For more detailed information refer to Powerplant Handbook H-8083-32-ATB, Chapter 10 p.36]

10-37) C.

Valve blow-by is indicated by a hissing or whistle when pulling the propeller through prior to starting the engine. It is caused by the valve not seating properly and should be corrected immediately to prevent valve failure and possible engine failure.

[For more detailed information refer to Powerplant Handbook H-8083-32-ATB, Chapter 10 p.40]

10-38) C.

When performing a differential compression test, turn the engine over by hand in the direction of rotation until the piston is at top dead center. This can be detected by a decrease in force required to move the propeller. If the engine is rotated past top dead center, the 15 to 20 psi from the differential tester tends to move the propeller in the direction of rotation.

[For more detailed information refer to Powerplant Handbook H-8083-32-ATB, Chapter 10 p.41]

10-39) AMP057
When performing a compression check, if low compression is obtained on a cylinder,

A. the cylinder must be removed and replaced.
B. a logbook entry must be made and the value accessed at the next 100 hour inspection.
C. rotate the engine with the starter or restart and run the engine and check the compression again.

10-40) AMP057
Staking a valve

A. should not be attempted on aircraft engines.
B. is an attempt to dislodge foreign material from the valve face/seat interface.
C. should be accomplished only by a qualified repair station.

10-41) AMP057
If air is heard coming from the crankcase breather or oil filler during a differential compression check, what is this an indication of?

A. Exhaust valve leakage.
B. Intake valve leakage.
C. Piston ring leakage.

10-42) AMP049
1. Cast iron piston rings may be used in chrome-plated cylinders.
2. Chrome plated rings may be used in plain steel cylinders.
Regarding the above statements,

A. only No. 1 is true.
B. neither No. 1 nor No. 2 is true.
C. both No. 1 and No. 2 are true.

10-43) AMP057
If an engine cylinder is to be removed, at what position in the cylinder should the piston be?

A. Bottom dead center.
B. Top dead center.
C. Halfway between top and bottom dead center.

10-44) AMP007
A cold cylinder check is performed

A. immediately after engine shutdown.
B. performed before start-up of an overhauled engine.
C. while the engine is running.

10-39) C.

Obtaining low compression on the first check of compression check is not automatically grounds for rejection of the cylinder. Debris between the valve face and the seat, for example, could be causing the low reading. If low compression is obtained on any cylinder, turn the engine through with the starter, or re-start, and run the engine to takeoff power and recheck the cylinder. If the compression is within limits, continue the cylinder in service.

[For more detailed information refer to Powerplant Handbook H-8083-32-ATB, Chapter 10 p.41]

10-40) B.

If low compression on a cylinder found during a compression check is not corrected by cranking the engine with the starter or re-running the engine, the rocker box cover should be removed and valve clearance should be checked. If clearance is within limits, stake the valves by placing a fiber drift on the rocker arm immediately over the valve stem and tapping it with a 1 to 2 pound hammer several times. This is an attempt to dislodge any foreign material that may be between the valve and the valve seat. After staking, rotate the engine with the starter and recheck compression.

[For more detailed information refer to Powerplant Handbook H-8083-32-ATB, Chapter 10 p.41]

10-41) C.

Cylinders having compression below minimum specified should be further checked to determine whether leakage is past the exhaust valve, intake valve, or piston. Excessive leakage can be detected (during compression check) past the piston rings by escaping air at the engine breather outlets or oil filler port.

[For more detailed information refer to Powerplant Handbook H-8083-32-ATB, Chapter 10 p.41]

10-42) C.

In some instances, air-cooled engines are equipped with chrome-plated cylinders. When installing a chrome-plated cylinder, do not use chrome-plated rings. The matched assembly (piston, piston rings, cylinder, cylinder head assembly, etc.) includes the correct piston rings for the cylinder. However, if a ring is needed, check the cylinder marking to determine which ring, chrome-plated or otherwise, is correct for replacement.

[For more detailed information refer to Powerplant Handbook H-8083-32-ATB, Chapter 10 p.42]

10-43) B.

When removing a cylinder from an engine, pushrods are removed by depressing the rocker arm. Before removing the pushrods, turn the crankshaft until the piston is at top dead center on the compression stroke. This relieves pressure on both the intake and exhaust rocker arms.

[For more detailed information refer to Powerplant Handbook H-8083-32-ATB, Chapter 10 p.42]

10-44) A.

When cylinder head temperatures have stabilized during run-up, stop the engine by moving the mixture control to the idle cutoff or full lean position. When the engine ceases firing, turn off both ignition and master switches. Record the cylinder head temperature indication on the gauge on the flight deck. As soon as the propeller has ceased rotating, apply the temperature sensing instrument to the cylinder heads and record the temperatures.

[For more detailed information refer to Powerplant Handbook H-8083-32-ATB, Chapter 10 p.44]

10-45) AMP069
Compressor field cleaning on turbine engines is performed primarily in order to

A. prevent engine oil contamination and subsequent engine bearing wear or damage.
B. facilitate flight line inspection of engine inlet and compressor areas for defects or FOD.
C. prevent engine performance degradation, increased fuel costs, and damage or corrosion to gas path surfaces.

10-46) AMP069
The blending of blades and vanes in a turbine engine

A. is usually accomplished only at engine overhaul.
B. should be performed parallel to the length of the blade using smooth contours to minimize stress points.
C. may sometimes be accomplished with the engine installed ordinarily using power tools.

10-47) AMP069
Turbine engine parts can be cleaned with

A. emulsion-type cleaners or chlorinated solvents.
B. mineral spirits.
C. soapy water and rinsed with clean water.

10-48) AMP069
Turbine engine components exposed to high temperatures generally may NOT be marked with
1. layout dye.
2. commercial felt tip marker.
3. wax or grease pencil.
4. chalk.
5. graphite lead pencil.

A. 1, 2, and 3.
B. 3 and 5.
C. 4 and 5.

10-49) AMP069
When cleaning turbine engine fuel nozzles, loosen carbon deposits

A. only with a stainless steel implement or wire brush.
B. before exposing to manufacturer recommended cleaning fluid.
C. with an approved cleaning product and remove softened deposits with a soft bristle brush.

10-50) AMP069
Where do stress rupture cracks on a turbine engine usually appear on turbine blades?

A. Across the blade root, parallel to the fir tree.
B. Along the leading edge or trailing edge at right angle to the edge length.
C. Along the leading edge, parallel to the edge.

10-45) C.
Accumulation of dirt on the compressor blades reduces the aerodynamic efficiency of the blades with resultant deterioration in engine performance. The efficiency of the blades is impaired by dirt deposits in a manner similar to that of an aircraft wing under icing conditions. Unsatisfactory acceleration and high exhaust gas temperature can result from foreign deposits on compressor components. An end result of foreign particles, if allowed to accumulate in sufficient quantity, would be [fuel] inefficiency and damage to the gas path surfaces of the engine.
[For more detailed information refer to Powerplant Handbook H-8083-32-ATB, Chapter 10 p.46]

10-46) B.
Whenever possible, stoning and local rework of the blade should be performed parallel to the length of the blade. Rework must be accomplished by hand using stones, files, or emery cloth. Do not use a power tool to buff the entire area of the blade. The surface finish in the repaired area must be comparable to that of a new blade.
[For more detailed information refer to Powerplant Handbook H-8083-32-ATB, Chapter 10 p.46]

10-47) A.
Turbine engine parts can be degreased by using emulsion-type cleaners or chlorinated solvents. The emulsion-type cleaners are safe for all metals since they are neutral and non-corrosive. Cleaning parts by the chlorinated solvent method leaves the parts absolutely dry. If they are not to be subjected to further cleaning operations, they should be sprayed with a corrosion preventative solution to protect them against rust or corrosion.
[For more detailed information refer to Powerplant Handbook H-8083-32-ATB, Chapter 10 p.49]

10-48) B.
Always refer to manufacturer's information for marking parts. However, in general, layout dye (lightly applied) or chalk may be used to mark parts that are directly exposed to the engine's gas path, such as turbine blades and discs, turbine vanes, and combustion chamber liners. A wax marking pencil may be used for parts not directly exposed to the gas path. Do not use a wax marking pencil on a liner surface or turbine rotor. The use of carbon alloy or metallic pencils is not recommended because of the possibility of causing intergranular corrosion attack that could result in a reduction in material strength and cracking.
[For more detailed information refer to Powerplant Handbook H-8083-32-ATB, Chapter 10 p.50]

10-49) C.
Clean all carbon deposits from the nozzles by washing with a cleaning fluid approved by the engine manufacturer and remove the softened deposits with a soft bristle brush. It is desirable to have filtered air passing through the nozzle during the cleaning operation to carry away deposits as they are loosened. Because the spray characteristics of the nozzle may become impaired, no attempt should be made to clean the nozzles by scraping with a hard implement or by rubbing with a wire brush.
[For more detailed information refer to Powerplant Handbook H-8083-32-ATB, Chapter 10 p.51]

10-50) B.
Stress rupture cracks usually appear as minute hairline cracks on or across the leading or trailing edge at a right angle to the edge length. Visible cracks may range in length from 1/16th inch upward.
[For more detailed information refer to Powerplant Handbook H-8083-32-ATB, Chapter 10 p.51]

10-51) AMP068
Turbine blades are generally more susceptible to operating damage than compressor blades because of

- A. higher centrifugal loading.
- B. exposure to high temperatures.
- C. high pressure and high velocity gas flow.

10-52) AMP069
When the leading edge of a first stage turbine blade is found to have stress rupture cracks, which of the following should be suspected?

- A. Faulty cooling shield.
- B. Over-temperature condition.
- C. Overspeed condition.

10-53) AMP069
Jet engine turbine blades removed for detailed inspection must be reinstalled in

- A. a specified slot 180° away.
- B. a specified slot 90° away in the direction of rotation.
- C. the same slot.

10-54) AMP069
Hot spots on the tail cone of a turbine engine exhaust

- A. indicate a problem in the combustion section of the engine.
- B. can glow red hot and light off any remaining fuel in the exhaust stream.
- C. may indicate damage to the turbine blades.

10-55) AMP068
The exhaust gas temperature (EGT) indicator on a gas turbine engine provides a relative indication of the

- A. turbine inlet temperature.
- B. temperature of the exhaust gases as they pass the exhaust cone.
- C. exhaust temperature.

10-56) AMP068
Which of the following is the ultimate limiting factor of turbine engine operation?

- A. Compressor inlet air temperature.
- B. Turbine inlet temperature.
- C. Burner can pressure.

10-57) AMP033
The engine pressure ratio (EPR) indicator is a direct indication of

- A. engine thrust being produced.
- B. pressure ratio between the front and aft end of the compressor.
- C. ratio of engine RPM to compressor pressure.

10-51) B.

Turbine blades are usually inspected and cleaned in the same manner as compressor blades. However, because of the extreme heat under which the turbine blades operate, they are more susceptible to damage.

[For more detailed information refer to Powerplant Handbook H-8083-32-ATB, Chapter 10 p.51]

10-52) B.

Do not confuse stress rupture cracks or deformation of the leading edge with foreign material impingement damage or with blending repairs to the blade. When any stress rupture cracks or deformation of the leading edges of the first stage turbine blades are found, an over-temperature condition must be suspected. Check the individual blades for stretch and the turbine disc for hardness and stretch.

[For more detailed information refer to Powerplant Handbook H-8083-32-ATB, Chapter 10 p.51]

10-53) C.

Blades removed for a detailed inspection or for a check of turbine disk stretch must be re-installed in the same slots from which they were removed. Number the blades prior to removal.

[For more detailed information refer to Powerplant Handbook H-8083-32-ATB, Chapter 10 p.51]

10-54) A.

The exhaust section of a turbine engine should be inspected for cracks, warping, buckling or hotspots. Hotspots on the tail cone are a good indication of a malfunctioning fuel nozzle or combustion chamber.

[For more detailed information refer to Powerplant Handbook H-8083-32-ATB, Chapter 10 p.55]

10-55) A.

The turbine inlet temperature is proportional to the energy available to turn the turbine. This means that the hotter the gases are that are entering the turbine section of the engine, the more power is available to turn the turbine wheel(s). The exhaust temperature is proportional to the turbine inlet temperature. Regardless of how or where the exhaust temperature is taken on the engine for the flight deck indication, this temperature is proportional to the temperature of the exhaust gases entering the first stage of the turbine inlet guide vanes. A higher EGT corresponds to a larger amount of energy to the turbine so it can turn the compressor faster.

[For more detailed information refer to Powerplant Handbook H-8083-32-ATB, Chapter 10 p.55]

10-56) B.

The hotter the gases are that are entering the turbine section, the more power is available to turn the turbine wheel. This increases engine output. However, a point exists when the turbine inlet guide vanes start to be damaged. The turbine inlet temperature and, thus, engine operation is limited by this.

[For more detailed information refer to Powerplant Handbook H-8083-32-ATB, Chapter 10 p.55]

10-57) A.

Engine pressure ratio (EPR) is an indication of the thrust being developed by a turbofan engine and is used to set power for takeoff on many types of turbine powered aircraft. It is instrumented by total pressure pickups in the engine inlet (Pt_2) and in the turbine exhaust (Pt_7). The indication is displayed on the flight deck by the EPR gauge which is used in making engine power settings.

[For more detailed information refer to Powerplant Handbook H-8083-32-ATB, Chapter 10 p.56]

10-58) AMP019

What is the primary purpose of the tachometer on an axial-compressor turbine engine.

   A. Monitor engine RPM during cruise conditions.
   B. It is the most accurate instrument for establishing thrust settings under all conditions.
   C. Monitor engine RPM during starting and to indicate overspeed conditions.

10-59) AMP009

In what units are turbine engine tachometers calibrated?

   A. Percent of engine RPM.
   B. Actual engine RPM.
   C. Percent of engine pressure ratio.

10-60) AMP068

Which of the following is used to monitor the mechanical integrity of the turbines, as well as to check engine operating conditions of a turbine engine?

   A. Engine oil pressure.
   B. Exhaust gas temperature.
   C. Engine pressure ratio.

10-61) AMP069

The abbreviation Pt7 is used in turbine engine terminology means

   A. the total inlet pressure.
   B. pressure and temperature at station No. 7.
   C. the total pressure at station No. 7.

10-62) AMP068

What is the first engine instrument indication of a successful start of a turbine engine?

   A. A rise in the engine fuel flow.
   B. A rise in oil pressure.
   C. A rise in the exhaust gas temperature.

10-63) AMP068

What instrument on a gas turbine engine should be monitored to minimize the possibility of a "hot" start?

   A. RPM indicator.
   B. Turbine inlet temperature.
   C. Torquemeter.

10-64) AMP068

When starting a turbine engine

   A. a hot start is indicated if the exhaust gas temperature exceeds specified limits.
   B. an excessively lean mixture is likely to cause a hot start.
   C. release the starter switch as soon as indication of light-off occurs.

10 - Engine Maintenance and Operation
Answers

10-58) C.
Turbofan engines with two spools or separate shafts, high pressure and low pressure spools, are generally referred to as N1 and N2, with each having its own indicator. The main purpose of the tachometer is to be able to monitor RPM under normal conditions, during engine start, and to indicate an overspeed condition, if one occurs.
[For more detailed information refer to Powerplant Handbook H-8083-32-ATB, Chapter 10 p.56]

10-59) A.
Turbine engine tachometers are usually calibrated in percent rpm so that various types of engines can be operated on the same basis of comparison. Also, turbine speeds are generally very high and the large numbers of RPM would make it confusing.
[For more detailed information refer to Powerplant Handbook H-8083-32-ATB, Chapter 10 p.56]

10-60) B.
Temperature is an engine operating limitation and is used to monitor the mechanical integrity of the turbines as well as to check engine operating condition. Temperature of the gases entering the first stage of turbine inlet guide vane is the important consideration but it is impractical to measure at this point in the engines. Rather, turbine outlet temperature, which is the exhaust gas temperature (EGT), is measured and monitor since it is directly proportional to turbine inlet temperature.
[For more detailed information refer to Powerplant Handbook H-8083-32-ATB, Chapter 10 p.56]

10-61) C.
The EPR gauge is instrumented by total pressure pickups since it is a ratio of the pressure at the inlet of the engine compared to the pressure at the outlet. On an actual turbine engine, it compares P_{t2} (inlet pressure) with P_{t7} (pressure at the turbine exhaust). Therefore, P_{t7} is used to mean the total pressure at station No. 7 which is in the turbine exhaust area of the engine.
[For more detailed information refer to Powerplant Handbook H-8083-32-ATB, Chapter 10 p.56]

10-62) C.
A successful start is noted first by a rise in exhaust gas temperature. If fuel does not start to burn inside the engine within a prescribed period of time, or if the exhaust gas starting temperature limit is exceeded (a hot start), the starting procedure should be aborted.
[For more detailed information refer to Powerplant Handbook H-8083-32-ATB, Chapter 10 p.58]

10-63) B.
During the start of a turbine engine, if the exhaust gas temperature limit is exceeded, a hot start will occur. Exhaust gas temperature is used in many turbine engines instead of turbine inlet temperature. It is proportional to turbine inlet temperature and, although lower, it provided surveillance over the engine's internal operating conditions. So while it is the EGT gauge that is monitored in engines without turbine inlet temperature gauges, it is the turbine inlet temperature that is of concern. Adhere to the manufacturer's start check list and limitations when operating any aircraft engine.
[For more detailed information refer to Powerplant Handbook H-8083-32-ATB, Chapter 10 p.56-58]

10-64) A.
If the exhaust gas starting temperature limit is exceeded, a hot start occurs. Hot starts are not common, but when they do occur, they can usually be stopped in time to avoid excessive temperature by observing the exhaust gas temperature constantly during the start and shutting down the engine immediately upon indication that the EGT starting limit is being exceeded.
[For more detailed information refer to Powerplant Handbook H-8083-32-ATB, Chapter 10 p.58]

10-65) AMP068

When starting a turbine engine, a hung start is indicated if the engine

- A. exhaust gas temperature exceeds specified limits.
- B. fails to reach idle RPM.
- C. RPM exceeds specified operating speed.

10-66) AMP068

What should be done initially if a turbine engine catches fire when starting?

- A. Turn off the fuel and continue engine rotation with the starter.
- B. Continue engine start rotation and discharge a fire extinguisher into the intake.
- C. Continue starting attempt in order to blow out the fire.

10-67) AMP068

What is the proper starting sequence of a turbojet engine?

- A. Ignition, starter, fuel.
- B. Starter, ignition, fuel.
- C. Starter, fuel, ignition.

10-68) AMP068

What effect does high atmospheric humidity have on the operation of a jet engine?

- A. Decreases engine pressure ratio.
- B. Decreases compressor and turbine RPM.
- C. Has little or no effect.

10-69) AMP068

A cool-off period prior to shutdown of a turbine engine is accomplished in order to

- A. allow the turbine wheel to cool before the case contracts around it.
- B. prevent vapor lock in the fuel control and/or fuel lines.
- C. prevent seizure of the engine bearings.

10-70) AMP068

Which two engine parameters on a turboprop engine are used to compute takeoff power from the ambient pressure and temperature prevailing at the time of takeoff?

- A. EGT and fuel flow.
- B. RPM and EGT.
- C. EGT and torquemeter pressure.

10-71) AMP068

What results if a turbine engine is operated with excessively high EGT?

- A. Damage to the turbine section and/or reduced turbine component life.
- B. Compressor overspeed and associated compressor blade damage.
- C. Lubricating oil vaporization and possible scoring of the main bearings.

10-65) B.

A hung start is when the engine lights off but the engine will not accelerate to idle RPM. Therefore, EGT and turbine inlet temperature gauges will show elevated levels but the engine tachometer will not indicate idle rpm.

[For more detailed information refer to Powerplant Handbook H-8083-32-ATB, Chapter 10 p.58]

10-66) A.

Initially, move the fuel shutoff lever to the OFF position if an engine fire occurs or if the engine fire warning light is illuminated during the starting cycle. Continue cranking or motoring the engine until the fire has been expelled from the engine. If this initial action does not extinguish the fire, on the ground, CO2 can be discharged into the engine inlet duct while the engine is being cranked.

[For more detailed information refer to Powerplant Handbook H-8083-32-ATB, Chapter 10 p.58]

10-67) B.

Always follow the manufacturer's starting checklist step by step when starting a turbine engine. However, the general starting sequence is: 1) Rotate the compressor with the starter; 2) Turn ON the ignition; and 3) Open the engine fuel valve, either by moving the throttle to idle or by moving a fuel shutoff lever to OPEN, or by turning a switch. Thus, STARTER, then IGNITION, then FUEL is the usual starting sequence of a turbojet engine.

[For more detailed information refer to Powerplant Handbook H-8083-32-ATB, Chapter 10 p.58]

10-68) C.

Relative humidity, which affects reciprocating engine power appreciably, has a negligible effect on turbine engine thrust. Therefore, relative humidity is not usually considered when computing thrust for takeoff or determining fuel flow and RPM for routine operation of a jet engine.

[For more detailed information refer to Powerplant Handbook H-8083-32-ATB, Chapter 10 p.60]

10-69) A.

When an engine has been operated at high power levels for extended periods, a cool down time should be allowed before shut down. It is recommended the engine be operated at below a low power setting, preferably at idle for a period of 5 minutes to prevent possible seizure of the rotors. The mass of the turbine rotor is much greater that the turbine case and the turbine case is exposed to cooling air from both inside and outside the engine. Consequently, the case and rotor(s) lose their residual heat at different rates after the engine is shut down. Without a cool-off period before shutdown, the case, cooling faster, tends to shrink upon the turbine wheels that are still rotating. Seizing is possible.

[For more detailed information refer to Powerplant Handbook H-8083-32-ATB, Chapter 10 p.60]

10-70) C.

On a turboprop engine, torquemeter pressure is approximately proportional to the total power output and, thus, is used as a measure of engine performance. The torquemeter pressure gauge reading during the takeoff engine check is an important value. It is usually necessary to compute the takeoff power in the same manner as is done for a turbojet engine. This computation is to determine the maximum allowable exhaust gas temperature and the torquemeter pressure that a normally functioning engine should produce for the ambient air temperature and barometric pressure prevailing at the time.

[For more detailed information refer to Powerplant Handbook H-8083-32-ATB, Chapter 10 p.60]

10-71) A.

Some of the most important factors affecting turbine engine life are EGT, engine cycles, and engine speed. Excess EGT of a few degrees reduces turbine component life. The exhaust gas temperature needs to be as high as possible without damaging the turbine section of the engine.

[For more detailed information refer to Powerplant Handbook H-8083-32-ATB, Chapter 10 p.62]

Applicants for powerplant certification are required to answer oral examination questions before, after, or in conjunction with the practical examination portion of the airman certification process. The oral examination is used to establish knowledge. The practical examination is used to establish skill, which is the application of knowledge. Use the following questions to prepare for the oral examination. The questions are examples aligned with Practical Test Standards subject matter from which the examiner will choose topics for oral examination.

10-1(O). What is the probable cause of hydraulic lock and how is it remedied?

10-2(O). What checks are necessary to verify proper operation of a reciprocating engine?

10-3(O). Explain the checks necessary to verify proper operation of propeller systems.

10-4(O). What is involved with the correct installation of piston rings and what results if the rings are incorrectly installed or are worn?

10-5(O). What are some procedures for inspecting various engine components during overhaul?

10-6(O). What are the procedures for reciprocating engine maintenance as they pertain to overhauling an engine?

10-7(O). What are some checks necessary to verify proper operation of a turbine engine?

10-8(O). What are some turbine engine troubleshooting procedures?

10-9(O). What are some turbine engine maintenance procedures?

10-10(O). What is the possible problem with an engine that indicates high EGT (exhaust gas temperature) for a particular EPR (engine pressure ratio)?

10-11(O). What are the typical parameters sought for oil pressure when starting a reciprocating aircraft engine?

10-12(O). Explain the operation of a temperature indicating system on a turbine engine.

10-13(O). What is the operation of a turbine engine tachometer?

10-14(O). How is an EGT System checked for proper operation?

10-15(O). What is EPR and how is it instrumented on a gas turbine engine?

10-16(O). What can be done to check the accuracy of a turbine engine tachometer?

10-1(O). Answer: Whenever a radial engine remains shut down for more than a few minutes, oil or fuel may drain into the combustion chambers or intake pipes of the lower, downward extending cylinders. This is known as hydraulic lock. As the piston moves toward top center in these cylinders, it will collide with these incompressible liquids. Severe damage can be caused. The liquid must be removed to remedy the hydraulic lock and make it safe to start the engine. This is done by removing either the front or rear spark plugs of the affected cylinders and pulling the engine through by hand in the normal direction of rotation. Then the spark plugs are reinstalled and the engine is started.
Reference: FAA-H-8083-30-ATB Page 10-26

10-2(O). Answer: A ground check or power check is performed to evaluate the functioning of the engine by comparing power input as measured by manifold pressure with power output as measured by RPM (or torque) and comparing these to known acceptable values. It also includes checking the powerplant and accessory equipment by ear, visual inspection, and by proper interpretation of instrument readings, control movements, and switch reactions. Fuel pressure and oil pressure checks must verify that these pressures are within established tolerances. A cylinder compression test can be performed if it is suspected that there is a problem with valves, pistons or piston rings. A magneto safety check exposes problems with the ignition system. Idle speed and idle mixture checks can also be performed although these relate more to the proper functioning of the fuel system than the engine itself just as the magneto check focuses more on ignition system integrity.
Reference: FAA-H-8083-30-ATB Page 10-26 to 10-40

10-3(O). Answer: The propeller must be checked to ensure proper operation of the pitch control and pitch change mechanism. The operation of a controllable pitch propeller is checked by the indications of the tachometer and manifold pressure gauge when the proper governor control is moved from one position to another. Each propeller requires a different procedure. The applicable manufacturer's instructions should be followed.
Reference: FAA-H-8083-30-ATB Page 10-28

10-4(O). Answer: Piston rings prevent leakage of gas pressure from the combustion chamber while lubricating the cylinder walls and reducing to a minimum the seepage of oil into the combustion chamber. Worn or broken piston rings can cause excessive oil consumption and loss of compression. Oil blow-by into the combustion chamber can lead to sticking valves, spark plug misfiring, as well as detonation or pre-ignition due to carbonization of the oil. During installation, the rings are place in the proper grooves facing the correct direction according to the engine manufacturer's instructions. The ring gaps are staggered around the piston. They are compressed with a ring compressor to the diameter of the piston as the cylinder is slid down around the piston making sure that the cylinder and piston plane remain the same. As the cylinder is lowered around the piston with a straight, even motion, it displaces the ring compressor as the rings slide into the bore. Rocking or forcing the cylinder over the piston and rings could cause a ring to escape from the ring compressor and expand or it could crack or chip a ring or damage the ring land.
[pages 10-14 to 43

10-5(O). Answer: There are 3 basic categories of inspection during overhaul: visual, structural non-destructive testing (NDT) and dimensional. The first inspection to be done is the visual inspection. A preliminary visual inspection should be performed before cleaning the parts since indications of failure may often be detected from the residual deposits of metallic particles in some recesses of the engine. Then, parts can be cleaned and visually inspected. Structural inspections can be performed on parts by methods such as magnetic particle inspection, dye penetrant, eddy current, ultra sound, and x-ray as specified by the manufacturer. Finally, using very accurate measuring equipment, each engine component can be dimensionally evaluated and compared to the service limits and tolerances set by the manufacturer.
Reference: FAA-H-8083-30-ATB Page 10-3

10-6(O). Answer: Aircraft engine maintenance practices, including overhaul, are performed at specified intervals established by the manufacturer. For an overhauled engine to be as airworthy as a new engine, worn and damaged parts must be detected and replaced. This is done by completely disassembling the engine. Visual, non-destructive, and dimensional inspections are performed. The manufacturer publishes inspection criterion and a new minimum and serviceable dimension for all critical component parts. Parts that do not meet these standards must be rejected for use in the engine. A major overhaul of an engine consists of the complete reconditioning of the powerplant. This includes disassembly of the crankcase for access and inspection/rework of the crankshaft and bearings. It is not a major repair and can be performed or supervised by a certified powerplant technician as long as the engine does not contain an internal supercharger or propeller reduction other than spur-type gears. At the time of an engine overhaul, all accessories are removed, overhauled, and tested in accordance with the accessory manufacturer's instructions.
Reference: FAA-H-8083-30-ATB Page 10-1 to 10-2

10-7(O). Answer: The manufacturer's operating instructions should be consulted before attempting to start and operate any turbine engine. Checking turbofan engines for proper operation consists primarily of simply reading the engine instruments and then comparing the value with those known to be correct for a particular operating condition. Be sure the engine and instrument indications have stabilized. Idling speed must be checked (tachometer) as well as oil pressure and EGT (exhaust gas temperature). Engine pressure ratio (EPR) measures thrust and is used to set takeoff power. It varies with ambient temperature and pressure. Takeoff thrust is checked by adjusting the throttle to obtain a single, predicted, indication on the EPR (engine pressure ratio) gauge. This can be computed from the takeoff thrust setting curve in the operations manual. It can be done at full power or when the throttle is set at the part power stop. If an engine develops the predicted thrust and if all the other engine instruments are indicating within their proper ranges, engine operation is considered satisfactory. On newer aircraft, performance is a function of the onboard computer. FADEC engines have means for checking the engine and displaying the results on the flight deck.
Reference: FAA-H-8083-30-ATB Page 10-56 to 10-58

10-8(O). Answer: Turbine engine troubleshooting should be performed in accordance with the engine manufacturer's instructions. Trouble shooting charts exist to guide the technician. Engine analyzers are manufactured that can assist with calibration and the accuracy of important engine parameter indicators such as RPM and EGT. Follow the analyzer manufacturer's instructions.
Reference: FAA-H-8083-30-ATB Page 10-60 to 10-66

10-9(O). Answer: The detailed procedures recommended by the engine manufacturer should be followed when performing inspections or maintenance on a turbine engine. Some common functions include periodic inspection, cleaning and repair of compressor components which can have performance reduction due being dirty and foreign object damage (FOD). Compressor blades, inducers, and guide vanes all may be damaged. The extent of the damage must be ascertained. Repairable damage limits set by the manufacturer must be adhered to and various NDT methods may need to be employed. The possibility exists to rework or blend out damage using stones usually blending parallel to the length of the component. Combustion section inspection and cleaning is very important since the serviceability of the combustion section is a controlling factor in the service life of a turbine engine. Inspection for hot spots, exhaust leaks and distortions can be done without opening the case. After the case has been opened, inspection for localized overheating, cracks, and excessive wear are important. Evidence of FOD can be found even in the combustion section. Hot section inspections, which include the turbine section components, usually are required at regular intervals. Follow the manufacturer's instructions for procedures and damage limits. This is applicable for fuel nozzles, turbine disks, blades, and guide vanes as well as the exhaust section components.
Reference: FAA-H-8083-30-ATB Page 10-46 to 10-55

10-10(O). Answer: The engine is likely out of trim. The accuracy of the EGT gauge/sensors could also be in question and should be checked.
Reference: FAA-H-8083-30-ATB Page 10-61 to 10-66

10-11(O). Answer: Oil pressure indication should occur within 30 seconds of start-up. Normal oil pressure indication should occur within 1 minute of start-up or the engine should be shut down.
Reference: FAA-H-8083-30-ATB Page 10-26 to 10-27

10-12(O). Answer: Temperature of turbine engine gases entering the first stage turbine inlet guide vanes is the most critical of all engine variables. In many engines, it is impractical to measure the temperature exactly at this point. Relative temperatures that are proportional to this temperature are measured instead. EGT, TGT, TOT, and TIT are all such indications. Accuracy of temperature indication in this portion of the engine is critical because if it is too high, the engine could be destroyed. If is too low, insufficient power will be developed. A series of individual thermocouple probes located around the engine section where the temperature is measured are connected to a gauge on the flight deck. The gauge shows the average temperature measured by the thermocouples. This assists in producing an accurate indication. This indication is so important that testing of the individual thermostats, the indicator, and the entire indicating system is done periodically. An analyzer test box capable of measuring the accuracy of all thermocouple components and the entire system is used.
Reference: FAA-H-8083-30-ATB Page 10-56

10-13(O). Answer: Gas turbine engine speeds are measured by the RPM of each turbine-compressor spool and are displayed on the flight deck. Percent of RPM is used rather than the actual RPM so that various types of engines can be operated on the same basis of comparison. Also, turbine engine speeds are very high and percent RPM simplifies monitoring. Some tachometers measure RPM using a rotating tachometer generator that is geared to the engine. The frequency of the generator output is proportional to the engine speed. Another (newer) type of tachometer uses a magnetic pickup that counts passing gear teeth edges, which are seen electrically as pulses of electrical power as they pass by the pick-up. By counting the number of pulses, the shaft RPM is obtained. Clearance between the gear teeth and the magnetic pickup must be maintained for accuracy.
Reference: FAA-H-8083-30-ATB Page 10-56 to 10-65

10-14(O). Answer: A calibrated test analyzer unit is used to check the EGT system and components for proper operation. The unit contains heater probes and built-in thermocouples against which the accuracy of the aircraft thermocouples is compared. The analyzer also is capable of checking the continuity of the system and the accuracy of the EGT indicator on the flight deck. Resistance and insulation checks are also made. Follow the instructions that come with the test analyzer unit being used.
Reference: FAA-H-8083-30-ATB Page 10-64 to 10-65

10-15(O). Answer: EPR stands for engine pressure ratio. It is an indication of thrust developed by a turbofan engine and is used to set power for takeoff on many types of aircraft. It is instrumented by total pressure pickups located in the engine inlet (P2) and in the turbine exhaust (P7). The indication is displayed on the flight deck on the EPR gauge, which is used in making engine power settings.
Reference: FAA-H-8083-30-ATB Page 10-56

10-16(O). Answer: A calibrated test analyzer unit can be used to check the tachometer of a turbine engine. The scale of the RPM check circuit is calibrated in percent RPM to correspond to the aircraft tachometer indicator. The aircraft tachometer and the RPM check circuit are connected in parallel and both are indicating during engine run-up. The RPM check circuit indication is compared with the aircraft tachometer indication to

Applicants for powerplant certification are required to demonstrate the ability to apply knowledge by performing maintenance related tasks for the examiner. The Practical Test Standards (PTS) list the subject areas from which the skill elements to be performed by the applicant are chosen. The following examples resemble tasks an examiner may ask an applicant to perform. The Performance Level required to be demonstrated for each skill element is listed. Consult the PTS for Level descriptions.

10-1(P). Given an actual aircraft engine or mockup, appropriate publications, and tooling inspect a reciprocating engine installation and record findings. [Level 3]

10-2(P). Given an actual aircraft engine or mockup, appropriate publications, and tooling inspect a turbine engine installation and record findings. [Level 3]

10-3(P). Given an actual aircraft engine or mockup, appropriate publications, and a bore scope inspect a turbine engine and record findings. [Level 3]

10-4(P). Given an actual aircraft engine or mockup, appropriate publications, and tooling determine the proper crankshaft flange run-out and record findings. [Level 3]

10-5(P). Given an actual aircraft engine or mockup, an airworthiness directive, and required tooling inspect an engine in accordance with the airworthiness directive and record findings. [Level 2]

10-6(P). Given an actual aircraft engine or mockup, appropriate publications, and tooling inspect a turbine engine compressor section and record findings. [Level 3]

10-7(P). Given an actual aircraft engine or mockup, appropriate publications, and tooling inspect a crankcase for cracks and record findings. [Level 3]

10-8(P). Given an actual aircraft engine or mockup, appropriate publications, and tooling inspect a crankshaft oil seal for leaks and record findings. [Level 3]

10-9(P). Given an actual aircraft engine or mockup, appropriate publications, and tooling complete an engine conformity inspection and record findings. [Level 3]

10-10(P). Given an actual aircraft engine or mockup, appropriate publications, and tooling complete an engine airworthiness inspection and record findings. [Level 3]

10-11(P). Given an actual aircraft engine or mockup, appropriate publications, and tooling perform an inspection on a mechanical and/or electrical temperature system and record findings. [Level 3]

10-12(P). Given an actual aircraft engine or mockup, appropriate publications, and tooling perform an inspection on a mechanical and/or electrical pressure system and record findings. [Level 3]

10-13(P). Given an actual aircraft engine or mockup, appropriate publications, and tooling perform an inspection on a mechanical and/or electrical RPM system and record findings. [Level 3]

10-14(P). Given an actual aircraft engine or mockup, appropriate publications, and tooling perform an inspection on a mechanical and/or electrical rate of flow system and record findings. [Level 3]

10-15(P). Given an actual aircraft engine or mockup, appropriate publications, and tooling verify the proper operation and marking of an indicating system and record findings. [Level 2]

10-16(P). Given an actual aircraft engine or mockup, appropriate publications, and tooling replace a temperature sending unit and record maintenance. [Level 3]

10-17(P). Given an actual aircraft engine or mockup, appropriate publications, and tooling troubleshoot an oil pressure indicating system and record findings. [Level 3]

10-18(P). Given an actual aircraft engine or mockup, appropriate publications, and tooling locate and inspect fuel flow components on an engine and record findings. [Level 2]

10-19(P). Given an actual aircraft engine or mockup, appropriate publications, and tooling replace an exhaust gas temperature (EGT) indication probe and record maintenance. [Level 3]

10-20(P). Given an actual aircraft engine or mockup, appropriate publications, and tooling troubleshoot a manifold pressure gage that is slow to indicate the correct reading and record findings. [Level 2]

10-21(P). Given an actual aircraft engine or mockup, appropriate publications, and tooling remove, inspect, and install fuel flow transmitter and record maintenance and findings. [Level 3]

Light-Sport Aircraft Engines

Types of Light-Sport and Experimental Engines, Opposed Engines, Direct Drive VW Engines, Maintenance, Lubrication, Preservation

11-1) AMG087
A light sport aircraft means an aircraft, other than rotorcraft or power-lift, that

    A. has a maximum occupancy of no more than four people.
    B. is powered by a single reciprocating engine if powered.
    C. has a maximum takeoff weight not exceeding 1000 pounds.

11-2) AMG066
A light sport aircraft engine

    A. must be certified by the FAA.
    B. normally meets FAA or ASTM standards.
    C. by definition, is not certified by the FAA.

11-3) AMG059
Who may perform an annual condition inspection on a light sport aircraft?

    A. Only an FAA certificated airframe and powerplant mechanic.
    B. The owner of the light sport aircraft who has completed the FAA approved training course for the aircraft in question.
    C. Only an FAA certified airframe and powerplant mechanic with an inspection authorization.

11-4) AMP056
Of the following, which are true of small, in-line, light-sport aircraft engines?
1. Water- cooled only.
2. Most are 2 cycle engines.
3. They have constant speed propellers.
4. Use a single crankshaft.
5. Are radial in design.

    A. 1, 2, and 5.
    B. 2, 4, and 5.
    C. 2 and 4.

11-5) AMP063
The Rotax 447, 503, and 582 engines all have breaker-less magneto capacitor discharge ignition systems, however, the larger engines have

    A. dual ignition for each cylinder.
    B. a standby secondary ignition that uses breaker ignition should the primary fail.
    C. have a single ignition system with a higher power output.

11-6) AMP027
A liquid cooling system is employed on the Rotax 582 series engine. Circulation of the coolant is accomplished by

    A. a ram air driven pump.
    B. the external oil/water dual pump.
    C. an integrated engine water pump.

11-1) B.

A light sport aircraft is an aircraft that has a single reciprocating engine if it is a powered aircraft. Its maximum seating capacity is no more than two people. The maximum takeoff weight of a light sport aircraft is no more than 1320 pounds for an aircraft not intended for operation on water; or 1430 pounds for an aircraft intended for operation on water.

[For more detailed information refer to Powerplant Handbook H-8083-32-ATB, Chapter 11 p.2]

11-2) B.

The manufacturer of a light sport aircraft engine ensures the reliability and durability of the product by design, research and testing. Although most of these engines are not certified by the FAA, close control of manufacturing and assembly procedures is generally maintained. Normally, each engine is tested before it leaves factory and meets certain American Society for Testing and Materials (ASTM) standards. Some engines used on light sport aircraft are certified by the FAA and these engines are maintained as per the manufacturer's instructions and Title 14 of the Code of Federal Regulations (14 CFR).

[For more detailed information refer to Powerplant Handbook H-8083-32-ATB, Chapter 11 p.2]

11-3) B.

The holder of a repairman certificate (light-sport aircraft) with an inspection rating, may perform the annual condition inspection on a light-sport aircraft that is owned by the holder, has been issued an experimental certificate for operating a light-sport aircraft under 14 CFR part 21, section 21.191(i), and is in the same class of light sport aircraft for which the holder has completed the required training.

[For more detailed information refer to Powerplant Handbook H-8083-32-ATB, Chapter 11 p.3]

11-4) C.

Light-sport/ultralight aircraft engines can be classified by several methods, such as by operating cycles, cylinder arrangement, and air or water cooled. An inline engine generally has two cylinders, is two cycle, and is available in several horsepower ranges. These engines may be either liquid cooled, air cooled, or a combination of both. They have only one crankshaft that drives the reduction gear box or propeller directly. Most of the other cylinder configurations used on light-sport aircraft are larger, horizontally opposed, ranging from two to six cylinders from several manufacturer's. The engines are either gear reduction or direct drive.

[For more detailed information refer to Powerplant Handbook H-8083-32-ATB, Chapter 11 p.4]

11-5) A.

The typical ignition system on the Rotax 447 and 503 is a breaker-less ignition with a dual ignition system used on the 503, and a single ignition system used on the 447 engine series. Both systems are of a magneto capacitor discharge design. The larger Rotax 582 also has a dual ignition using breaker-less magneto capacitor discharge design.

[For more detailed information refer to Powerplant Handbook H-8083-32-ATB, Chapter 11 p.5]

11-6) C.

The cooling system of a Rotax 582 engine is in a two circuit arrangement. The cooling liquid is supplied by an integrated pump in the engine through the cylinders and the cylinder head to the radiator. An expansion tank, radiator, and overflow bottle work together to remove vapor and allow for expansion of the coolant.

[For more detailed information refer to Powerplant Handbook H-8083-32-ATB, Chapter 11 p.5-6]

11-7) AMP030
Being two-stroke cycle engines, light-sport aircraft engines operate on a mix of oil and gasoline that is delivered to the carburetor via gravity feed, or

    A.   use an oil-free piston design.
    B.   use an oil injection system.
    C.   mix the oil and gas in the carburetor.

11-8) AMP039
The typical fuel to oil ratio for a two-stroke cycle light-sport aircraft engine is

    A.   50 to 1.
    B.   25 to 1.
    C.   10 to 1.

11-9) AMP027
The Rotax 914 engine is a lightweight, four cylinder opposed engine that

    A.   is water cooled.
    B.   is air cooled.
    C.   has water cooled heads and air cooled cylinder barrels.

11-10) AMP063
The breaker-less capacitor discharge ignition systems with integrated generators used on most Rotax engines

    A.   require battery power to function.
    B.   are completely free of maintenance.
    C.   must have clearances checked every 100 hours.

11-11) AMP050
A unique manufacturing feature of the Jabiru light-sport engines is

    A.   most parts are machined from solid material.
    B.   mostly titanium is utilized.
    C.   that a great amount of aluminum is used to keep weight to a minimum.

11-12) AMP008
The HKS 700T, the Jabiru 2200, and 3300 all share what common feature?

    A.   They are four stroke engines.
    B.   They are two stroke engines.
    C.   They are all FAA certified engines.

11-13) AMP056
Which of the following light-sport aircraft engines begin as automobile engine which are then remanufactured and modified for aircraft use?
1. HKS 700T
2. Jabiru 3300
3. Revmaster R2300
4. Aeromax Aviation 100IFB
5. Great Plains 2276
6. Continental 0-200

    A.   2, 3, 4, and 5.
    B.   4, 5, and 6.
    C.   3, 4, and 5.

11-7) B.
Some light-sport aircraft engines use oil injection systems that use an oil pump driven by the crankshaft via the pump gear that feeds the engine with the correct amount of fresh oil. The oil pump is a piston-type pump with a metering system. Diffuser jets in the intake inject pump supplied two-stroke oil with the exact proportioned quantity needed. The oil quantity in the oil tank must be checked before operating the engine as the oil is consumed during operation and needs to be replenished regularly.
[For more detailed information refer to Powerplant Handbook H-8083-32-ATB, Chapter 11 p.6]

11-8) A.
Generally, smaller two-cycle engines are designed to run on a mixture of gasoline and 2 percent oil that is premixed before supplying the fuel tank. Therefore, the engines are planned to run on a gasoline–oil mixture of 50:1.
[For more detailed information refer to Powerplant Handbook H-8083-32-ATB, Chapter 11 p.6-7]

11-9) C.
The cooling system of the Rotax 914 is designed for liquid cooling of the cylinder heads and ram-air cooling of the cylinders.
[For more detailed information refer to Powerplant Handbook H-8083-32-ATB, Chapter 11 p.7]

11-10) B.
Most Rotax engines are equipped with a dual ignition unit that uses breaker-less, capacitor discharge design with an integrated generator. The ignition unit is completely free of maintenance and needs no external power. Two independent charging coils located on the generator stator supply one ignition circuit each. The energy is stored in capacitors of the electronic modules. At the moment of ignition, two each of the four external trigger coils actuate the discharge of the capacitors via the primary circuit of the dual ignition coils. A fifth trigger coil is used to provide a revolution counter signal.
[For more detailed information refer to Powerplant Handbook H-8083-32-ATB, Chapter 11 p.8]

11-11) A.
Jabiru engines use the latest manufacturing techniques. All Jabiru engines are manufactured, assembled and run on a dynamometer, and calibrated before delivery. The crankcase halves, cylinder heads, crankshaft, starter motor housing, gearbox cover, together with many smaller components are machined from solid material. The sump (oil pan) is the only casting. The cylinders are machined from bar 4140 chrome molybdenum alloy steel as are the crankshaft and camshaft.
[For more detailed information refer to Powerplant Handbook H-8083-32-ATB, Chapter 11 p.10-11]

11-12) A.
The larger light-sport aircraft engines, generally opposed four and six cylinder models, are 4 stroke cycle engines. HKS and Jabiru engines are not FAA certified.
[For more detailed information refer to Powerplant Handbook H-8083-32-ATB, Chapter 11 p.10-12]

11-13) C.
Many engines used on light sport aircraft are engines originally designed for use in automobiles. The Aeromax Aviation 100IFB was originally a General Motors Corvair engine. Many modifications and new parts, including a specially made integral front bearing (IFB) allow the manufacturer to take advantage of this engine's opposed six-cylinder configuration. Revmaster and Great Plains both use Volkswagon automobile engines. The Continental, Jabiru and HKS engines are designed and purpose built for aircraft.
[For more detailed information refer to Powerplant Handbook H-8083-32-ATB, Chapter 11 p.10-16]

11-14) AMP060

Great Plains engines for light sport aircraft are

  A. completely assembles in the manufacturer's facility.
  B. assembled in the field from manufacturer kits or by the manufacturer.
  C. are certified by the FAA.

11-15) AMP056

In addition to its FAA certified engines, Lycoming Engines produces an experimental, non-certified version of its O-233 series engine for light sport aircraft. It features

  A. capability of running on AVGAS or unleaded automotive fuel.
  B. breaker ignition.
  C. high performance but lower time between overhaul.

11-16) AMP058

Maintenance and inspections on light-sport aircraft

  A. are set up by the owner operator.
  B. are less detailed than with certified aircraft.
  C. must be recorded in the aircraft maintenance logbook.

11-17) AMP023

On a light-sport aircraft with two carburetors, carburetor synchronization must be performed as follows:

  A. pneumatic synchronization first, then mechanical synchronization.
  B. mechanical synchronization first, the pneumatic synchronization.
  C. perform mechanical and pneumatic synchronization with the compensating tube connected.

11-18) AMP023

In addition to idle speed adjustment during synchronization,

  A. full takeoff RMP must be able to be obtained.
  B. mixture must be check with full carburetor heat ON.
  C. cruise RPM and mixture must be verified.

11-19) AMP031

Prior to an oil level check on a dry sump engine,

  A. motor the engine with the starter to ensure even distribution.
  B. disconnect the ignition switch.
  C. turn the propeller by hand several times to pump the oil from the engine to the oil tank.

11-20) AMP007

In addition to changing oil regularly, the condition of an engine can be

  A. improved by reducing the maximum RPM of operations.
  B. detected with an ultra-sound inspection.
  C. discerned by the amount of metal chips found on the magnetic chip detector.

11 - Light-Sport Aircraft Engines
Answers

11-14) B.
Great Plains is a company that specializes in the conversion of Volkswagon automobile engines for use in aircraft. They offer kits with instructions for the aviator to build up an engine in the field. They will also build the engine for the customer is so chosen. Great Plains offers engine kits for all Type One Volkswagon engines ranging from 1600cc up through 2276cc (cubic centimeters).
[For more detailed information refer to Powerplant Handbook H-8083-32-ATB, Chapter 11 p.15]

11-15) A.
The Lycoming 0-233 series light sport aircraft engine is light and capable of running on AVGAS or unleaded automotive fuel. It features dual CDI spark ignition, an optimized oil sump, a streamlined accessory housing, hydraulically adjusted tappets, a lightweight starter, and a lightweight alternator with integral voltage regulator. It has proven a very reliable engine with a TBO of 2400 hours.
[For more detailed information refer to Powerplant Handbook H-8083-32-ATB, Chapter 11 p.16]

11-16) C.
Most light-sport aircraft engines require a definite time interval between overhauls. This is specified or implied by the engine manufacturer. Checks and maintenance that are performed should be accomplished in accordance with a maintenance checklist and all actions should be recorded in the aircraft maintenance logbook by the person or company performing the work.
[For more detailed information refer to Powerplant Handbook H-8083-32-ATB, Chapter 11 p.17]

11-17) B.
Mechanical synchronization always is performed first when synchronizing carburetors. Then, the two carburetors are adjusted to equal flow rates at idle by use of a suitable flow meter or vacuum gauges. The compensating tube between the carburetors is typically removed to install the gauges.
[For more detailed information refer to Powerplant Handbook H-8083-32-ATB, Chapter 11 p.18]

11-18) A.
Once the proper idling speed has been established, it is necessary to check the operating range above the idle speed. First, establish that the engine is developing full takeoff performance or takeoff RPM when selected on the flight deck. Then, the setting of the operating range (idle to full throttle) can be checked or adjusted.
[For more detailed information refer to Powerplant Handbook H-8083-32-ATB, Chapter 11 p.19]

11-19) C.
Before checking the engine oil level, make sure that there is not excess residual oil in the crankcase. Prior to oil level check, turn the propeller several times by hand in the direction of engine rotation to pump all of the oil from the engine to the oil tank. This process is complete when air flows back to the oil tank.
[For more detailed information refer to Powerplant Handbook H-8083-32-ATB, Chapter 11 p.20]

11-20) C.
The engine's magnetic chip detector should be removed and inspected for the accumulation of magnetic particles. This inspection is important because it allows conclusions to be drawn on the internal condition of the gearbox and engine, and it reveals information about possible damage. If a significant amount of metal chips are detected, the engine must be inspected, repaired or overhauled.
[For more detailed information refer to Powerplant Handbook H-8083-32-ATB, Chapter 11 p.21]

Applicants for powerplant certification are required to answer oral examination questions before, after, or in conjunction with the practical examination portion of the airman certification process. The oral examination is used to establish knowledge. The practical examination is used to establish skill, which is the application of knowledge. Use the following questions to prepare for the oral examination. The questions are examples aligned with Practical Test Standards subject matter from which the examiner will choose topics for oral examination.

Note: The FAA has not yet released PRACTICAL TEST STANDARDS for light-sport aircraft engines. The following questions are anticipated to satisfy such standards once released by the FAA.

11-1(O). Name some characteristics and types of light-sport aircraft engines.

11-2(O). How is maintenance recording accomplished on a light-sport aircraft?

11-3(O). What type of oil system is often found on light-sport aircraft engines and what should be done before checking the oil level?

11-4(O). In what way does the certified technician deviate from manufacturer's instructions when maintaining a light-sport aircraft engine?

11-1(O). Light sport aircraft engines can be classified in many ways. They are usually in-line or opposed in cylinder configuration. Both two-cycle and four-cycle engine are used. Cooling can be liquid-cooled or air-cooled or a combination of both. There is only one crankshaft. Fixed pitch or ground adjustable propellers are used with the exception of an auto-feathering propeller being allowable on a glider. The engines for light-sport aircraft come in various sizes. They utilize various fuels from automobile gas to 100LL– the manufacturer specified fuel is required. Ignition is usually breaker-less capacitor-discharge type. Turbo charging is possible. Some engine are converted automobile engines.
Reference: H-8083-32-ATB Page 11-4 to 11-16

11-2(O). Maintenance requirements and recording on light-sport aircraft is very similar to that of aircraft certified in the standard aircraft category. Manufacturer's checklists and instructions are always used and required. Checklists and work orders for inspections and work accomplished must be recorded and kept in the maintenance records as well as recorded in the logbook. The technician must sign these records. It is the responsibility of the owner operator to store and maintain these records. Execution of service bulletins must also be entered in the logbook.
Reference: H-8083-32-ATB Page 11-17

11-3(O). Dry sump oil systems are common on light-sport aircraft engines. Two-cycle engines are often used on light-sport aircraft. These engines use oil mixed with the fuel to lubricate the engine. On some models, the oil is mixed with the fuel before it is poured into the fuel tank. However, on other models, the dry sump reservoir feeds an oil injection system that supplies the engine with the required lubrication oil. Usually, oil metering is directed in relation to throttle position supplying more oil when engine speed is high. By turning the engine through by hand before checking the oil quantity in the reservoir, residual oil in the system can be returned to establish an accurate quantity level.
Reference: H-8083-32-ATB Page 11-6 to 11-21

11-4(O). The powerplant technician must not deviate from the manufacturer's instructions for maintenance of a light-sport aircraft engine. The technician should maintain the aircraft according to manufacturer's schedules and specifications.
Reference: H-8083-32-ATB Page 11-3 to 11-23

Applicants for powerplant certification are required to demonstrate the ability to apply knowledge by performing maintenance related tasks for the examiner. The Practical Test Standards (PTS) list the subject areas from which the skill elements to be performed by the applicant are chosen. The following examples resemble tasks an examiner may ask an applicant to perform. The Performance Level required to be demonstrated for each skill element is listed. Consult the PTS for Level descriptions.

11-1(P). Given an actual aircraft engine or mockup, appropriate publications, and tooling, inspect a light-sport aircraft engine installation and record findings. [Level 3]

11-2(P). Given an actual aircraft engine or mockup, appropriate publications, and tooling, inspect the automatic lubrication system on a light-sport aircraft engine. [Level 3]

11-3(P). Given an actual aircraft engine or mockup, appropriate publications, and tooling, inspect excess pressure valve operation and the cooling system for proper operation and cooling on a light-sport aircraft engine and record findings. [Level 3]

11-4(P). Given an actual aircraft engine or mockup, appropriate publications, and tooling determine the proper crankshaft flange run-out on a light-sport aircraft engine and record findings. [Level 3]

11-5(P). Given an actual aircraft engine or mockup, an airworthiness directive, and required tooling inspect a light-sport aircraft engine installation in accordance with the airworthiness directive and record findings. [Level 2]

11-6(P). Given an actual aircraft engine or mockup, appropriate publications, and tooling check and adjust carburetor synchronization of a light-sport aircraft engine and record findings and maintenance performed. [Level 3]

11-7(P). Given an actual aircraft engine or mockup, appropriate publications, and tooling, inspect Bowden cables for proper routing, actuation and lubrication on a light-sport aircraft engine and recording record findings and maintenance performed. [Level 3]

11-8(P). Given an actual aircraft engine or mockup, appropriate publications, and tooling, perform an oil change on a light-sport aircraft engine and record findings and maintenance performed. [Level 3]

11-9(P). Given an actual aircraft engine or mockup, appropriate publications, and tooling, inspect the magnetic plug on a light-sport aircraft engine for accumulation of metallic chips and record findings. [Level 3]

11- 10(P). Given an actual aircraft engine or mockup, appropriate publications, and tooling, inspect the fuel system pressure control and return lines on a light-sport aircraft engine for proper operation and record findings. [Level 3]

11-11(P). Given an actual aircraft engine or mockup, appropriate publications, and tooling, perform a frictional torque check in free rotation of the overload clutch on a light-sport aircraft engine and record findings. [Level 3]

11-12(P). Given an actual aircraft engine or mockup, appropriate publications, and tooling, perform a cylinder compression check on a light-sport aircraft engine system and record findings. [Level 3]

Aviation Mechanic Powerplant

Practical Test Standards FAA-S-8081-28, Effective June 1, 2003
With changes 1 and 2

A. RECIPROCATING ENGINES

REFERENCES: AC 65-12A; JSPT.

Objective. To determine that the applicant:

1. Exhibits knowledge of at least two of the following—
    a. reciprocating engine theory of operation.
    b. basic radial engine design, components, and/or operation.
    c. firing order of a reciprocating engine.
    d. probable cause and removal of a hydraulic lock.
    e. valve adjustment on a radial engine.
    f. purpose of master and/or articulating rods.
    g. checks necessary to verify proper operation of a reciprocating engine.
    h. induction system leak indications.
    i. reciprocating engine maintenance procedures.
    j. procedures for inspecting various engine components during an overhaul.
    k. correct installation of piston rings and results of incorrectly installed or worn rings.
    l. purpose/function/operation of various reciprocating engine components, including, but not limited to, any of the following: crankshaft dynamic dampers, multiple springs for valves, piston rings, and reduction gearing.

2. N/A

3. Demonstrates the ability to perform at least one of the following—
    a. measure the valve clearance on a reciprocating aircraft engine when the lifters are deflated. (Level 2)
    b. accomplish a compression test, and note all findings. (Level 3)
    c. inspect engine control cables and/ or push-pull tubes for proper rigging. (Level 3)
    d. inspect ring gap, install piston rings on a piston, and install an aircraft engine cylinder. (Level 3)
    e. dimensionally inspect an aircraft engine component. (Level 3)
    f. replace/install one or more aircraft engine components. (Level 3)

B. TURBINE ENGINES

Objective. To determine that the applicant:

1. Exhibits knowledge of at least two of the following—
    a. turbine engine theory of operation.
    b. checks necessary to verify proper operation.
    c. turbine engine troubleshooting procedures.
    d. procedures required after the installation of a turbine engine.
    e. causes for turbine engine performance loss.

    f.   purpose/function/operation of various turbine engine components.

    g.   turbine engine maintenance procedures.

2. N/A

3. Demonstrates the ability to perform at least one of the following:

    a.   repair a turbine engine compressor blade by blending. (Level 3)

    b.   remove and/or install a turbine engine component. (Level 3)

    c.   determine cycle life remaining between overhaul of a turbine engine life limited component. (Level 2)

    d.   check rigging of a turbine engine inlet guide vane system. (Level 3)

    e.   measure compressor or turbine blade clearance. (Level 3)

    f.   troubleshoot a turbine engine. (Level 3)

    g.   locate and identify turbine engine components. (Level 2)

    h.   inspect turbine engine components. (Level 3)

NOTE: T. AUXILIARY POWER UNITS may be tested at the same time as AREA B. No further testing of auxiliary power units is required.

C. ENGINE INSPECTION
*Core competency element
REFERENCES: AC 43.13-1B; 14 CFR part 43.
Objective. To determine that the applicant:

1. Exhibits knowledge of at least two of the following—

    a.   the use of a type certificate data sheet (TCDS) to identify engine accessories.

    b.   requirements for the installation or modification in accordance with a supplemental type certificate (STC).

    c.   procedures for accomplishing a 100-hour inspection in accordance with the manufacturer's instruction.

    d.   compliance with airworthiness directives.

    e.   changes to an inspection program due to a change or modification required by airworthiness directive or service bulletin.

    f.   determination of life limited parts.

    g.   inspection required after a potentially damaging event, including but not limited to any of the following: sudden stoppage, overspeed, or overtemperature.

2. *Demonstrates the ability to perform inspection of a reciprocating and/or turbine engine installation in accordance with the manufacturer's instructions. (Level 3)

3. Demonstrates the ability to perform at least one of the following—

    a.   inspect a turbine engine using a bore scope. (Level 3)

    b.   determine proper crankshaft flange run-out. (Level 3)

    c.   inspect an engine in accordance with applicable airworthiness directive. (Level 2)

    d.   inspect a turbine engine compressor section. (Level 3)

    e.   inspect a crankcase for cracks. (Level 3)

    f.   inspect a crankshaft oil seal for leaks. (Level 3)

    g.   engine conformity inspection. (Level 3)

    h.   engine airworthiness inspection. (Level 3)

SECTION V—POWERPLANT SYSTEMS AND COMPONENTS

H. ENGINE INSTRUMENT SYSTEMS
*Core competency element
REFERENCES: AGTP; AC 65-15A.
Objective. To determine that the applicant:

1. Exhibits knowledge of at least two of the following—
   a. troubleshoot a fuel flow and/or low fuel pressure indicating system.
   b. the operation of a fuel flow indicating system and where it is connected to the engine.
   c. the operation of a temperature indicating system.
   d. the operation of a pressure indicating system.
   e. the operation of an RPM indicating system.
   f. required checks to verify proper operation of a temperature indicating system.
   g. required checks to verify proper operation of a pressure indicating system.
   h. required checks to verify proper operation of an RPM indicating system.
   i. the operation of a manifold pressure gage and where it actually connects to an engine.

2. *Demonstrates the ability to perform inspection of engine electrical and/or mechanical instrument systems to include at least one of the following (Level 3)—
   a. temperature.
   b. pressure.
   c. RPM.
   d. rate of flow.

3. Demonstrates the ability to perform at least one of the following—
   a. verify proper operation and marking of an indicating system. (Level 2)
   b. replace a temperature sending unit. (Level 3)
   c. remove, inspect, and install fuel flow transmitter. (Level 3)
   d. troubleshoot an oil pressure indicating system. (Level 3)
   e. locate and inspect fuel flow components on an engine. (Level 2)
   f. replace an exhaust gas temperature (EGT) indication probe. (Level 3)
   g. troubleshoot a manifold pressure gage that is slow to indicate the correct reading. (Level 2)

I. ENGINE FIRE PROTECTION SYSTEMS

REFERENCES: AP; JSPT.
Objective. To determine that the applicant:

1. Exhibits knowledge of at least two of the following—
   a. checks to verify proper operation of an engine fire detection and/or extinguishing system.
   b. troubleshoots an engine fire detection and/or extinguishing system.
   c. inspection requirements for an engine fire extinguisher squib and safety practices/precautions.
   d. components and/or operation of an engine fire detection and/or extinguishing system.
   e. engine fire detection and/or extinguishing system maintenance procedures.

2. N/A

3. Demonstrates the ability to perform at least one of the following:

    a.   check an engine fire detection and/or extinguishing system for proper operation. (Level 2)

    b.   accomplish weight and pressure inspection of an engine fire bottle, and verify hydrostatic inspection date. (Level 2)

    c.   repair an engine fire detector heat sensing loop malfunction. (Level 3)

    d.   check operation of firewall shut-off valve after a fire handle is pulled. (Level 2)

    e.   troubleshoot an engine fire detection or extinguishing system. (Level 2)

    f.   inspect an engine fire detection or extinguishing system. (Level 2)

J. ENGINE ELECTRICAL SYSTEMS
REFERENCES: AP; JSPT.

Objective. To determine that the applicant:

1. Exhibits knowledge of at least two of the following—

    a.   generator rating and performance data location.

    b.   operation of a turbine engine starter-generator.

    c.   the procedure for locating the correct electrical cable/wire size needed to fabricate a replacement cable/wire.

    d.   installation practices for wires running close to exhaust stacks or heating ducts.

    e.   operation of engine electrical system components.

    f.   types of and/or components of D.C. motors.

    g.   inspection and/or replacement of starter-generator brushes.

2. N/A

3. Demonstrates the ability to perform at least one of the following—

    a.   flash a generator field. (Level 3)

    b.   install an engine driven generator or alternator. (Level 3)

    c.   use of an engine electrical wiring schematic. (Level 2)

    d.   accomplish the installation of a tach generator. (Level 3)

    e.   fabricate an electrical system cable. (Level 3)

    f.   repair a damaged engine electrical system wire. (Level 3)

    g.   replace and check a current limiter. (Level 3)

    h.   check/service/adjust one or more engine electrical system components. (Level 3)

    i.   troubleshoot an engine electrical system component. (Level 3)

K. LUBRICATION SYSTEMS
REFERENCES: JSPT; AP.

Objective. To determine that the applicant:

1. Exhibits knowledge of at least two of the following—

    a.   differences between straight mineral oil, ashless dispersant oil, and synthetic oil.

    b.   types of oil used for different climates.

    c.   functions of an engine oil.

    d.   identification and selection of proper lubricants.

    e.   servicing of the lubrication system.

    f.   the reasons for changing engine lubricating oil at specified intervals.

    g.   the purpose and operation of an oil/air separator.

    h.   reasons for excessive oil consumption without evidence of oil leaks in a reciprocating and/or turbine aircraft engine.

2. N/A

3. Demonstrates the ability to perform at least one of the following—

    a.   inspect an engine lubrication system to ensure continued operation. (Level 3)

    b.   inspect oil lines and filter/screen for leaks. (Level 3)

    c.   replace a defective oil cooler or oil cooler component. (Level 3)

    d.   replace a gasket or seal in the oil system, and accomplish a leak check. (Level 3)

    e.   adjust oil pressure. (Level 3)

    f.   change engine oil, inspect screen(s) and/or filter, and leak check the engine. (Level 3)

    g.   pre-oil an engine. (Level 2)

L. IGNITION AND STARTING SYSTEMS
*Core competency element
REFERENCE: AP.
Objective. To determine that the applicant:

1. Exhibits knowledge of at least two of the following—

    a.   troubleshooting a reciprocating and/or turbine engine ignition system.

    b.   replacement of an exciter box and safety concerns if the box is damaged.

    c.   troubleshooting a starter system.

    d.   checking a starter system for proper operation.

    e.   the operation of a pneumatic starting system.

    f.   reasons for the starter dropout function of a starter generator or pneumatic starter.

    g.   the purpose of a shear section in a starter output shaft.

    h.   purpose of checking a p-lead for proper ground.

    i.   inspection and servicing of an igniter and/or spark plug.

    j.   magneto systems, components, and operation.

    k.   function/operation of a magneto switch and p-lead circuit.

    l.   high and low tension ignition systems.

2. *Demonstrates the ability to perform at least one of the following (Level 3)—

    a.   check engine timing.

    b.   check a magneto switch for proper operation.

    c.   inspect a turbine engine ignition system for proper installation.

    d.   inspect a starter/generator for proper installation.

    e.   inspect magneto points.

3. Demonstrates the ability to perform at least one of the following—

    a.   install a magneto, and set timing on an aircraft engine. (Level 3)

b. repair an engine ignition and/or starter system. (Level 3)
c. remove, inspect, and install turbine engine igniter plugs, and perform a functional check of the igniter system. (Level 3)
d. inspect generator or starter-generator brushes. (Level 3)
e. install brushes in a starter or starter-generator. (Level 3)
f. install breaker points in a magneto and internally time the magneto. (Level 3)
g. repair an engine direct drive electric starter. (Level 3)
h. inspect and test an ignition harness with a high tension lead tester. (Level 3)
i. inspect and/or service and install aircraft spark plugs. (Level 3)
j. bench test an ignition system component. (Level 2)

M. FUEL METERING SYSTEMS
REFERENCE: AP.
Objective. To determine that the applicant:

1. Exhibits knowledge of at least two of the following—
   a. troubleshooting an engine that indicates high exhaust gas temperature (EGT) for a particular engine pressure ratio (EPR).
   b. purpose of an acceleration check after a trim check.
   c. reasons an engine would require a trim check.
   d. purpose of the part power stop on some engines when accomplishing engine trim procedure.
   e. procedure required to adjust (trim) a fuel control unit (FCU).
   f. possible reasons for fuel running out of a carburetor throttle body.
   g. indications that would result if the mixture is improperly adjusted.
   h. procedure for checking idle mixture on a reciprocating engine.
   i. possible causes for poor engine acceleration, engine backfiring or missing when the throttle is advanced.
   j. types and operation of various fuel metering systems.
   k. fuel metering system components.

2. N/A

3. Demonstrates the ability to perform at least one of the following—
   a. remove and install the accelerating pump in a float-type carburetor. (Level 3)
   b. check and adjust the float level of a float-type carburetor. (Level 3)
   c. check the needle and seat in a float-type carburetor for proper operation. (Level 2)
   d. check a fuel injection nozzle for proper spray pattern, and install a fuel injector nozzle. (Level 2)
   e. check and adjust idle mixture. (Level 3)
   f. install a turbine engine fuel nozzle. (Level 3)
   g. locate and identify various fuel metering system components. (Level 2)
   h. service a carburetor fuel screen. (Level 3)

N. ENGINE FUEL SYSTEMS

*Core competency element

REFERENCES: AP; JSPT.

Objective. To determine that the applicant:

1. Exhibits knowledge of at least two of the following—
    a. inspection requirements for an engine fuel system.
    b. checks of fuel systems to verify proper operation.
    c. troubleshooting an engine fuel system.
    d. procedure for inspection of an engine driven fuel pump for leaks and security.
    e. function and/or operation of one or more types of fuel pumps.
    f. function and/or operation of one or more types of fuel valves.
    g. function and/or operation of engine fuel filters.

2. *Demonstrates the ability to perform at least one of the following (Level 3)—
    a. check a fuel selector valve for proper operation.
    b. inspect an engine fuel filter assembly for leaks.
    c. inspect a repair to an engine fuel system.

3. Demonstrates the ability to perform at least one of the following—
    a. check a fuel boost pump for proper operation. (Level 3)
    b. repair fuel selector valve. (Level 3)
    c. inspect a main fuel filter assembly for leaks. (Level 3)
    d. check the operation of a remotely located fuel valve. (Level 3)
    e. locate and identify a turbine engine fuel heater. (Level 2)
    f. service an engine fuel strainer. (Level 3)
    g. inspect an engine driven fuel pump for leaks and security, and perform an engine fuel pressure check. (Level 3)
    h. repair an engine fuel system or system component. (Level 3)
    i. troubleshoot a fuel pressure system. (Level 3)

O. INDUCTION AND ENGINE AIRFLOW SYSTEMS

*Core competency element

REFERENCES: JSPT; AP.

Objective. To determine that the applicant:

1. Exhibits knowledge of at least two of the following—
    a. inspection procedures for engine ice control systems and/or carburetor air intake and induction manifolds.
    b. operation of an alternate air valve, both automatic and manual heat systems.
    c. troubleshooting ice control systems.
    d. explain how a carburetor heat system operates and the procedure to verify proper operation.
    e. effect(s) on an aircraft engine if the carburetor heat control is improperly adjusted.
    f. causes and effects of induction system ice.
    g. function and operation of one or more types of supercharging systems and components.

2. *Demonstrates the ability to perform inspection of engine induction or airflow system to include at least one of the following (Level 3)—
    a.   engine ice control system.
    b.   induction manifolds.

3. Demonstrates the ability to perform at least one of the following—
    a.   repair a defective condition in a carburetor heat box. (Level 3)
    b.   check proper operation of an engine anti-ice system. (Level 3)
    c.   rig a carburetor heat box. (Level 3)
    d.   inspect an induction system. (Level 3)
    e.   replace an induction system manifold gasket and/or induction tube. (Level 3)
    f.   service an induction system air filter. (Level 3)
    g.   trouble shoot an engine malfunction resulting from a defective induction or supercharging system. (Level 3)

P. ENGINE COOLING SYSTEMS
REFERENCES: AC 65-12A; AP.
Objective. To determine that the applicant:

1. Exhibits knowledge of at least two of the following—
    a.   required inspection on an engine cooling system.
    b.   operation of cowl flaps, and how cooling is accomplished.
    c.   how turbine engine cooling is accomplished.
    d.   cooling of engine bearings and other parts on turbine engines.
    e.   the importance of proper engine baffle and seal installation.
    f.   the operation of a heat exchanger.
    g.   the function and operation of an augmentor cooling system.
    h.   rotorcraft engine cooling systems.

2. N/A

3. Demonstrate the ability to perform at least one of the following—
    a.   inspect an engine cooling system. (Level 3)
    b.   check cowl flap operation and inspect rigging. (Level 3)
    c.   repair one or more cylinder cooling fins. (Level 3)
    d.   repair an engine pressure baffle plate. (Level 3)
    e.   inspect a heat exchanger. (Level 3)
    f.   troubleshoot an engine cooling system. (Level 3)
    g.   locate and identify rotorcraft cooling system components. (Level 2)

Q. ENGINE EXHAUST AND REVERSER SYSTEMS
*Core competency element
REFERENCES: AC 43.13-1B, AC 65-12A; AGTP.
Objective. To determine that the applicant:

1. Exhibits knowledge of at least two of the following—
    a. exhaust leak indications and/or methods of detection.
    b. thrust reverser system operation and components.
    c. differences between a cascade and a mechanical blockage door thrust reverser.
    d. hazards of exhaust system failure.
    e. effects of using improper materials to mark on exhaust system components.
    f. function and operation of various exhaust system components.

2. *Demonstrates the ability to perform inspection of engine exhaust system and/or turbocharger system. (Level 3)

3. Demonstrates the ability to perform at least one of the following—
    a. determine if components of an exhaust system are serviceable. (Level 2)
    b. show the procedures to accomplish a pressurization check of an exhaust system. (Level 2)
    c. repair one or more exhaust system components. (Level 3)
    d. check engine exhaust system for proper operation. (Level 3)
    e. replace one or more exhaust gaskets. (Level 3)
    f. install an engine exhaust system. (Level 3)
    g. check a turbocharger and waste gate system for proper operation. (Level 3)
    h. troubleshoot and/or repair a turbine engine thrust reverser system and/or system component(s). (Level 3)

R. PROPELLERS
*Core competency element
REFERENCES: AP; AC 43.13-1B.
Objective. To determine that the applicant:

1. Exhibits knowledge of at least two of the following—
    a. propeller theory of operation.
    b. checks necessary to verify proper operation of propeller systems.
    c. procedures for proper application of propeller lubricants.
    d. installation or removal of a propeller.
    e. measurement of blade angle with a propeller protractor.
    f. repairs classified as major repairs on an aluminum propeller.
    g. reference data for reducing the diameter of a type certificated propeller.
    h. operation of propeller system component(s).
    i. propeller governor components and operation.
    j. theory and operation of various types of constant speed propellers.
    k. function and operation of propeller synchronizing systems.
    l. function and operation of propeller ice control systems.

2. *Demonstrates the ability to perform both of the following—
    a. inspection of a propeller installation, and make a minor repair on an aluminum propeller. (Level 3)
    b. determine what minor propeller alterations are acceptable using the appropriate type certificate data sheet. (Level 2)

3. Demonstrates the ability to perform at least one of the following—
   a.   service a constant speed propeller with lubricant. (Level 2)
   b.   use a propeller protractor to determine correct blade angle. (Level 3)
   c.   leak check a constant speed propeller installation. (Level 3)
   d.   install a fixed pitch propeller and check the tip tracking. (Level 3)
   e.   inspect a spinner/ bulkhead for defects and proper alignment and installation. (Level 3)
   f.   dye-penetrant inspection to determine the amount of propeller damage. (Level 2)
   g.   inspect and/or adjust a propeller governor. (Level 3)
   h.   inspect a wood propeller. (Level 3)
   i.   troubleshoot a propeller system. (Level 3)

S. TURBINE POWERED AUXILIARY POWER UNITS

REFERENCE: AP.

Objective. To determine that the applicant:

1. Exhibits knowledge of at least two of the following:
   a.   inspection to ensure proper operation of turbine driven auxiliary power unit.
   b.   replacement procedure for an igniter plug.
   c.   servicing an auxiliary power unit.
   d.   troubleshooting an auxiliary power unit.
   e.   function and operation of auxiliary power unit(s).

NOTE: Subject area T, AUXILIARY POWER UNITS, may be tested at the same time as AREA B, TURBINE ENGINES.
No further testing of auxiliary power units is required.